However, tradition aside, the choice of surname is as open to parents as the choice of given name. There's a huge number of titles to add to our personal names. <u>All have interesting histories,</u> such as how Mrs once said nothing about a woman's age or marital status.

Finally, HELLO, MY NAME IS looks at professional names used by authors and actors. The most famous stage name is Marilyn Monroe—though Norma Jean Baker wasn't impressed: 'I don't even know how to spell Marilyn' was her first reaction.

HELL

my name is

HELLO

my name is …

The remarkable story of personal names

Neil Burdess

SANDSTONEPRESS
HIGHLAND | SCOTLAND

First published in Great Britain
Sandstone Press Ltd
Dochcarty Road
Dingwall
Ross-shire
IV15 9UG
Scotland.

www.sandstonepress.com

The publisher acknowledges support from Creative Scotland
towards publication of this volume.

ISBN: 978-1-910985-32-8
ISBNe: 978-1-910985-33-5

Cover design by Mark Ecob, London
Typeset by Iolaire Typesetting, Newtonmore.
Printed and bound by Ozgraf, Poland

For Lynne & Win, John & Susie, Michael & Karina,
Dorothy & George, Mary & John

I acknowledge the generous support of Deakin University.

CONTENTS

ABOUT THE BOOK

So, you're thinking, what's *Hello, My Name Is: The Remarkable Story of Personal Names* about? First, let me explain what it's *not* about. I'm sure you've seen some of those baby name books that are designed to help parents-to-be to choose a name. There are not quite as many baby name books as there are baby names—but there are hundreds of them (books that is). Some now specialise: astrological names, science fiction names, names with only a certain number of letters, and you can even buy books that list names by *last* letter rather than first. So, if you're about to become a parent and are name shopping, then you have a wide choice of books.

However, *Hello, My Name Is: The Remarkable Story of Personal Names* isn't yet another baby name book. Instead, it looks more generally at the fascinating subject of personal names. Of course, everyone is particularly interested in his or her own name. Dale Carnegie, author of one of the most popular and influential books ever written, *How to Win Friends and Influence People*, points out that 'a person's name is to that person the sweetest and most important sound'. However, interest in personal names does not end there. Your name is just one in a whole ocean of names, many of which have a fascinating story to tell. For example, you may have kept up with the Kardashian sisters—Kourtney, Kimberly and Khloé (not forgetting half-sisters Kendall and Kylie). Their mother, Kris, chose names starting with the letter *K* to help unite the family, but she wasn't the first parent to think along these lines. In fact, *1500 years ago*

Anglo Saxon rulers in England used exactly the same naming technique to cement ties within the family at a time when surnames weren't used. For example, King Merewalh of Mercia had six children, whose names all started with the letter *M*. Amazingly, all three daughters became saints—a feat the Kardashian sisters are unlikely to equal.

There are five main parts to the book. Part 1 is 'The Remarkable Story of Personal Names'. It's the broadest, setting the scene for the more detailed stuff to follow. For example, why are names important? Would Barack Obama be exactly the same person if his name was 'Barry Dunham', as he might have been had circumstances been just a little different? Your name is part of your identity, and so if your name changes, do you change as well? There are plenty of people who use a name change as part of a makeover, with the new name being symbolic of becoming a new person. The other chapter in this part of the book asks whether the way we go about naming children in English-speaking countries is the 'natural' way. The answer is definitely not. There are wide variations between societies about when a child is given a name, who has the right to name a child, how the name is chosen, and what name is given.

Part 2 is 'The Story of Given Names'. Some governments require parents to choose from a list of approved names. But in English-speaking countries, parents can give pretty much any name to their child. As a result, there are tens of thousands of given names—one book lists an incredible *140,000*, from Aabha to Zywona for girls, and from Aaban to Zy-Yon for boys. I've managed to group these given names into just a handful of categories, starting with traditional names that go back many centuries, and ending with new names from new words. This section also looks at the influences on name givers as they choose a particular name from the many thousands available. Some are obvious. For example, the sex of the baby will be the first thing that many parents take into account. However, this wasn't always the case. Only a few hundred years ago many names were used for both boys and girls. For example, in the sixteenth century it wasn't unusual for both bride and groom to be called Richard or Philip—and they definitely weren't gay marriages. Other influences on name giving are less obvious, such as how names trickle down from the rich to the poor, and how there are fashions in names, just as there are fashions in clothes.

Part 3 is 'The Story of Family Names'. Family names, or surnames, are handed down from one generation to the next, and in Britain they go back nearly one thousand years. Before surnames there were by-names, which were not inherited. For example, Tom the blacksmith might be called Tom Smith; but if Tom's son, Dick, was a miller, then he might be Dick Miller. Over the centuries, surnames have risen and fallen. Smith is the undisputed top surname in both the US and Britain—though it doesn't even make the Top Ten in Wales where, of course, Jones is the unchallenged number 1. Some surnames are becoming less common, most obviously ones often seen as embarrassing, such as Smellie, Daft, Balls and Bottom, names which in the past had different, unexceptional meanings. More generally, migrants from non-English-speaking countries traditionally changed their surnames in the hope that it would help them fit more easily into their new country. The most dramatic example is the complete disappearance from US telephone directories of the surname Hitler in the run-up to World War Two. Ironically, the American Hitlers were mainly Jewish migrants who had fled earlier persecution in Europe. This part of the book also looks at the custom of a wife changing her surname to that of her husband. Back in the mid-nineteenth century, when the ownership of slaves was still legal in the US, members of a women's rights group agreed that 'the slavery and degradation of women proceeds from the institution of marriage'. It was no coincidence, they said, that both slaves and wives lost their original names. Slavery is long gone, but most women still change their name when they marry.

Part 4 is 'The Story of Name Titles'. Here, the focus is on the titles we so often attach to personal names. Most widely used, of course, are the social titles Mr, Mrs, Miss and Ms. Originally, Mrs was used to denote high social status rather than marital status or age. This is why one of the daughters of seventeenth century English poet John Milton is described on her tombstone as 'Mrs Kathern Milton'—and she was less than six months old when she died. More recently, the title Ms as a replacement for Miss and Mrs generated a lot of heated discussion. Sometimes the heat drove out common-sense, such as the argument put forward by one New York academic that the Miss and Mrs titles have 'evolutionary value', and that the very future of the species might be threatened if a man can't tell by her title if a woman is unmarried, and so 'eligible for his overtures'.

Part 5 is 'The Story of Professional Names'. In some jobs, it has long been standard practice to adopt a different name to suit the new professional role. An excellent example is the role of head of the Roman Catholic Church, with popes taking on a new papal name after their election. So, when Jorge Mario Bergoglio was elected in 2013, he became Pope Francis. This part of the book focuses on two professions, authors and actors, looking at their pen names and stage names. The use of stage names was once a common practice, though is now fairly unusual. For example, in the middle of the twentieth century, Norma Jeane Dougherty agreed, rather reluctantly, to become Marilyn Monroe—'I don't even know how to spell Marilyn!' was her first reaction. However, by the end of the twentieth century there was no similar pressure placed on Charlize Theron to replace her South African birth name with a stage name.

So, that's a taste of what's in store when you read *Hello, My Name Is: The Remarkable Story of Personal Names*. I've very much enjoyed writing it, and I'm pretty sure you'll enjoy reading it.

ABOUT THE AUTHOR

Hello. My name is Dr Neil Burdess. Now in some cultures, there's a belief that once you tell other people your name, then they have power over you. I don't go along with that idea, but I do know that my name gives you a good deal of information about me.

First, there's the title that goes in front of a person's name. These days the tendency is to informality, and so we use titles such as Mr, Ms and Dr less and less. This is very different from the way things were done in the past. For example, you may have heard the opening lines of Jane Austen's 1813 novel *Pride and Prejudice*: 'It is a truth universally acknowledged, that a single man in possession of a good fortune, must be in want of a wife.' The paragraph ends with Mrs Bennet telling her husband: 'My dear Mr. Bennet … have you heard that Netherfield Park is let at last?' Throughout the book, the married couple address each other as 'Mr Bennet' and 'Mrs Bennet', even in private. Of course, we don't know whether this applied even in the bedroom, as the novel definitely doesn't go there, but I wouldn't be surprised if it did.

Other titles refer to a person's occupation, rank or qualification. For example, in English-speaking countries, we use the title *Dr* for two main groups. The first group that automatically springs to mind are medical practitioners. The second group are people with a doctoral degree, who are often university teachers. In fact, the term *doctor* means 'teacher' in Latin. It's possible that a medical doctor might write a book like this one, but if you had to choose, medical practitioner or university teacher, you would almost certainly say that the author was a university teacher. (You'd be right—medicos are *far* too busy healing the sick and making money.)

What does my first name tell you? Like most first names, *Neil* is gender-specific—you know I'm a man. Indeed, if you look at the 100 most popular boys' and girls' names in the US over the last century, you'll find that no name appears in both lists. One of the reasons for this is the long-established custom of adapting boys' names for use by girls. For example, five of the top 100 girls' names (Jane, Janet, Janice, Jean, Joan) all originate from one boys' name, John.

Less obviously, knowing my first name puts you in a better position to guess my age. This is because, as with clothes and music, there are fashions in names. These days, Neil is not a name you hear much. Historically, the name was most popular in Britain in the 1960s and '70s when it was in the top 25 names, but it's been going downhill pretty much ever since. Even the fact that the first man on the moon was a Neil was not enough to stop the downward slide. The name now languishes in the bottom half of the 1000 most popular boys' names. Of course, the chances are that you didn't know these details—neither did I until I looked them up. But if asked, you'd probably say that Neil is not a fashionable name now, and you might guess that I'd be at least middle aged. (Right again.)

Now that you know my first name's Neil, are you in any better position to identify my ethnic (i.e. cultural) background? A quick search would tell you that Neil is an anglicised version of the Gaelic name Niall, which from the Middle Ages appears mainly in Ireland, Scotland, and northern England. So perhaps the name might indicate a family background from this area. (It does.)

The next bit of detective work is based on what's *not* in my name. I remember once going to donate blood, and having to fill in the inevitable registration form. Of course, the first question asked for my name. I filled in the box for my first name, and the one for my last name, but the box for a middle name proved a problem, as I don't have one. 'But the computer won't accept you if I leave this box empty,' explained the helpful receptionist. As I wanted to be a blood donor, I suggested we add the middle 'name' *Na*. It actually stood for *Not applicable*—but the computer was happy. Almost certainly, the software used by the receptionist came from the United States where traditionally almost everyone has a middle name. Because I don't have a middle name, you might well guess that I'm not American. (You'd be right.)

And what about the surname, *Burdess*? It's certainly not a name you come across very often, even when you include the various alternative spellings: Birdis, Bourdas, Bourdice, Bourdis, Burdas, Burdass, Burdis and Burdus. One explanation is that, like so many others, the surname refers to a certain type of employment—though the link is not as clear as in Butcher, Baker and Miller. Burdess was a nickname for English merchants who imported wine from the French city of Bordeaux, the name being an anglicisation of Bordeaux. It was first recorded as Burdeus in the thirteenth century in north-east England, and this region is still the surname's 'hot spot' (well, the slightly warm spot). So, there is some evidence that a person with the surname Burdess is most likely to originate from the north of England. (I do.)

This discussion assumes that Neil Burdess is my real name, although authors sometimes replace their own names with pen names, a nineteenth century term that's still going strong, though you rarely see a pen now. For example, American novelist Stephen King has used the pen name Richard Bachman, and British author J.K. Rowling sometimes uses the pen name Robert Galbraith. But if I am using a pen name, with a whole universe of possible names why on earth would I choose *Neil Burdess*? The only reason that comes to mind is that it places me alphabetically on the bookshelves very close to one of my favourite writers, the best-selling Bill Bryson. Coming that close to Bill is surely no bad thing. It occurs to me that if a publisher accepts my manuscript (as must have happened if you're reading this book) they might advise me to change my real name to a more 'sellable' pen name. *William Brice* comes to mind—or is that a bit too much like Bill Bryson? And if I do use a pen name, I'll have to start this introduction all over again…

PART ONE...

The remarkable story of personal names

ONE

___

I'm Tom. You're Dick. She's Harriet

Names, identity and identification

Although animals such as chimpanzees and dolphins have a very basic ability to use symbols to communicate with each other, the use of language is something only humans possess. Today, there are about 7000 languages, and each one includes personal names to identify people. Names are so important that the United Nations Convention on the Rights of the Child says that from birth each child has the right to a name. One British judge recently ruled that a five-month-old baby boy should be taken from his parents in part because they refused to give him a name.

Why are names important? The question is not new. Over 2,000 years ago, the Greek philosopher Plato wondered whether a name has some natural link to the person it relates to, or whether it is just a randomly chosen word that takes on meaning only through use. Unfortunately, philosophers have not been able to agree on the answer to Plato's question. So, we can't say whether the 44th US President is who he is in part because he's called *Barack Obama*, or whether he would be exactly the same person if his name were, say, *Barry Dunham*. Barry was his nickname until he was a young man when he decided he wanted people to use his real name. Dunham was his mother's maiden name. She and her husband divorced when Barack was only three years old. If she had gone back to using her maiden name, it's possible that she could have called her son Dunham. Perhaps in an alternative universe there's a President

Hello, My Name Is . . .

Barry Dunham—or perhaps Barack Obama became president in part *because* of his name.

Most of us are strongly attached to our names. We might opt for a shortened version of a first name or possibly use a nickname, but you don't often meet people who have changed their names because they don't like the one they've got. You may have needed to introduce someone but couldn't remember his or her name—and become extremely embarrassed as a result. In fact, forgetting someone's name came out first in one survey of our most embarrassing moments. We know how upset the person will be that we've forgotten their name—what Dale Carnegie calls their 'sweetest and most important sound'.

Dale Carnegie goes so far as to say that 'We should be aware of the *magic* contained in a name'. Perhaps unintentionally, his use of the word 'magic' hits the nail on the head in the sense that for long periods of human history there has been the belief that a person's name has supernatural properties. One ancient belief was that telling someone your name made you vulnerable to evil magic. This led the ancient Egyptians to have two names: a public name that they could use without fear of magic because it wasn't their real name; and their true name known only to a handful of people. One famous study of magic and religion lists many societies in the nineteenth century that still practised this taboo on the use of personal names. And the taboo persisted well into the twentieth century in small, traditional societies.

Most people would say that in the twenty-first century these are just bizarre customs of bygone days. There's no *magic* in names these days. Yet, today there are many baby name books that tell you the meaning of each name. For example, Alan and Alana come from Gaelic words meaning *beautiful* and *happy*. You could argue that the fact so many would-be parents consult baby name books for the meaning of names shows that belief in the magic of names has not disappeared—name a baby Alan or Alana and you increase its chances of being beautiful and happy.

Here's another example of the 'magic' in names. *Numerology* is the study of numbers to tell the future. One branch of numerology turns your name into a number that is then interpreted to see what your name says about you. One way of turning names into numbers uses the position of each letter in the alphabet. For example, A is the first letter, and is numbered 1, B is second and numbered 2, and so on until the letter I, which is ninth in the alphabet and numbered 9. The 1 to 9 sequence is repeated from J to R, and starts again at S. The table below shows the number associated with each letter.

A	B	C	D	E	F	G	H	I	J	K	L	M	N	O	P	Q	R	S	T	U	V	W	X	Y	Z
1	2	3	4	5	6	7	8	9	1	2	3	4	5	6	7	8	9	1	2	3	4	5	6	7	8

Take Elvis Presley's first name, convert each letter to a number (E=5, L=3, V=4, I=9, S=1), and then add the numbers (5+3+4+9+1=22). Numerologists then 'interpret' these numbers. One numerologist's prediction for someone who is a number '22', like Elvis, is that they can expect to live an exciting life if they take their chances—which Elvis obviously did. Mind you, as a 'Neil' I'm also a number 22, and that's about all Elvis and I have in common. (If you're interested in an interpretation of your number, there are *lots* of websites when you google 'numerology'.)

To many people, numerology belongs to a time when people argued about how many angels could dance on a pinhead. However, just like astrology, numerology is alive and well today—just browse the New Age shelves in any large bookshop. You'll find, among many, many others, *The Complete Idiot's Guide to Numerology* (perhaps the title says it all). It includes the chapter 'Names by the numbers: choosing the name that's right for you, your child, your company—anyone or anything you'd like to name!'. Having said this, I wonder if you were tempted to work out your own number and check online to see what it 'means' (just as I did).

Ren Lexander takes another approach to names. In his *Secret Meaning of Names* he focuses on parents, suggesting that the name they give their child is 'not a neutral label' but 'a condensed transmission from the subconscious of the parents' which 'contains coded messages about parental hopes, expectations and fears'. And because these messages are repeated to the child every time the name is said, they can 'shape the child's character and so their life'. He sums up his basic approach saying that 'a name "sounds right" to a parent because there are subconscious associations with other words in the language'. Apparently, Ren Lexander has helped many hundreds of clients to 'decode' their names—and often choose new ones. In fact, he changed his own name from Garry to Ren. 'Garry' was almost 'carry', and he felt that his parents had picked him out as the son who would 'carry' or look after the family. Instead, he chose a new name, Ren. At first, he wasn't sure why, but then realised that Ren is close to René, meaning reborn, and Ren in Japanese means lotus blossom, the symbol of enlightenment.

Roy Feinson uses a different approach in his book, subtitled *The Dynamic Interplay of Names and Destiny*. He suggests that 'words evolve into our language and culture because the very sounds of these words evoke a particular emotional resonance'. Not only that, the pronunciation of the name 'requires a specific distortion of the speaker's face, which reinforces the emotional response of the listener'. Feinson suggests that 'reactions to these sounds in our own name can affect our self-image and the expectations others have of us'. To give an example, the sound of the letter 'm' is one of the first uttered by babies wanting mother's breast milk, and the sound is the first in the word for 'mother' in many languages (e.g. mama, mère, mutter). Feinson gets into his stride when looking at the shape of the letter 'm', saying 'the two prominently rounded forms are reminiscent of female mammary glands'. Perhaps that's why Norma Jeane Dougherty became one of the most iconic figures of the twentieth century—but only after she changed her name to Marilyn Monroe.

Bruce Lansky doesn't go down quite the same path as Roy Feinson, but he does agree that our name can affect our self-image and our image among other people. His best-selling book, subtitled *What Impression Will Your Baby's Name Make?*, uses the results from a huge survey to find the most common images people have about popular names. For example, he says that if you want people to think that your baby son is good-natured, then it's best to call him Desmond, Paddy or Ricky.

If you want to give the impression that he's a generous person, you should call him Bill, Kelvin or Moses. But exactly what first impression a name gives can change over time. A friend of mine told me recently that when her son was born, around 1980, she thought Bart was an excellent name—but ten years later along came *The Simpsons,* and Bart's image has not been the same since. Nevertheless, the idea of the importance of names on first impressions has proved popular with parents, who have bought Bruce Lansky's book in the hundreds of thousands.

Novelists are very aware of the importance of first impressions when deciding on the names of their characters. Charles Dickens was so concerned about selecting the right name for each of his characters that he made a habit of collecting potential names for use in his novels. There are nearly one thousand named characters in Dickens' work, including unforgettable names such as Edwin Drood (a character in *The Mystery of Edwin Drood*), Thomas Gradgrind (*Hard Times*), Uriah Heep (*David Copperfield*), Ebeneezer Scrooge (*A Christmas Carol*) and Wackford Squeers (*Nicholas Nickleby*). According to Harry Stone, Dickens agonised over the names of his chief characters, especially when they were also the title of the book. For example, he toyed with the names Chuzzletoe, Chuzzlebog, Chubblewig and Chuzzlewig before deciding on *Martin Chuzzlewit*. He strongly believed that there was a right name for a character: 'the name that conveyed the outward show and inward mystery ... the name which revealed and yet concealed.' So, when deciding on the name of the *David Copperfield* character that would become Mr Murdstone, Dickens' first thought was to emphasize the hardness of the man by giving him the name 'Mr Harden'. When he started to link the character to murder, he noted two other names, 'Murdle' and 'Murden', but felt that both names were unsatisfactory as neither highlighted the hardness of the character. Dickens ended up calling him 'Murdstone', clearly combining the ideas of murder and hardness.

Not everyone agreed with Dickens' technique of so explicitly revealing personality traits through a character's name. According to Daniel Stashower's biography of Arthur Conan Doyle, the creator of Sherlock Holmes felt that Dickens' fictional names were often a 'blot' on his work:

5

'I think that if he had dropped all the Turveydrops and Tittletits and the other extraordinary names he gave to people, he would have made his work more realistic'. Not surprisingly, Doyle gave his famous detective the unrevealing surname Holmes rather than a more Dickensian name, such as Sharp or Wiseman. But he balanced this common surname with a very uncommon given name, Sherlock, to match the great detective's decidedly uncommon personality.

Modern authors are also greatly concerned about the names of their fictional characters. Best-selling British novelist David Lodge points out that, to keep readers reading, a book needs to draw them quickly into the fictional world of the author. And it's not easy when there's a lot of information for a new reader to absorb. One way to make this task easier is to give characters names that, while sounding natural, nevertheless 'fit' the personality of each of the characters. So, in his novel *Nice Work* he named the main male character Vic Wilcox 'to suggest, beneath the ordinariness and Englishness of the name, a rather aggressive, even coarse masculinity (by association with *victor, will* and *cock*)'. He named the main female character Robin Penrose. He chose her surname 'for its contrasting connotations of literature and beauty (*pen* and *rose*)'; and her unisex first name allowed a twist in the plot, with Wilcox expecting to meet a male Dr Robin Penrose. I must admit that I read the novel without consciously making these links—but as David Lodge says, 'such suggestions are supposed to work subliminally on the reader's consciousness'.

If anything, the problems novelists face in keeping readers reading pale into insignificance compared to those faced by TV scriptwriters. They need to keep viewers viewing even though their work has to compete with many distractions—phones, children, pets, and so on. Once again, one of the ways to make the characters as clear as possible is by giving them names that 'fit' the fictional role. For example, in the classic TV series *M*A*S*H*, you wouldn't mix up the arrogant Charles Emerson Winchester III and the wisecracking Hawkeye Pierce.

The media delight in highlighting examples of people whose names seem to fit perfectly with their job. For example, I've a newspaper article headed

'Mr A Pothecary is a chemist', which is based on the traditional name for a dispensing chemist in a hospital being an apothecary (perhaps it was a slow news day). Wags have used a bit of lateral thinking to extend the idea for comic effect. There's the American scientist named Doom who helped create the first atomic bomb. Unfortunately, he didn't have a PhD and so wasn't Dr Doom. Buzz Aldrin was the second man to walk on the moon; his mother's maiden name was Marion Moon (though he didn't tell NASA because 'someone would think I was trying to get favored treatment' in his jokey comment). My favourite is the two medical researchers, A.J. Splatt and D. Weedon, who wrote about incontinence. Strictly speaking, names originating in non-English speaking countries don't really count—but I still like the Belgian soccer player called Mark De Man (who does play mainly in defence), and the Dutch urologist called Dr Dik Kok. Not surprisingly, psychologists have a term for this matching of name and occupation. They call it *nominative determinism* and it's backed up by some pretty strong research evidence.

One study of nearly a quarter of a million people in Germany was published under the title 'It pays to be Herr Kaiser'. It found that people with 'noble-sounding surnames' such as *Kaiser* (Emperor), *König* (King) and *Fürst* (Prince) were more likely to hold higher status jobs than those with family names that referred to 'common occupations' such as *Koch* (Cook) and *Bauer* (Farmer). One possible explanation is that 'a person with a name strongly linked to a high-status role may be seen as more worthy of occupying a managerial position than a person whose name is linked to a low-status role or to no role at all'. (Just as, other things being equal, tall people are more likely to be successful at work than short people.) It's also possible that 'bearing a noble name shapes *self*-perception, which may lead people with such names ... to actively pursue high-status jobs'. In other words, it's about *identity:* what others think about us, and what we think about ourselves.

More generally, other psychological studies have found that people with easy-to-pronounce names are evaluated more positively than those with difficult-to-pronounce names. Psychologists call it *processing fluency.* One of the consequences of this is that people with easier to pronounce names are more successful both at work and socially. For example, lawyers with easier to pronounce names tend to hold more senior positions in their law firms.

There's also been a good deal of study on people's initials. Some psychologists have found that people with positive initials such as VIP and WIN live longer than those with negative initials such as ASS and PIG, with the negative group having more deaths from causes that have obvious psychological components such as suicides and accidents. Others have found that some people seem to be so attached to the letters in their own names that they are likely to settle in cities with matching initials; are more likely to marry others whose first or last names resemble their own; and tend to pursue careers with matching initials (e.g. people named Dennis or Denise are over-represented among dentists). It's possible that, without necessarily being aware of it, some people are so full of their own importance that they are attracted to people, places and things that remind them of themselves. Psychologists call it *implicit egotism*.

But other research results seem unexplainable by mainstream science (except that they must happen just by chance). For example, how do you explain the fact that students whose names begin with the letters A or B are more likely to get A's or B's for their assignments, whereas students whose names start with C or D are more likely to get C's or D's?

*

From the beginning of human history, it has been useful for people in the family or clan to refer to specific people by name. When the number of people in the group was small, each person was identified exactly by a single name. However, when the population increased faster than the name pool, one name became shared by several people. People then specified *which* William or Alice by describing them in some way, perhaps by referring to their parents, their job, or their appearance. Eventually, these informal descriptions became formalised as societies became bigger and more bureaucratic, and surnames began to be used. In *really* large organisations, names are often supplemented by identification numbers. For example, Prince Harry has the ID 564673 in the British Army.

The earliest well-documented example occurred as far back as 6000 years ago when the Qin dynasty in China attempted to name and register each person. Previously, only members of the elite had surnames. The government extended this to everyone so that they could be identified, allowing authorities to be more in control of collecting taxes, conscripting soldiers, running the criminal justice system, tracking property ownership, and keeping a close eye on potentially troublesome individuals, in particular members of ethnic minority groups. It was also hoped that if members of minority groups adopted mainstream names, it might encourage them to identify more with the majority culture—and thus become less of a political threat. Identification *and* identity are therefore both important.

A century after their successful conquest of England in 1066, the Normans turned their attention to Ireland. Although initially successful, control of Ireland from London tended to wax and wane, especially outside the region around Dublin known as the *Pale* (hence the phrase 'beyond the Pale'). Over time, many Norman lords became largely independent of London, and often adopted Irish customs, including speaking Gaelic and taking Irish names. The government in London became so concerned that a fourteenth century law required every Englishman in Ireland to use the English language and have an English name. In the mid-fifteenth century the English parliament focused on the native Irish population living around Dublin, directing each Irishman to adopt an English surname—or have his goods seized. In the mid-sixteenth century the English government had a third go. Shane O'Neill, the Earl of Tyrone, caused so many problems for the English Crown that Queen Elizabeth I banned anyone from using the name O'Neill on punishment of death and forfeiture of property. However, none of these three attempts at controlling names in Ireland was successful. Elizabeth I would not be amused to find that in the reign of her namesake, Elizabeth II, there was a Northern Ireland first minister called O'Neill, and the name was one of the top ten Irish surnames.

As governments became more sophisticated, they became more successful at controlling names. For example, Jews in Europe had kept their traditional system of patronymics, such as *David ben Joseph* (David, son of Joseph) or *Miriam bat Aaron* (Miriam, daughter of Aaron). The only ones with surnames were those named Cohen and Levi, which are priestly names. After a census in the Holy Roman Empire in central Europe in the 1780s highlighted this, the emperor ordered all Jews to give themselves surnames. Some adopted place names (e.g. *Berlin*), others occupational names (e.g. *Goldschmitt*—goldsmith), some nicknames (e.g. *Gross*—big) and so on. A century or so later, the US government issued a similar decree, requiring American Indians to abandon their traditional naming system and adopt the same system of surnames as the rest of the American population.

Knowing the names of everyone in their jurisdiction was also important in the colonies that many European states set up. For example, in the mid nineteenth century, the governor of the Spanish colony of the Philippines decided to draw up a register of the population under his control. The problem was that generally Filipinos didn't use surnames, so he set about drawing up a list not only of Spanish surnames, but also words related to plants, animals, geology, geography and the arts, which local authorities then used to give permanent surnames to people in their locality. Each district governor was given a few pages from the alphabetical list, resulting in whole towns being given surnames beginning with the same letter.

In the aftermath of World War I, Mustafa Kemal Atatürk became the first President of Turkey. He saw that his role was to create a modern European nation-state—and names had an important role to play. Traditionally, citizens of Turkey did not use an inherited family name, instead using a patronymic system. For example, male Turks used their father's name followed by *-oğlu* ('son of') before their given name (e.g. Mustafa-oğlu Mehmet—Mehmet, son of Mustafa). Following the introduction of the Surname Law of 1934, everyone in Turkey had to adopt a Turkish word as a surname. As happened in Europe many centuries earlier, many Turkish people took their job title as their family name (e.g. rug makers took the surname Halici, and smiths became Demirci). For Atatürk, the use of hereditary family names meant that the process of government was more efficient because record keeping was easier. More importantly, Atatürk saw it as a way to unite the country by encouraging everyone to see themselves first and foremost as Turkish. The downside was that some members of ethnic minority groups resented being forced to adopt Turkish names—and they now want their original names back.

At about the same time, the Nazi government in Germany introduced the notorious Nazi name decrees. Unlike Turkish law, which was designed to bring people together, the basic underlying principle of the Nazi law was to separate people by race. In large part, the name decrees were designed to identify German Jews, who Hitler defined as anyone with at least one Jewish grandparent. The Nazi government published a list of 185 male and 91 female given names that they regarded as Jewish—though leaving out Jewish names that were also traditionally popular among non-Jews, especially those used by Nazi leaders. For example, the name *Joseph* was not on the list as it was the preferred given name of the Minister of Propaganda, Joseph Goebbels. Of course, many German Jews did not have a name that was on the official list. In this case, Jewish males had to add the name *Israel* as a middle name, and Jewish females had to add the middle name *Sarah*. The basic purpose of the name decrees was to enable Germans avoid any dealings with Jews.

A final, much less extreme example goes back to central Africa in the early 1970s. At this time, the former Belgian Congo, now the newly independent Republic of the Congo, was headed by a ruthless despot, Joseph-Desiré Mobutu, who ruled for over thirty years. In the 1970s in an attempt to create a stronger national identity, he began his *authenticity* policy, designed to substitute African culture for anything that reflected the country's colonial past. Place names and personal names were one part of this policy. He changed the name of the country from Congo to *Zaire*, the name of the capital from Léopoldville to *Kinshasa*, and his own name from Joseph-Desiré Mobutu to *Mobutu Sese Seko Nkuku Ngbendu Wa Za Banga,* meaning 'The all-powerful warrior who goes from conquest to conquest, leaving fire in his wake'. (Clearly, modesty was not one of Mobutu's virtues.) He used his own name change to encourage every other Zairian with a western name to adopt an African name. He also encouraged Zairians to address each other as *Citizen* rather than the standard French title *Monsieur* or *Madame*. The policy petered out in the early 1980s.

Nowadays we assume that our government knows everyone's name. This was brought home to me a few years ago when local newspapers reported that a gunman was captured after killing a security guard at an abortion clinic in Melbourne. He refused to tell the police and courts his name, and the following day a newspaper headline read 'Police plea: do you know this man?'. The next day's headline was 'Identity of accused remains a mystery'; and the day after that it was 'Clinic accused baffles millions'. A week later police still didn't know the name of the accused, who the media now referred to as 'Mr X'. The case was 'unprecedented' said the detective leading the investigation. Eventually, more than a fortnight after the crime, people in a small town in another state recognised his picture, and gave Mr X a name. But the fact that someone had been able to hide his name from the authorities for so long was generally seen as incredible.

The government of modern China has an even bigger problem keeping track of nearly one and a half *billion* citizens (1,500,000,000 seems much bigger). Rather than helping solve the problem, computers seem to have made matters worse as they can read only 32,000 of the 55,000 written Chinese characters. This means that the millions of citizens whose names include obscure characters can't get a computer-readable identity card unless they adopt more common names.

No matter what the language, for a bureaucratic system to work well, people have to spell their names consistently. However, consistent spelling came about only fairly recently in the English language. For example, Shakespeare didn't spell his name the same way twice in any of his six known signatures. Even in his will he signed himself *Shakspere* at one point, and *Shakspeare* at another. Surprisingly, one spelling he never used was what we now regard as the 'correct' one, *Shakespeare*. Such inconsistency is not surprising when you consider that the first noteworthy English dictionary was not published until the middle of the eighteenth century, almost 150 years after Shakespeare died. It's only in the last 150 years that people have begun to spell their own names with any consistency.

Today, of course, the authorities take a very dim view if we misspell our name on official documents as computer systems are based on consistency. I'm reminded of a terrorist attempting to blow up a plane on which he was a passenger on Christmas Day, 2009. US authorities didn't pick him up because his name on their terrorist database had a different spelling from the name on the plane's passenger list. Spelling becomes particularly tricky when a name has to be translated from a different alphabet. For example, the Saudi Arabian who for several years was the world's most wanted terrorist was known by different US government agencies as 'Osama bin Laden', 'Usama bin Laden', and 'Usama Bin Ladin'.

The difficulties of governments dealing with people from different cultures extend beyond spelling issues. As we'll see in the next chapter, the naming system used in English-speaking countries is only one of a wide variety of possibilities. How do government administrators deal with people who have only a single name, or who don't have a surname, or whose 'last' name is the one they list first? To make sure that administrators can identify these people correctly, they need to be aware of different naming practices.

If a society becomes very big, then personal names, even those with two or three parts, become less useful as identification labels. Smith is the most common surname in the US, and Jacob is a very common first name, so it's likely that in a single year about 300 new Jacob Smiths will join the many older Jacob Smiths. As a consequence, the US government relies on national identification *numbers* to track citizens. The US Social Security number is a nine-digit number (e.g. 123-45-6789) that has now become a de facto ID number, with the Social Security Administration advising card-holders to take it with them when going for a new job, opening a new bank account, or obtaining benefits from government agencies.

When you go to see government officials, they will address you by name even if they track you on the computer system by your ID number. In contrast, prison officials have traditionally used prisoners' ID numbers, even when talking to them face-to-face, and insisted that prisoners refer to each other by their number. Evidence for this occurs in some very unexpected places—such as the lyrics to Elvis Presley's 1957 hit record *Jailhouse Rock:* 'Number 47 said to number 3/You're the cutest jailbird I ever did see' (a pretty risqué lyric for the 1950s). Elvis himself was number 6239 in the movie. Of course, the use of numbers rather than names in prisons has less to do with identifying prisoners, and more to do with dehumanising them as part of their punishment. Prison haircuts, prison uniforms and prison numbers are all ways to show prisoners that they no longer have individual identities. If you don't have a name, you're a nobody.

Totalitarian regimes know this well. In the labour camps of Soviet Russia, a number was sewn on each prisoner's clothes, as described by Nobel Prize winner Alexander Solzhenitsyn in his novel *One Day in the Life of Ivan Denisovich.* In the concentration camps of Nazi Germany, prisoners were tattooed with a number. The significance comes across starkly in the memories of one survivor. During his family's 4½ years in appalling conditions in a Jewish ghetto, his mother assured her son that as long as he had his name he was still a human being. So, when he arrived in Auschwitz concentration camp and was tattooed with a number, he began to cry because the Nazis told him that he was now not a name but a number.

TWO

Bart Simpson, Bart Homerson and Bart bin Homer

Names and naming around the world

In modern societies, we expect a child to be given a name almost immediately after birth, but what about more traditional societies? Richard Alford's study of traditional societies still in existence in the mid-twentieth century found that naming a baby soon after birth was the most common practice, but it certainly wasn't the only one. In societies where infant mortality was high, adults often didn't name babies until it was clear that they would live through infancy. For example, children were named only when they reached a particular life-stage, such as when they could crawl, when they were weaned, or when their first tooth appeared. The thinking was that the family might grieve less if an unnamed child died. Other societies waited until a child's physique or personality was clear so that the name could reflect this characteristic. Finally, some societies put off naming babies for supernatural reasons, believing that harmful spirits were less likely to notice an unnamed child.

Even in modern societies, the idea of announcing a child's name immediately after birth is not a universal practice. For example, in Iceland a baby's name is not announced until the official naming ceremony. As parents legally have up to six months to register a baby's name, there can be a long period before the name becomes known. Before the naming ceremony, only the parents know the name—even grandparents and siblings are kept in the dark. Until then, the baby is called *drengur*

15

or *Gunnarsson* if he's a boy, and *stúlka* or *Gunnarsdóttir* if she's a girl. If the parents don't want to divulge the sex, they can call the baby *elskan*, an affectionate term meaning sweetheart.

In our society, naming a child is usually the joint responsibility of the mother and father. In contrast, in ancient times often only mothers named their children. The birth of Biblical strongman Samson is described in the Old Testament as follows: 'And the woman bare a son, and called his name Samson' (Judges 13:24). (Samson, you might recall, grew up to have tremendous strength—which he lost when the devious Delilah cut off his hair while he slept.) This name giving role was just one aspect of the dominant position of women in many ancient societies. Marriage agreements in ancient Egypt clearly show this, one husband-to-be declaring to his bride that after marriage she would 'assumest full power over me'.

In part, women's dominant social position was because of the widespread belief that men played no part in conceiving babies. Instead, pregnancy was seen as the result of eating special foods, bathing in the sea or, most importantly, the work of spirits. This lack of understanding about sex and pregnancy, particularly by men, in ancient hunter-gatherer societies is not surprising. After all, sex doesn't always result in pregnancy, and when it does the biological father could well have moved on as in many prehistoric societies sexual liaisons were short-lived. Also important is the fact that only women kept calendar records, which would allow them to see the nine-month pattern between sex and childbirth. It followed that if men played no part in conceiving babies, they had no part in naming babies. This was the exclusive role of mothers.

Over the centuries societies that were once controlled by women (called *matriarchal* societies) gradually changed, and became controlled by men (*patriarchal* societies). Part of this social change involved a change in the way human reproduction was understood. Instead of being superfluous in the creation of babies, men now saw themselves as having the starring role, by providing the seeds of life. In contrast, they saw women as simply providing the receptacles of men's seeds. Not surprising, therefore, in traditional societies still in existence in the mid-twentieth century, it was *fathers alone* who were most likely to be name givers.

People in modern English-speaking countries today see the name of a baby as being the choice of the parents. Society has no part to play except when parents choose what are generally regarded as completely unsuitable names. However, this idea that society should step in only in the most extreme cases certainly doesn't apply across all cultures and all times. Richard Alford's study of traditional societies still in existence in the mid-twentieth century found that there was a completely free-choice system of naming in only half of them. In the rest, there were various restrictions on the name-givers. Some traditional societies fixed children's names according to the circumstances of their birth. For example, one society used seven specific names depending on whether the child was the couple's first, second, and so on. If the couple had more than seven children, the sequence of names started again, with the eighth and subsequent children's names having a prefix meaning 'little'. Elsewhere, birth order determined which relative the child was named after. For example, the first son was named after his paternal grandfather, and the first daughter after her maternal grandmother.

Yet another fixed system relied on when a child was born. For example, some West African societies used a 'day name' that reflected the day of the week on which a birth occurred. People from West Africa were often part of the transatlantic slave trade to America from the sixteenth to nineteenth centuries, and West African slaves continued using day names. There is an echo of this naming practice in the classic novel *Robinson Crusoe*, which is set in the slave trade era. In fact, in the early part of the novel Crusoe himself is at first a slave and later a slave-owner. After saving a man from cannibals, Robinson Crusoe 'let him know his name should be Friday, which was the day I saved his life'. Not surprisingly, Robinson Crusoe at first saw Friday more as a slave than as a companion.

In societies that believed in reincarnation, the names of ancestors were called out one by one until the baby cried, smiled or laughed. This indicated which ancestor had returned, and so the child was given that ancestor's name. In another society, there was a list of approved names remembered by the 'keeper of names', and a child could not be given the name of any living person.

There are echoes of some of these traditional practices in more modern European customs. Lists of approved names were used in many parts of Europe when the Christian churches played a major role in naming children. In the time before state registration of births, names were officially recognised by church baptism. To help cement the position of Christianity in society, churches instructed their members to give children the names of saints when they were baptised. This became formal Roman Catholic Church law in the sixteenth century. The Church's justification was that some of the goodness of each saint would also appear in the character of the saint's namesakes. The Church also argued that the children would be watched over by their saint and protected from harm. Where the influence of the Roman Catholic Church was strong, this law had a major impact. For example, in parts of France in 1700, virtually all first names in general use were saints' names.

The influence of the Christian churches on naming continued into the twentieth century, though the interpretation of what was an appropriate name became more flexible. A 1950s guide for Roman Catholic priests gave the following advice: 'The name given in Baptism should be a Christian name. If the parish priest cannot induce the parents to do so, he should add the name of some saint to that suggested by the parents and enter both in the baptismal register'. Presumably, this was easier to do when parents were illiterate, and so couldn't read the baptismal register. In the 1980s, church law was made even more flexible. Parents, godparents and priests were advised simply 'to take care that a name foreign to Christian sensibility is not given'. Apparently not enough parents followed the Church's advice. So, in 2011 Pope Benedict XVI warned against giving children celebrity-inspired names, urging them instead to find their inspiration in the Bible.

In Spain and Portugal, the traditionally strong influence of the Roman Catholic Church was made even stronger by right-wing governments in the twentieth century. Under legislation enacted by Spanish dictator General Franco, only Christian and traditional Spanish names were allowed. In particular, the name Maria, in honour of the Virgin Mary, became by far the most popular name for girls. It can even form part of a boy's name; for example, José Maria honours both Joseph and Mary, the parents of Jesus.

Giving children the names of saints had an added benefit to the Christian churches, which saw the long-established tradition of celebrating birthdays as a left-over from pre-Christian times. In fact, originally the Church ignored even Christ's birthday, and later arbitrarily chose a late December date in order to Christianize the ancient festival to the Roman god Saturn. Instead of celebrating birthdays, people were encouraged to celebrate the saint whose name they carried. Each saint has an annual feast day; for example, Saint Victor's Day is the 20th of April in Spain. As a result, Spanish boys named Victor celebrate their saint's *name day* on the 20th of April. An alternative church strategy was to encourage parents to choose a saint whose name day was the same as the child's birthday. In this way, name day celebrations coincided with birthday celebrations—and eventually might supersede them. Of course, the churches weren't able to replace birthdays with name days, but many parts of Europe still celebrate name days in addition to birthdays.

Some modern societies still use lists of names. In Denmark there are 9000 officially approved boys' names (ranging from Ab to Zygmund) and 12,000 officially approved girls' names (ranging from Abbelone to Zyhrie). The modern Danish equivalent of the traditional 'keeper of names' are academics at Copenhagen University who must decide on the appropriateness of a chosen name that isn't on the official list.

There are two main reasons for having an official list of approved names. First, it helps protect Danish children from being burdened with preposterous or silly names. Secondly, personal names are an important element in what it means to be 'Danish'; limiting the pool of names is thus one way to preserve Danish culture. The issue of preserving local culture is also the main reason for the very similar naming system used in Iceland, a very small country with a distinctive way of life that Icelanders are keen to preserve. Recently, the first name Magnus was rejected by the Icelandic Naming Committee as incorrect in terms of the general rules of the Icelandic language. But Magnús (note the accent) *is* an approved Icelandic name.

In Saudi Arabia, rather than a list of allowed names, there's a list of *disallowed* names that new parents are prohibited from giving their children. Published in 2014, the list includes names that go against Saudi Arabian culture. Most controversial are names that are banned because they offend religious sensibilities. One example is *Abdul Nabi* because it can be interpreted as 'Worshipper of the Prophet'—but only God can be worshipped. The ban is controversial because the meaning of the name is open to more than one interpretation. The ruling royal family were also keen to ban names that they regard as their sole preserve, such as *Malek* meaning 'King', and *Malika* meaning 'Queen'. Names that are clearly non-Saudi, such as Linda, Alice and Sandy, also make the list of disallowed names, though it's unclear why, for example, Belinda, Alicia and Randy aren't also banned. As there are so many names that are foreign to Saudi culture, it makes the Icelandic and Danish option of drawing up a list of *approved* names look more practical.

We expect the name on a birth registration to have at least a first name, and a last name that is usually the father's last name; there's also the possibility of one or more middle names. But the number of names each person has is closely related to the number of people living in the same society. Richard Alford found that two in every five societies used just a single name to identify people. The smallest and simplest societies were most likely to use only one name. After all, if someone's life is lived largely among a small number of other people, they are unlikely to need more than one name for identification purposes. In addition, many of these societies relied on gathering wild plants or hunting wild animals rather than agriculture. As a result, these hunting and gathering societies were less concerned with the inheritance of land—and thus less likely than agricultural societies to use names to show family membership and inheritance rights.

Simple names are one example of *unstructured names*, so called because there is no structural link in the names of family members. For example, today on the Indonesian island of Java, the father might be called Hadiman, the mother Yolanda Pramudita Sulastri, and the daughter Ami Prasang. Not surprisingly, unstructured names like these can cause confusion in English-speaking countries where the custom of having given names and a surname is deeply entrenched. To get around what they see as the problem of someone having only one name, English-speaking administrators might use the single name as both a first and last name. Thus, a man with the single name Hadiman becomes 'Hadiman Hadiman'.

Of course, in the twenty-first century, most people live in large-scale societies and have two or three names, one of which connects them to a larger family group. But the form that these names take varies enormously from culture to culture. For example, the US cartoon character Bart Simpson, son of Homer Simpson, would be 'Simpson Bart' in China, 'Bart Homerovich Simpson' in Russia, 'Bart Homerson' in Iceland, and 'Bart bin Homer' in some Arabic-speaking areas.

It's clear from these (rather silly) examples that even the English terms 'first name', 'middle name' and 'last name' don't always apply. Instead, the general term *given names* is used for those names that are given to the child at birth. The names that link people to other members of their family are *family names* or *surnames*.

People in English-speaking countries expect given names to come before family names. It is also common in northern and western Europe (e.g. France, Netherlands, Germany) and generally is called the *western order* of names. However, the term is a bit misleading because this name order is also widespread in Asia, occurring for example in parts of Iran, India and Indonesia. It is also the standard name order among Swahili-speaking people in Africa, and in many of the island nations of the South Pacific.

Placing the more individual given names first may in part reflect the more individualistic culture of many western countries. In contrast, in more family-focused cultures the family name comes first, followed by the given names. This *eastern order* of names is used by speakers of Mandarin, Cantonese and Hakka in China, as well as among native speakers in Japan, North Korea, South Korea and Vietnam. However, the term 'eastern order' is also not entirely correct, with people in several countries in Europe (e.g. Serbia, Croatia, Romania) placing family names before given names.

The names of the late Chinese leader Mao Zedong and the Chinese tennis player Li Na are in conventional eastern order with their family name coming first. To refer to them as 'Chairman Zedong' or 'Ms Na' would be like referring to David Cameron as 'Prime Minister David'. Names are a perennial problem for students from cultures that use the eastern order of names when they come to study in an English-speaking country. For example, recently I received an email headed 'Hello Burdess' from a new Chinese student who had not yet come to grips with (to her) our strange naming practices. What makes the English naming system even more confusing is the fact that whenever we create lists of names, we usually order them by *family* name, and usually place the family name before the given names in each entry on the list.

It's not just name order that can vary. Although several countries in Eastern Europe use the western order for names, the endings of family names differ between males and females. Most married women in Russia take their husband's family name, but usually add a feminine ending. So when Olga marries Boris Ivanov, she becomes Olga Ivanova, changing her husband's family name, Ivanov, to its feminine form, Ivanova.

Russian naming practices have an added twist. In Chapter 1, I mentioned the Russian novel *One Day in the Life of Ivan Denisovich*, but when you start reading, the main character is called Shukhov. It's not until well into the novel that someone addresses Shukhov as 'Ivan Denisovich', followed by a comment about addressing people 'by their patronymic'. In Russia, a *patronymic* is a middle name based on your father's given name. So, the name Ivan Denisovich tells you that Ivan is the son of (*ovich*) Denis. Shukhov is his family name, and the character's full name therefore is Ivan Denisovich Shukhov. If Ivan had an unmarried sister called Katya, her full name would be Katya Denisovna Shukhov, the patronymic taking on a female ending (*ovna*) and meaning 'Katya, daughter of Denis'.

Patronymics are even more important in the small European country of Iceland where they have been used instead of family names for many centuries. For example, Leif Eriksson was probably the first European to land in North America, in about 1000 AD (almost five centuries before Christopher Columbus). He was the son of another explorer, Erik the Red, hence the patronymic Eriksson, 'son of Erik'. Erik the Red also had a daughter, whose full name was Freydís Eríksdóttir, meaning 'Freydís, daughter (*dóttir*) of Erik'. One thousand years later, the same system of patronymics is still in use in Iceland. Icelandic performer Björk has the patronymic Guðmundsdóttir, meaning 'daughter of Guðmundur'. Incidentally, Icelanders use only given names when addressing someone, either formally or informally, so Björk is her real name, not a stage name. Icelandic law also allows children to be named after their mother, a system known as *matronymics*. Soccer fans may have heard of Heidar Helguson, a former Icelandic international footballer, who is named after his mother, Helga ('Heidar, son of Helga').

Iceland is now the only European country that still uses a parent's given name rather than a family name. However, systems that incorporate the given names of male ancestors are widespread in other parts of the world, including Bangladesh, Iran and Ethiopia, and in parts of the Arab-speaking world. The best-known example is Saudi Arabian-born Osama bin Laden, who for many years headed the FBI's 'Most Wanted Terrorists' list, with a reward of $25 million on his head. Osama's grandfather was Awad bin Laden, meaning Awad, son of Laden; and Osama's father was Mohammed bin Awad bin Laden (Mohammed, son of Awad, son of Laden). In turn, Osama's full name was Osama bin Mohammed bin Awad bin Laden (Osama, son of Mohammed, son of Awad, son of Laden). As 'bin Laden' is, strictly speaking, not a family name, he was more correctly known as 'Osama' or 'Osama bin Laden' rather than 'bin Laden'. If he had a sister called Fatimah, she would be Fatimah binti Laden, 'Fatimah, daughter of Laden'. In fact, Osama was the only child born before his parents divorced—though he had over 50 half-brothers and half-sisters.

Spain, Portugal and their former colonies in Central America, South America and Africa all use naming systems that incorporate the *mother's* family name, though the ordering of the parents' family names varies. For example, the full name of Spanish artist Pablo Picasso is Pablo Diego José Francisco de Paula Juan Nepomuceno María de los Remedios Cipriano de la Santísima Trinidad Ruiz Picasso. His final name, *Picasso,* is his mother's family name, and the one before it, *Ruiz,* is his father's family name, as is the Spanish naming custom. The other names honour various saints and relatives—his parents were clearly a very religious, family-orientated couple! A more recent, slightly different, example is Spanish tennis player Rafa Nadal, whose full name is Rafael Nadal Parera. Like Picasso, Rafael's name includes his father's family name, *Nadal* (his father is Sebastián Nadal) and his mother's family name, *Parera* (his mother is Ana María Parera). Unlike Picasso, the tennis player dropped his mother's family name in everyday life, to become Rafa Nadal.

Staying with sport, probably the world's most famous soccer player is the legendary Pelé. He was born in Brazil, the largest of Portugal's former colonies. Pelé is the nickname of Edison Arantes do Nascimento (which is a bit harder for football fans to chant). Following Portuguese naming conventions, his first name is his given name, Edison (after the US inventor Thomas Edison). Then there's his mother's family name, Arantes (his mother was Maria Celeste Arantes); and finally there's his father's family name, do Nascimento (his father was João Ramos do Nascimento).

Pelé's name includes one given name and two family names, but things can get a bit more complicated than this as parents can choose *two* given names and *four* family names. For example, imagine that Pelé's parents could not decide whether to call him Edison or Alexander (after the Scottish inventor Alexander Graham Bell). If so, they could have given their son both names. And if they wanted to remember the family names

24

of both sets of maternal grandparents (Celeste and Arantes) and both sets of paternal grandparents (Ramos and do Nascimento), then Pelé's full name would have been Edison Alexander Celeste Arantes Ramos do Nascimento—and his nickname would have been even more welcomed by Brazilian football fans.

*

Personal names are universal, and are important in terms of our own identity—what we think about ourselves and what others think about us. Names are also important in terms of identification—how other people can identify us in the crowd of people that make up modern society. There are also huge differences between cultures in the way we name people. The way we name people in English-speaking societies today is by no means the 'natural' way. But to look in detail at naming practices around the world would need a whole series of books. So, the rest of '*Hello, My Name* ...' *Is* focuses almost entirely on English-speaking countries. As with many aspects of a culture, how we go about naming people today has long historical roots, and so we need to look back in time to understand the present. This applies particularly to the oldest element of the naming system, our given names.

PART TWO...

The story of given names

THREE

Thomas, Tom and Tommee

Traditional given names and those based on them

Given names are the names we are given when we are born. In English-speaking countries given names are often called 'first names' because we put them before our surnames. However, in many parts of the world given names come *after* surnames, and so the term 'given names' helps avoid confusion. Traditionally, given names in English-speaking countries were known as 'Christian names', which was appropriate when virtually all were formally given and recorded in a Christian church. Today, while many people's given names are also Christian names, many other people are members of different religions, or none, and so the term is not generally applicable.

There are thousands of given names. Each year in Britain over 60,000 different names are registered; in the US a total of over 1.25 million names have been used since records began. In theory, it's possible for parents to choose virtually any combination of letters as a given name for their child. To take just one example, there are almost twelve million ways to order five letters selected from our 26-letter alphabet—and officials might reject only a handful as offensive. (I might be better off choosing four-letter words, though even these wouldn't make much of a dent in the almost half a million possibilities). In theory, then, parents with a liking for names with five letters could name their child anything from Aaaaa to Zzzzz. Of course, I've been careful to use the phrase 'in theory', and clearly almost all the twelve million five-letter 'names' would never enter the heads of prospective parents. Having said that, recently over a hundred American baby girls were named *Abcde*, and half a dozen boys were named *Zzyzx*.

I've divided these thousands of given names into three groups. First, there are traditional given names, which have been used for several centuries (e.g. Thomas, Richard, Henry). Second, there are given names based on traditional names, many of which have also been around for many centuries (e.g. Tom, Dick, Harry), but others are fairly recent (e.g. Tommee, Rikki, Harye). And third, there are non-traditional given names that are more modern, and stem from a range of sources of inspiration. This chapter focuses on names like Thomas, Tom and Tommee.

✻

The names below are those given most often to boys and girls in the US in the last 100 years.

James	John	Robert	Michael	William	David	Richard	Joseph	Charles	Thomas
Mary	Patricia	Jennifer	Elizabeth	Linda	Barbara	Susan	Margaret	Jessica	Sarah

All the boys' names are traditional. David, Joseph, Michael, James, John and Thomas are from the Bible, the first three being in the Old Testament. The origins of the four non-Biblical names, Robert, William, Richard and Charles, are a bit more recent, but are also lost in the mists of time, going back to before the Norman conquest of England in 1066.

Traditional names also make up most of the girls' list. Mary, Elizabeth, Susan and Sarah are all Biblical: Mary was the mother of Jesus; Elizabeth was the mother of John the Baptist; Susan was a disciple of Jesus; and Sarah was the wife of Abraham. Although not in the Bible, the names Barbara and Margaret go back almost as far. They are the names of early Christian saints, both of whom have violent legends associated with their sainthood. Barbara was beheaded by her father who, in turn, was struck down by God with a bolt of lightning. Because she refused to give up Christianity, Margaret was tortured and then put to death—but not before she had thwarted the Devil in the shape of a dragon. Another traditional name on the girls' list is Jennifer, which is a Cornish version of the name Guinevere, the unfaithful queen of the legendary King Arthur.

You can group traditional English names according to the historical period they come from. First, there's the Anglo-Saxon period, which lasted for several hundred years until the Norman Conquest of England in 1066. Secondly, there's the 500 years following the Norman Conquest. Thirdly, there's the period after the Protestant Reformation in the 1500s, when Henry VIII broke from the Roman Catholic Church to create an independent Church of England.

Of course, names are just one element of language. Over the last 1000 years, the English language has changed a lot, and personal names are no exception. Before the Norman Conquest in 1066, the language Anglo-Saxon settlers in England used was Old English. This language had more in common with Old German than modern English, the Anglo-Saxons having come from what is now northern Germany. For example, *Beowulf* is an epic poem from Anglo-Saxon times. (J.R.R. Tolkien, author of *Lord of the Rings*, was a leading *Beowulf* expert.) The opening lines of *Beowulf* in Old English are as follows: 'Hwæt! We Gardena in geardagum, þeodcyninga, þrym gefrunon, hu ða æþelingas ellen fremedon.' In contrast, the modern English translation goes like this: 'Lo! praise of the prowess of people-kings of spear-armed Danes, in days long sped, we have heard and what honour the athelings won!' Clearly, the Old English version bears little resemblance to the modern English translation.

You'll notice from the *Beowulf* quote that even the Old English alphabet was different from today's. For example, the letter *æ* (*Æ* in upper case) came between A and B, and was widely used in Anglo-Saxon names, including kings Æthelwulf, Æthelbald and Æthelred; and queens Æthelflæd, Ælfthryth and Ælfgifu. Names starting with Æthel were common among Anglo-Saxon royalty because it means 'noble'. But even Anglo-Saxon names that are made up only from today's alphabet, such as Eadred, Eadwig, Eadgifu and Ecgwynn, are not what we would recognise as given names today.

On the other hand, considering that the Anglo-Saxon period in English history began about 1500 years ago and ended nearly 1000 years ago, the more surprising thing is that quite a lot of Old English names *are* still in use. Some have been modernised over time—for example, Ælfræd became Alfred—but the original names are still recognisable. Alfred, the king who burned the cakes according to legend, had a son named Edward, a grandson named Edmund, and a great-grandson named Edgar, all Anglo-Saxon kings. Other Anglo-Saxon male names include Alvin, Alwin, Chad, Cuthbert, Dunstan, Godwin, Harold, Oswald and Wilfred. There aren't as many recognisable female names, but they include Audrey, Edith, Ethel, Hilda and Mildred.

Much less familiar Anglo-Saxon names still make it into at least one baby name book, including Egbert and Ethelwulf (even the most ambitious name-giver would flinch at using Æthelwulf). Among female names, there's Godiva, who according to legend rode naked through the streets of Coventry. Although this ride was in a good cause, it probably helps explain why there's no record of parents registering the name recently. Also listed are Eacnung, Eadburga and Eadlin, though I suspect that the author of *The Complete Book of Baby Names* was casting around for names to make up her claim of '100,001+ best baby names'.

The arrival of the invaders led by William, Duke of Normandy, had a huge impact on all aspects of life in England, and personal names were no exception. In fact, names changed more dramatically after the Conquest than at any time before or since. For example, surveys done in Winchester, the capital of England in Anglo-Saxon times, showed that just before the Norman Conquest 85 per cent of men's names were Old English, the favourite names being Godwin and Alwin. Less than fifty years later, the proportion had dropped to 30 per cent, and 150 years after the Conquest only five per cent of names were Old English. By then, the favourites were Norman, particularly Robert and William.

The reasons for these changes are not hard to find. First, King William replaced virtually all the Anglo-Saxon aristocracy with Norman lords. Many of the more prominent Anglo-Saxons, those who had not fled or been sold into slavery overseas, attempted to show loyalty to the new king by giving Norman names to their children, and it's this group of Anglo-Saxons who would be most likely to appear on the various surviving lists of names. More generally, one of the main ways in which naming patterns change over time is by poorer people copying the names of the rich. Eventually, even the landless peasants adopted Norman names. So great was the pressure to conform that early in the twelfth century, a boy from Northumbria was being bullied at school because he was named *Tostig*. Only half a century earlier, Tostig was a high status Anglo-Saxon name. In fact, the last Anglo-Saxon king of England, Harold, had a brother named Tostig, who was Earl of Northumbria. Harold was defeated by William at the Battle of Hastings. Not surprisingly, the young Tostig changed his name to William.

The name changes were made easier because many of the names used by the Normans were originally Old German or Norse names—the same sources as for many Old English names. For example, King William's name comes from the Germanic *Wil* meaning 'will' or 'desire', and *helm* meaning 'helmet' or 'protection'. One of the clearest ways of highlighting your loyalty to the new Norman regime was to name your son after the king, and in the first century after the Conquest, William was the most popular male name. Other obvious choices for boys were the names of King William's sons, Robert, Richard and Henry (William's fourth son was named after his father). Richard and Henry in particular were ideal names for kings. In Old German, Richard meant 'power' (*Ric*) and 'strong' or 'hardy' (*hard*); and Henry meant 'home' (*Haim*) and 'power' (*ric*). Other male names of Germanic origin introduced into England by the Normans include Albert, Arnold, Bernard, Gerald, Gilbert, Herbert, Hubert, Hugh, Humphrey, Leonard, Leopold, Ralph, Raymond, Roger, Roderick, Roland and Walter.

A similar story also applies to the female side of William's family. His wife was called Matilda, which was the name of an early German queen. And three of his daughters, Adelaide, Matilda and Adela, also had names of Germanic origin. Other female names introduced into England by the Normans included Gertrude, Ida, Rosalind and Rosamund.

Only Cecily, William's oldest daughter, didn't fit this general naming pattern. Her name came from the second-century Christian martyr, St Cecilia of Rome, the patron saint of music. The influence of the Roman Catholic Church grew considerably in Britain in the twelfth and thirteenth centuries, resulting in the greatly increased use of the names of saints. These included saints who appear in the Bible, and other saints who were canonised by the Roman Catholic Church because of their exceptional holiness. For example, Mary and Elizabeth are biblical saints, and Agnes, Margaret and Katherine are saints who do not appear in the Bible. All five names first appear as English given names in a 30-year period starting in the late 1100s. For boys, the names of biblical saints occur only rarely in King William's *Domesday Book*, a list of landholders in England completed in 1086. For example, John and Peter are each listed only a dozen times, and Andrew, Matthew, James and Simon occur only once or twice. The names of biblical saints Luke, Bartholomew, Philip, Paul, Thomas and Michael don't appear in records for another century.

Once established, religious names quickly became popular for both boys and girls. By the mid-1500s, religious names made up about half of all baptisms, with John and Thomas being the most popular, Thomas perhaps benefiting from the popularity of Thomas Becket, an early English martyr and saint. Among girls, the influence of the Roman Catholic Church was even greater, with over eight out of ten baptisms using religious names, equally divided between non-biblical saints such as Agnes, Katherine and Margaret, and saints from the New Testament, such as Elizabeth, Mary and Joan. Names from the Old Testament of the Bible were rarely used.

*

In the 1530s, Henry VIII formally separated church affairs in England from the Roman Catholic Church by establishing the Church of

England, with himself as Supreme Head rather than the pope in Rome. This led to widespread political and social change, including the use of given names. Not surprisingly, those names most closely associated with Catholicism quickly fell out of favour. These included all the saints who don't appear in the Bible but who had been canonised by the Roman Catholic Church. This had most impact on female names, with the rapid decline in the popularity of names such as Barbara, Margaret, Dorothy, Agnes and Katherine. Many male names also lost favour because of their Catholic origins. For example, Austin, Christopher, Denis, Martin and Valentine virtually disappeared in the sixteenth century. In fact, although the names John and Thomas continued to be popular, many other New Testament names were felt to be too closely associated with what was scornfully called 'popery', and so became much less popular.

The establishment of the Church of England coincided with the publication in 1535 of the first modern English translation of both the Old and New Testaments of the Bible. Other translations quickly followed, culminating in the 'Authorized Version' or 'King James Bible' in 1611. The Protestant reform movement stressed the central importance of the Bible, and the new English translations meant that many more people could read the Bible themselves. It also meant that they had access to the large stock of names from the Old Testament—from Aaron to Zechariah, and Abigail to Zipporah. These names had the added attraction that they were much less associated with 'popery' than many New Testament names. As a result, Old Testament names became much more common during the late sixteenth and seventeenth centuries, especially among girls. During this period the percentage of girls baptised with Old Testament names rose from about 20 per cent to 50 per cent.

Of these Old Testament names, Sarah was undoubtedly the greatest success story. From not being in the top 50 names in the mid 1500s, Sarah rose to challenge the long-standing dominance of Mary, Elizabeth and Anne by the late 1600s. But Old Testament boys' names struggled to make any dent in the popularity of more traditional names. The top five places were monopolised by John, Thomas, William, Richard and Robert; and Edward, James, George and Henry usually made up the next four places. However, two Old Testament names, Samuel and Joseph, sneaked into the top 10 during the seventeenth century.

The fact that a name appears in the Bible was not enough in itself. As the sixteenth century clergyman Thomas Cartwright helpfully explained, they had to be names of people who were 'godly and virtuous'—like Sarah and Joseph. Sarah was the wife of Abraham, the first of the Jewish patriarchs. She was also the great-grandmother of Joseph, who became a favourite of the Egyptian pharaoh after interpreting his dream about seven fat cows and seven thin cows. It was Joseph who encouraged the Israelites to settle in Egypt. However, while Sarah and Joseph were seen by Thomas Cartwright as godly and virtuous, the same could not be said of names such as Cain, Jezebel, Eve and Judas—Eve, for example, for her part in the Garden of Eden story; and Judas because of his betrayal of Jesus. As a consequence, such names never became popular.

The use of Old Testament names was particularly taken up by the Puritans, a Protestant group who felt that the new Church of England was still too much like the old Church of Rome. Many Puritans left England for greater religious freedom in America and, like the Jews, saw themselves as a chosen people going to a new Promised Land. As a consequence, they felt it was right for them to use Jewish names from the Old Testament. In the early 1600s, ninety per cent of children born in Boston had biblical names—in effect, the Bible became a giant book of baby names. Old Testament names such as Samuel, Isaac, Sarah and Hannah became popular, competing in popularity with John, Thomas, Mary and Elizabeth. Old Testament names came to be seen as especially American, with famous examples including Abraham Lincoln, Noah Webster and Benjamin Franklin. Old Testament names have retained their popularity in the US, especially for boys, with nine of the fifty most popular boys' names over the last 100 years being from the Old Testament (Michael, David, Joseph, Daniel, Joshua, Jacob, Jonathan, Samuel, Benjamin). Four of the top fifty girls' names are from the Old Testament (Sarah, Deborah, Ruth, Rachel).

✳

A second large group of given names include those based on traditional names. These include *short forms* or *pet names*, such as Tom for Thomas, Dick for Richard, and Harriet for Henrietta. Some short forms have been around almost as long as the full names. When the Normans introduced the name Richard to England in the eleventh century, the native Anglo-Saxons had trouble getting their tongues around the Norman pronunciation—and the name Dick was born. Often, the original aim of the short form was to help people identify exactly who they were talking about at a time when the number of given names was limited and the use of family names was not in general use. As a result, many traditional names have several long-established short forms. For example, as well as Dick, long-established short forms of Richard include Dicky, Rick, Ricky, Rich and Richie. More recently, name-givers are using even more alternative spellings, such as Ricki, Riki, Riky and Rikki.

It may be that many of these alternative spellings are in fact errors on the part of the person registering the name. Incredibly, one British study found that almost one fifth of parents had misspelled their child's name on the birth register. However, they rarely become public knowledge, unlike the mistake recently revealed by actress Keira Knightley. She was meant to be *Kiera*, but her mother got the spelling wrong when she registered her daughter's name as *Keira*. Recently, a total of about 500 girls in Britain were registered in one year as either Keira or Kiera, with about three in four having the Keira Knightley spelling. I wonder how many spelling mistakes there are in these registrations—and how many are *based* on a spelling mistake … Increasingly, registration authorities are recognising that these sorts of errors occur, and have a 'cooling off' period during which time parents can change their minds and alter the registered name. My favourite story comes from Leicester Town Hall. A father came in to register his son's name, but later that day the mother called to say that her husband had got confused and given their new son the same name as their older son. Could they change it please?

Elizabeth is the girl's name that has probably given rise to the most generally recognised short forms: Bess, Bessie, Bessy, Bet, Beth, Betsy, Bette, Betty, Buffy, Eliza, Elspet, Elspeth, Elspie, Elsa, Elsie, Libby, Lilibet,

Lisa, Liza, Lisbet, Lisbeth, Liz, Liza, Lizbet, Lizbeth, Lizzie, Lizzy and Tetty. (Queen Elizabeth II was called Lilibet when a child.) In addition, because many traditional English names have their origin in continental Europe, very similar names are often used in other countries. These continental names are sometimes used by English-speaking parents who want to give their child a traditional name but with a slightly exotic flavour. So, for example, there's Elisabeth, the common European spelling; and there are short forms, such as Elise from France, Bettina from Italy, and Isabella from Spain. Sometimes, people become familiar with the short form, but forget the original. This may have happened with the name Linda, which is one of the Top Ten most popular girls' names in the US over the last century. The name Linda may have started life in the nineteenth century as a short form of Belinda. Or possibly not—etymologists, who study the history of names, tell us that the name has 'uncertain etymology'. (In other words, they don't know.)

Although short forms of names have been around for many centuries, they have not always been seen as 'legitimate' names among more conservative groups. For example, a friend of mine attended a Catholic school in New Zealand in the 1960s. One day, a teacher was going round the class asking the children for their fathers' names (I've no idea why). On being asked, my friend truthfully replied 'Harry, sir'. 'You mean *Henry*', replied the teacher. 'No sir, it's Harry', responded my friend. 'Come out here, boy!' cried the teacher—and my unfortunate friend ended up being caned for 'impudence'. The cane-wielding teacher obviously couldn't get his head around the idea that any father could have been registered with the short-form name Harry. He would have been thinking back to the time when a Catholic priest would do his best to make sure that none of his parishioners used an unsuitable short form of a name—even writing down the traditional name in the register if he knew the parents couldn't read.

Patricia is another name on the Top Ten list of most popular US names that I've not yet mentioned. General use of the name dates back to the 1880s when one of Queen Victoria's grandchildren was born on St Patrick's Day. She was named Princess Patricia, which is the feminised form of Patrick. (In Latin, *patricius* means patrician, or nobleman; *patricia* is a noblewoman—an ideal name for a princess.) The practice of changing male names to produce female names goes back a long way. One reason for this is that traditionally a common source of inspiration for parents has been the names of saints, especially those found in the Bible. Because these include many more men than women, in the Middle Ages it was common for women to have what we now see as men's names. So, for example, Church records show that in 1588 Richard Smerdon married Richard Palke. In fact, in the mid 1500's, Richard was in the top 50 names for *both* boys and girls. Other names commonly used for girls include Philip, Nicholas, Alexander, Gilbert, Basil, Simon, Robert and James, though the church records are sometimes a bit deceiving because when the priest recorded a name he did so in Latin and, following the rules of Latin grammar, wrote the name with a feminine ending. So, Philip became *Philippa*, Alexander became *Alexandra* and Nicholas became *Nicholaa*. However, these girls were known and baptised as Philip, Alexander, Nicholas and so on. It wasn't until much later that the written forms became regular girls' names.

More generally, it has long been a common practice to add extra letters (called a *suffix*) to the end of an existing male name to create a new female name. For example, there's Adrian/Adrienne, Brian/Brianna, Charles/Charlotte, and so on through the alphabet. It's easy to see the link between each of the pairs of names just mentioned, but sometimes the boy's name has been changed so much that the original is no longer clear. For example, Jane, Janet, Janette, Janice, Janis, Jayne, Jean, Jeanne, Jeannette, Joan, Joanne, and Johanna all originate from the name John. As well as changing male names to female names, suffixes can also change traditional female names into new ones. Overall, there are a dozen or more different suffixes. They include the Latin suffix *a*, as in Anna; the French suffixes *e* and *ette*, as in Anne and Annette; and the Spanish suffix *ita*, as in Anita.

Another way to create new names from old is to blend all or part of two existing names. This is particularly common with girls' names. Mary is one of the most popular ways to start a blended name. Mary-ellen, Marilyn and Mariangela are just a few possibilities. A popular way to end a blended name is to use the name Ann, Anne or Anna, such as Leann, Marianne and Joanna. Combining only part of one or both names results in what are called *collision names* such as Marylou, Katelyn and Cheryl (a collision of Cherry and Beryl). Probably the best-known example at the moment is Charlize Theron, the Oscar-winning movie star, whose given name combines those of her father (Charles) and her grandmother (Elizabeth). Sometimes, the collision can be so drastic as to pretty much destroy the original names. For example, Tiger Woods' real given name is *Eldrick*, which was coined by his mother because it began with an E (after Earl, his father) and ended with a K (after Kultida, his mother).

For parents who are less concerned with the sound of the name, and more with its spelling, then a straightforward way to create a new name from an old one is to use some creative spelling. For example, one baby name book lists over 40 different spellings for Alison (including Aleason, Allysyne and Alyzyne), all the way through the alphabet to over 40 spellings for Zachary (including Xachary, Zachkarrie and Zakry).

Another naming ploy is to follow the lead of a Scotsman who, over a century ago, registered his daughter's name as *Adnil*. According to one report, 'Her mother's name was Linda. At the time of her birth the child's parents were not on very good terms, and the father, in a moment of freakishness [a marvellous phrase], inverted the mother's name with the above result'. One inverted name that is very popular today is *Nevaeh*—which is Heaven spelled backwards. From being pretty much non-existent before the year 2000, it had an incredible surge in popularity and has been in the top 50 names for nearly a decade in the US. In Britain there was a similar though less pronounced trend. Nevaeh was not registered in the year 2000, but since then has gradually increased in popularity, and has almost squeezed into the top 100 names in the last few years. (However, this rapid rise in popularity didn't happen with the name Heaven over the same period in either the US or UK.) Apart from Nevaeh, most other inverted names, such as *Nomar* (Ramon backwards), *Legna* (Angel), *Nivek* (Kevin) and *Lamaj* (Jamal), have been used by only a handful of parents, though *Semaj* (James) has been in the US top 1000 boys' names for a decade or so. Of course, spelling words backwards generally doesn't work. Even Nevaeh begs the question about how you pronounce it.

A slightly more complex route is to take a name and then make anagrams by re-arranging the letters. If you start with a four-letter name like Lisa, there are 24 ways to order the letters:

Lisa	Lais	Lasi	Lias	Lsai	Lsia	Ials	Iasl	Ilas	Ilsa	Isal	Isla
Sail	Sali	Sial	Sila	Slai	Slia	Ails	Aisl	Alis	Alsi	Asil	Asli

But if you really want a never-before-used name, you still would need to be careful. One of the biggest lists of names I've come across in print is Janet Schwegel's *Baby Name Countdown*. Among its 140,000 registered names, I found eight of the 24 letter combinations from the above list. There were five girls' names (Ilsa, Isla, Sila, Alis, Asli) and three boys' names (Lias, Ilas, Asil). But even when you get rid of these registered names plus the unpronounceable options, it still leaves several possible unique names, including Isal, Sail and Lasi.

Easier, perhaps, is to take an established name and change the initial letter. For example, Harry is a very popular British boys' name. Changing the first letter gives you three more standard names (Barry, Garry, Larry); six others that are less recognisable but have been registered occasionally (Carry, Darry, Karry, Marry, Parry, Zarry); and two alternative registered spellings for the same-sounding name (Jarrie, Quari). But the technique still generates several possible new names, such as Farry, Sarry and Varry.

One final group is made up of given names that originally were *family* names. There are now hundreds of names like this, from Allan to Zane, with the majority used as boys' names. The practice began around the time of Shakespeare in the late 1500s among members of the peerage—dukes, marquises, earls, viscounts and barons. Money was the main reason for choosing these family names. In most cases, the child's mother was an heiress to her father's estate, and the use of her family name as the child's given name helped ensure that the inheritance was not lost. In other cases, prestige more than money was the prime reason for the child's given name. The fabulously named Scroop Egerton, Earl of Bridgewater, got his name to highlight his connection to the Scrope (pronounced *scroop*) family, which traces its origins to before the Norman Conquest.

Like many social customs, it was not long before using family names as given names was taken up more widely: 'Surnames of honourable and worshipfull families are given now to mean mens children for Christian names' is how William Camden bluntly described the custom in 1605. (Though his comment probably didn't offend many people as only members of 'honourable and worshipfull families' would have been able to read in 1605.) At first, this more widespread use of a family name as a given name was so that children of low status parents might benefit from having a high status name. The given name Percy was taken from the Percy family, whose sons have been Earls of Northumberland since the fourteenth century; and the given name Howard came from the family name Howard, whose sons have been Dukes of Norfolk since the fifteenth century.

One of the best-known examples of a surname used as a given name is Robinson Crusoe (though, like me, you probably think of the world's most famous castaway as a single word, *Robinsoncrusoe*). Daniel Defoe's novel, set in William Camden's lifetime in the early seventeenth century, begins by explaining that the hero's father married his mother 'whose relations were named Robinson, a very good family in that country, and from whom I was called Robinson'. Giving his son an established family name was particularly important as his father was an immigrant from Germany. He originally used his German family name, Kreutznaer, but after the birth of his son changed from Kreutznaer to Crusoe. (*The Life and Adventures of Robinson Kreutznaer* doesn't roll off the tongue quite as well...)

Over time, of course, the prestige status of the family name generally became lost, and now there are only a handful of historical figures that most people still associate with a high status historical figure—Nelson,

Lincoln and Washington come to mind. However, the problem of fame being short-lived does not apply to surnames based on old-fashioned trades, such as Mason, Tyler, Cooper and Taylor, or to Celtic names like Logan, Mackenzie and Cameron (the UK's most popular). During the twentieth century, family names like these have become increasingly popular as given names for both boys (e.g. Logan, Mason) and girls (e.g. Madison, Taylor). American singer-songwriter Taylor Swift is probably the highest profile celebrity with this sort of given name. Her parents named her after another US singer, James Taylor.

FOUR

Tuesday, Daisy and Imunique

Non-traditional given names

A traditional name often has a meaning once we translate it from its original language. For example, Amy comes from a French word meaning 'beloved'; Brian from an Irish word meaning 'noble'; and Clare from a Latin word meaning 'bright'. The list goes on through the alphabet to Zoe, a Greek word meaning 'life'. Over time, we have forgotten the original meaning of most traditional given names, which we see simply as names. Partly to get around this problem with traditional names, parents began to use Standard English words to say something explicitly about their child. The idea goes back to the 'virtue' names of the sixteenth century. It gained strength in the nineteenth century when Victorian parents began to find inspiration in the wonders of nature, and wanted to use the baby's name to commemorate the time and place of the baby's birth. The idea spread like wildfire near the close of the twentieth century, as it became increasingly common for parents to choose very unusual names in order to make their children stand out in a crowd. This chapter looks in detail at these types of non-traditional names.

Virtue names use Standard English words to explicitly say something about the personal qualities that parents hope their children will show. They go back to the sixteenth century Puritans, who wanted to mark off their children from what they saw as the godless masses. They also wanted to remind their children of their duty to God. So, they began to coin names such as Faith, Hope, Charity, Patience, Mercy, Joy and

Chastity. Some parents went further and gave their children slogan names such as *Be-faithful*, *Search-the-scriptures* and *Fight-the-good-fight-of-faith*. One Puritan father, John Barebone, named his two sons *Fear-God* and *Praise-God* because, according to the Church of England Prayer Book, married couples should bring up their children 'in the *fear*... and *praise* of God'. On the other hand, Puritan ministers regarded abandoned babies who were born outside marriage as being the result of a lack of virtue, and gave them names such as *Forsaken* and *Flie-fornication*.

Not surprisingly, the fashion for slogan names didn't last long. For example, Geoffrey Parry, a seventeenth century Puritan, named his own son *Love God* Parry, but Love God decided that his son would have a less religious name—and, a bit surprisingly, called him simply *Love* Parry. The next several generations continued with this unusual given name, the best known (or least unknown) being the impressively-named Sir Thomas Duncombe Love Jones-Parry, a nineteenth century Welsh politician.

Today, Love is a rare name in the US and UK, and is given almost exclusively to girls, but Grace and Faith are still in the US and UK top 100 girls' names. The long-neglected virtue name Chastity was boosted in 1969 when high-profile celebrities Sonny and Cher Bono named their daughter Chastity. By 1972 the name had gone from being virtually unused to being in the top 1000 list, where it remained for the next two decades. Readers of British crime novels may recall Colin Dexter's Chief Inspector Morse, who appeared in a dozen books. Morse's mother was a Puritan, and he was given the virtue name Endeavour—which he kept a closely guarded secret until almost the last book, preferring to be called simply *Morse*, or joking that his first name was *Inspector*. A recent TV British series about a young Detective Constable Morse is called *Endeavour*—though he's already 'Morse' to his friends and colleagues.

A final example of a virtue name is *Messiah*, which has been in the US top 1000 boys' names for the last decade, increasing steadily in popularity over that time. However, the name did not go down well with one Tennessee judge, who ordered a boy's name be changed from Messiah to Martin because, she said, Messiah belonged to only one person, Jesus Christ. The judge ended up losing her job for showing religious bias. In fact, according to one legal authority even if the child had been called Adolf Hitler, the judge still couldn't change it as it would be viewpoint discriminatory under the First Amendment. The argument is that if parents can choose to name a child after Franklin Roosevelt or Winston Churchill, they should also be able to name him after Adolf Hitler.

Another long-established source of inspiration for names is the timing of a child's birth. Historically, names such as Christmas, Epiphany, Easter and Whitsun were used to highlight when a child was born in the Christian calendar. A much more recent non-religious option is to name a child using the season of birth: Spring, Summer, Autumn (but not Fall) and Winter. A general interest in seasonal names started in the US in the 1970s, when for a couple of years all four were popular girls' names. However, only Autumn has retained its popularity among American parents into the twenty-first century, perhaps because of its added British flavour. In contrast, in Britain, Summer is currently the only popular seasonal name. The lack of interest in the given name Winter on both sides of the Atlantic is not surprising considering its chilly associations. As for the name Spring, it may be that girls who are born in that season are more likely to be named after a specific month of the year.

April, May and June are the most popular months used as given names, which is not surprising given that these months in the northern hemisphere mark the onset of spring and the coming of summer. April and June began to be widely used as names for girls only in the twentieth century, but the name May goes back to the nineteenth century when it was both a popular short form of Margaret and Mary, and one of the popular flower names. February is often the coldest month in the northern hemisphere, and is the least popular as a name. Even in the Hollywood movie industry, renowned for its unusual names, there is no actor with the given name February. At the moment, January Jones is probably the best-known celebrity with a month-name. January is her real name—and yes, in case you're wondering, she *was* born in January.

Finally in this discussion of names inspired by the time of birth, there are those names based on days of the week. As an earlier chapter points out, *day-names* are common in some cultures. A very old English rhyme goes like this: *Monday's child is fair of face, Tuesday's child is full of grace, Wednesday's child is full of woe, Thursday's child has far to go, Friday's child is loving and giving, Saturday's child works hard for its living, and a child that's born on the Sabbath day is fair and wise and good and gay.* Despite the clearly favourable predictions for children born on certain days, day-names have not found much favour in English-speaking countries. Even the most popular, Tuesday, Sunday and (despite the old verse) Wednesday, are fairly uncommon girls' names. The only reasonably well-known actress with a day name is Tuesday Weld—though her real name is Susan, and she was born on a Friday. Nicole Kidman and Keith Urban's first daughter is called Sunday because it was the day of the week the parents always spent together.

It's also possible to give a name that commemorates a significant *place*—perhaps where a baby was conceived, where the mother first discovered she was pregnant, or where the baby was born. The practice is not new. Charles Dickens' *Bleak House*, published in the 1850s, includes Mr and Mrs Bagnet, whose children were named Quebec, Malta and Woolwich, from the military bases where Mr Bagnet had worked. Rudyard Kipling (1865-1936), one of the most popular British writers of his time, was named after Rudyard Lake in Staffordshire where his parents went courting before they were married.

More generally, nineteenth century births aboard ship were commonplace among migrants travelling to the New World. Parents sometimes named those babies after the ship. For example, if any Australian reader has a relative named Oceana in their family tree, it's likely that she was born on the good ship *Oceana*, en route from London to Sydney. Or if there are American readers with a relative named Indiana, it's possible that she was born on the migrant ship *Indiana* between Liverpool and New York. But the idea goes much further back than the nineteenth century. For example, in 1620 the *Mayflower* took Pilgrims across the Atlantic Ocean to set up the Plymouth Colony in America. A baby boy was born during the voyage, and his parents named him Oceanus, the Latin word for 'ocean'. Another baby was born when the *Mayflower* was docked outside Plymouth Colony. His parents called him Peregrine, after their peregrination or pilgrimage to the New World. The name was particularly appropriate as it is based on the Latin word *peregrinus*, meaning 'foreigner' or 'stranger', which the Pilgrims certainly were in America.

An infamous modern example of commemorating the place where a baby was conceived comes (probably) from the anonymous New Zealand parent who registered the name *Number 16 Bus Shelter*. A famous modern example is when celebrities David and Victoria Beckham named their son *Brooklyn*, the name of the New York City borough where, so the story goes, they found out about the pregnancy. However, it might simply have been a bit of a coincidence, as they seem to have settled on the name somewhat earlier. Recently, I've come across a baby named Uber after he was born in an Uber car en route to the hospital.

These days, baby name books often have a 'place name' list. Laura Wattenberg, the author of one such list, declares with perhaps just a hint of exaggeration that 'The boundary between place names and personal names is disappearing, and the range of geographic choices grows every day.' She lists boys' names from Austin to Zaire, and girls' names from Abilene to Zaria (unless you're familiar with the geography of Nigeria, you'll need an atlas to find Zaria). Of course, you don't need to have any special connection to a place in order to like its name and give it to your baby. For example, Brooklyn is more popular in the United States as a whole than in its native New York City. It may be that, like the Beckhams, many visitors were in Brooklyn when they found out about the pregnancy—but I doubt it. Similarly, Austin is the only place name to appear in the boys' top hundred names in the US. Austin is the capital of Texas, but the name is no more popular in Texas than in the country as a whole. By the way, I've just found out that a name I mentioned earlier,

Zzyzx, is actually a place in the Mohave Desert in California—though we'll never know whether the handful of US parents had this place in mind when they named their sons Zzyzx.

Another source of inspiration for given names is what we might call the wonders of nature. For example, in the late nineteenth century flower names began to be given to girls. The earliest were Rose and Lily, though experts believe that they may have had a more complicated history. For example, Rose might come from an Old German word *hros* meaning 'horse'. Whatever the origins, these names spearheaded a huge interest in giving botanical names to girls. The list includes Columbine, Daffodil, Daisy, Fern, Gloxinia, Hazel, Holly, Iris, Ivy, Marigold, May, Myrtle, Olive, Poppy, Primrose, Prunella, Viola, Violet and a bunch of others.

A few flower names have recently become popular again. Lily is one of the most popular girls' name in Britain, particularly after you add together the different spellings of the name: Lily, Lilly, Lillie, Lili and Lilli. Poppy, Daisy, Holly, Rosie and Jasmine are also top 50 names. This trend can also be seen among a number of celebrities (not forgetting their spouses), such as Dandelion, daughter of Keith Richards; Peaches Honeyblossom, daughter of Bob Geldof; Bluebell, daughter of Geri Halliwell; Apple, daughter of Gwyneth Paltrow; Willow, daughter of Will Smith; Willow Sage, daughter of Pink; Blue Ivy, daughter of Beyoncé; and Petal Blossom Rainbow, daughter of Jamie Oliver (and sister to Poppy Honey Rosie, Daisy Boo Pamela, and Buddy Bear Maurice—the Olivers clearly *are* inspired by nature).

The nineteenth century also saw a trend to using jewels as girls' given names. The traditional name Margaret means 'pearl' in the original Greek, and an increasing number of parents chose to use Pearl directly. Other jewel names followed, including Ruby, Opal, Crystal, Jet, Amethyst and Beryl. The only one of these that is popular today is Ruby, which is a top 20 girls' name in Britain. Other jewel names that are occasionally seen today include Pearl, Amber, Jade, Diamond and Emerald.

Other than flowers and jewels, nature has not generally inspired name givers. There are none in the US top 100, though Brooke does make it into the British top 100. Other names associated with nature, such as River, Lake, Rain, Storm, Snow, Ocean, Dale, Glen, Dawn and Rainbow (my favourite) are given only occasionally. Certainly, names associated with nature are not a mainstream choice.

Names related to animals such as Wolf, Bear and Eagle are also rare. Even golfer Tiger Woods' nickname has encouraged only a few dozen parents—presumably keen golfers—to name their son Tiger. Interestingly, the popularity of the name *increased* after the news of Woods' extra-marital affairs. (Or perhaps the name had nothing to do with golf.) The nearest we get to a popular animal-related name is Leo, which is from the Latin word for lion; there's also several related names, such as Leon, Leonard, Leonel and Lionel (all in the top 1000 US boys' names). Some of these go back many centuries. In the fifth century, Leo I was the first of 13 popes named Leo. Leonard was introduced into England after the Norman Conquest. Bird names—including Robin, Raven, Teal, Swift, Sparrow, Lark, Hawk and Dove—are also rarely a source of inspiration for name givers. Robin is undoubtedly the oldest, originally being a short form of Robert. Currently, Raven is the most popular bird name in the US, but it's registered only a few hundred times each year, almost exclusively as a girl's name.

A very different source of inspiration are brand names, when children are named after prized possessions. The argument is that these names telegraph our desire for material or social success. Diane Stafford's baby name book has a list of 'Brand-name babies', though oddly it includes Kimberly (as in Clark) and John (as in Deere). But how many parents would name their daughter Kimberly after paper products, or their son John after tractors?

However, what about brand names where the link to prized possessions is much clearer—for example, Dior, Chanel and Armani (all high-fashion clothing), Lexus (luxury cars) or Rolex (luxury watches)? It turns out that very few parents use these brand names. In fact, each year in the US and Britain combined, parents register fewer than 2000 babies with one of these five brand names. At first glance, 2000 might seem a lot, but to put it into perspective, this is out of a total of nearly five million births. Only Chanel made it into the top 1000 girls' names in both countries. The only evidence of an increase in children being named after personal possessions is in the use of Armani as a boy's name in the US: it just sneaked into the top 1000 names in 1994, has risen steadily since then, and is now in the top 500.

Undoubtedly a major inspiration for given names in the last few decades is the desire by many parents to make their children stand out in a crowd by giving them a unique name. It's part of a much larger process that social scientists call *individualization*. At one time, this would mean checking out names in newspapers and magazines, and reviewing the names of people you knew personally. In the past, parents wanting a rare or unique name for their daughter might have decided to call her Unique because they personally knew no one else with that name. Today, parents have access to huge amounts of information about names available on the Internet and in baby name books. As a result, they know that *hundreds* of parents have already had the same idea, and named their daughter Unique. In fact, it has been in the US top 1000 girls' names recently. This then has resulted in the registration of similar but different names such as Amunique, Eunique, Omunique, Uniqua, Younique, Yunique and Imunique (my favourite). Unfortunately, none of these names is actually unique—if it were then, for reasons of privacy, it wouldn't be published in an official list.

Apart from varying the spelling of existing names (something looked at in Chapter 3), there are two alternative ways to come up with a distinctive name—finding new sources of inspiration, and creating completely new words. Both the British and US official lists of very unusual names have more girls' names than boys' names, showing that parents are less conservative when naming their daughters. In the US, there are 2800 names given to only five girls, and 2000 names given to only five boys. In Britain, about 1800 names were each given to only three girls, and 1400 given to only three boys. This has been true for hundreds of years. In fact, in *1281* the Archbishop of Canterbury warned priests against what he termed 'frivolous' names, the warning applying especially to the baptism of girls.

Looking through the British and US official lists of rare names, I found that many come into categories mentioned earlier. For example, there were plenty of traditional names with creative spellings, such as Dayzi, Jakk, Ysobella and Maksimilian; and traditional names that have been used as the foundation of new names, such as Kamarianna, Tyquavious and Floella. Puritan virtue names are echoed in the names Comfort, Delight, Peace, Prosper and Righteous. Perhaps commemorating the timing of a baby's birth are the names Oktober and Sunday. Place names were also prominent (sometimes with imaginative spellings) such as Havanna, Nigeria, Parris and Tennessee. A different way to re-use a traditional name is to make it cross the gender divide, such as Carlos and Gideon for girls, or Wendy and Lily for boys. There was a sprinkling of names from current, historical and literary figures, including Beckham, Rembrandt, Huckleberry and Nero. Perhaps the wonders of nature get a mention in names such as Island, Quince, Oceana and Alp. But completely new sources of inspiration such as Velvet, Mystery and Wing are quite rare.

In theory, the number of possible new names from completely new words runs into the millions because parents in English-speaking countries are largely free to register almost any combination of letters—hence the one hundred baby girls called *Abcde* in the US in the last few years. (If you're wondering why it's exclusively a female name, you'll need to turn to Chapter 10.) However, rare names include very few completely new words. My list of 'new names' originally included Bubacarr, Chuma, En, Fenris, Helo, Malala, Labeeba, Rem and Rubaab—but later I found that Chuma, Fenris, Rem and Malala are not new names at all: Chuma is a place in Bolivia, Fenris is a monstrous wolf in Norse mythology, Malala is an Afghani folk hero, and Rem is (among other things) an Egyptian god. And, of course, the names Bubacarr, En, Helo, Labeeba and Rubaab may be names from other cultures that I'm not familiar with.

Of course, it's only when the parents are celebrities that we find out why they have chosen unusual names. Although celebrities are often much maligned for their choice of weird and wacky baby names, many of them are simply following a long-established tradition of looking to other cultures for inspiration for a name. For example, Michael Hutchence and Paula Yates named their daughter *Hiraani*, a Polynesian word meaning 'Princess of the beautiful sky'; Halle Berry's daughter's name is *Nahla*, or honeybee in Arabic; and Katie Holmes and Tom Cruise named their daughter *Suri,* a Hebrew word meaning princess. Very occasionally, the inspiration for an unusual name is clearer, such as the name Malala. Malala Yousafzai was shot by the Taliban in Pakistan after speaking out in favour of schooling for girls; she survived only after surgery at a British hospital. She went on to become a leading figure in a global campaign for female education, and received a Nobel Peace Prize when she was still a teenager. It's very likely that some parents will have named their daughter after her. It may be that when her story becomes better known following the 2015 documentary *He Named Me Malala*, Malala will become more popular in the UK and US.

So, very few names seem to be completely new words—at least those names on official lists. Perhaps new words appear more often on the lists of very rare or unique names that the authorities don't publish. In Britain, less than ten per cent of children are given either a unique name or one that is shared with just one other child. But these names make up over four-fifths of all registered names. If anything, unique and rare names are even more widespread in the US, especially among the African American population. I can't find any national data, but state authorities occasionally give researchers access to birth records. They found that well over half of African American babies in Illinois were given unique names; in California 30 per cent of African American girls and 15 per cent of boys had unique names.

However, it's only the children of celebrities whose rare or unique names become widely known. For example, rock musician Frank Zappa and his wife named their son *Dweezil* after his wife's 'funny-looking little toe'. Not long after, musician David Bowie named his son Zowie (though he now goes by the name Duncan Jones). A more recent example is *Tu* Morrow, daughter of TV star Rob Morrow and his wife, actress

Debbon Ayer. 'She is debonaire!' exclaimed Rob Morrow to *People* magazine's Mike Lipton. 'And if we have a son, I want to name him Bone [Morrow], but I don't think Debbon will let me.' (Thank goodness for that.) Somehow, completely artificial names often end up sounding, well, artificial—including Adgurtha, Erdix, Golfyne, Irastus, Nopie, Ozno, Phaoose, Rabbidge and Urian. Or perhaps they sound odd simply because we're not used to them.

Laura Wattenberg's baby name book helps readers get around the twin issues of newness and pronunciation by providing forty building blocks, consisting of 17 beginning blocks (e.g. *Am, Jay, Ty*), 9 middle blocks (e.g. *ber, n, s*), and 14 end blocks (e.g. *a, en, y*). So, you can have 2142 names (17 x 9 x 14), including *Ambera, Jaynen,* and *Tysy*. The trouble is that 2142 possible names are nothing like enough to ensure that the name you come up with will be unique. For parents who *really* want a new name, the baby book suggests grabbing some Scrabble tiles and designing your own name—which I suspect is a lot easier said than done.

For *very* well-heeled parents who can't be bothered with grabbing Scrabble tiles, there's always the option of employing a naming agency. They are well established for product names as they help companies avoid embarrassing translation problems, such as when the Swedish company IKEA called a new children's mobile workbench 'Fartfull'—meaning *speedy* in Swedish. At least one company has expanded its role to include children's names. The Swiss Erfolgswelle naming agency proudly proclaims: 'Would you like to find a unique name for your unborn child? A wonderful first name that sounds so good that it just had to be invented? A brand-new name with an exciting derivation and unmistakable history? We will create one for you.' Among the features the agency's 'creative team' takes into consideration when devising given names are uniqueness, sound, rhythm, meaning, harmony with the family name and translation issues. The only downside is that is costs £20,000.

Of course, inventing a new name that sounds good is somewhat easier if you're a literary genius. You may remember the list of the most popular names in the US over the last 100 years that appeared in Chapter

3. Jessica is the only name from this list that I've not yet mentioned. William Shakespeare coined the name Jessica for the daughter of Shylock in *The Merchant of Venice*. He also invented the name Miranda, the heroine of *The Tempest*. Similarly, Jonathan Swift (best known today for *Gulliver's Travels*) used the name Vanessa in a poem published in 1713. As I'm on a literary roll, here's a few more. Amelia originated in English novelist Henry Fielding's 1751 novel of the same name. The name Cedric appears for the first time in Sir Walter Scott's 1819 novel *Ivanhoe*. The name Cora occurs for the first time in *The Last of the Mohicans* (1826) by American novelist James Fenimore Cooper. The name Lorna was created by English author R.D. Blackmore for his 1869 novel *Lorna Doone*. And the name Wendy first appeared in J.M. Barrie's 1904 play *Peter Pan*.

No fictional names from the last 100 years have become established as mainstream names. Fantasy and science fiction are the genres most likely to use new names. However, the most long-established fantasy series, Tolkien's *Lord of the Rings*, first published in the 1950s, has made no impact on the popular baby name lists in either the US or Britain. Only one girl's name, Arwen, was given by more than a handful of parents. Parents of boys are always more cautious about giving their sons unusual names, and perhaps the names of the main male *Lord of the Rings* characters, Frodo, Gandalf and Bilbo, are just *too* unusual.

Most recently, *Game of Thrones* has been a huge hit both in print and on television. Although perhaps not quite in the same literary league as Shakespeare or Tolkien, George R.R. Martin, the author of *Game of Thrones*, has devised several new names that have been taken up by fans. Most popular is Arya, from Martin's character Arya Stark, whose independent and wild-spirited personality must have helped put her name into the top 500 both in the US and Britain. (In contrast, Arya's more demure sister, Sansa, has been almost totally ignored by parents.) Another popular name from the show is Khaleesi, which is a title meaning *Queen*. It's a top 1000 name in Britain and the US. So, it's possible that in 100 years' time Arya and Khaleesi will be standard names, like Wendy and Jessica.

FIVE

Tarquin Fin-tim-lin-bin-whin-bim-lim-bus-stop-F'tang-F'tang-Olé-Biscuitbarrel

Who are the name givers?

After the Norman Conquest in 1066, the Roman Catholic Church became more influential in English life, including who could name a baby. For several centuries, the Roman Catholic Church in Europe had performed infant baptism, the idea being that every child needed *two* births, a natural birth and a spiritual birth. To cement this, there developed the idea that there had to be two kinds of parents, natural parents and spiritual parents. So, with the Church's strong support, natural parents began to invite outsiders to act as spiritual parents, or *godparents*. Amongst other duties, godparents were expected to play a major role in the baptism ceremony. During this ceremony, the priest asked the godparents to name the child, after which it was baptised using that name.

The link between the baptism ceremony and giving the child a name was fully established by the tenth century, and it then became customary for the senior godparent (there were usually three) to choose the child's name. Often the godparent gave his or her own name. This custom was followed in England for several centuries and William Shakespeare's 1592 play *Richard III* refers to the custom. Richard's brother George believes that King Edward IV has imprisoned him 'Because my name is George'. This is because of a nasty rumour (started by Richard) that someone whose name starts with *G* will murder the king's heirs. Richard tells brother George that instead of imprisoning him, the king should 'commit your godfathers', as they were responsible for naming him George. (Spoiler alert … The conniving Richard eventually comes to a sticky end.)

Naming by godparents was not confined to the royal family. In fact, parish registers in the late 1500s show that over three-quarters of boys and over two-fifths of girls were named after their godparents. By comparison only a handful of both boys and girls were named after their parents. The custom of godparents using their own names for their godchildren explains why families sometimes had two (or more) children with the same name—the children had the same godparent. It also explains why in the 1540s a *daughter* of the Right Hon Sir Anthony Denny was baptised as Douglas, after her godmother Lady Margaret Douglas.

The establishment of the Church of England in the 1530s led to many changes as the new Church distanced itself from the old Church of Rome. As well as changes in the popularity of names given at baptism, there were also changes to the baptism ceremony itself. For the first time both parents were able to attend a baptism, and thus were in a better position to influence the name given to their child. Puritans were the keenest to break with Roman Catholic traditions, including the role of godparents at baptisms. Puritan parents preferred to name their own children, often with virtue names such as Hope, Charity and Be-faithful. Although the Puritans did not succeed in encouraging many others to use these names, they did succeed in speeding up the process of name giving passing from godparents to parents. By the mid-1700s in Britain less than a third of boys and only a quarter of girls were named after their godparents, and the proportions kept falling with the start of the Industrial Revolution in the late 1700s. The introduction of state registration of births in Britain in the 1830s was the final blow to the traditional naming role of godparents.

However, one family that did continue the tradition of naming by godparents was the British royal family. The given names of Queen Victoria were Alexandrina Victoria. They were not chosen by her parents, but were announced at the baptism ceremony in 1819 by the child's uncle and senior godparent, the Prince Regent (the *de facto* king, because of the madness of his father, George III). Given the record-breaking length of Queen Victoria's reign, it's ironic that, because of family rivalries, the Prince Regent turned down the request of the baby's parents to name her Elizabeth because he didn't want his niece to bear any of the traditional names of the English Royal Family.

A decade later, when it became clear that, because of deaths elsewhere in the royal family, the young princess was going to be the next queen, there was pressure placed on her mother by the new king, William IV, to change Victoria's name to a more traditional English one, such as Elizabeth or Charlotte. However, Victoria's mother dug her heels in (after all, both mother and daughter were named Victoria) and the name change didn't go ahead. Much later, Queen Victoria, in turn, insisted that the godson who was most likely to become king be called Albert Victor. Her hope was that Britain would have a King Albert. However, Prince Albert Victor died even before his grandmother, Queen Victoria.

＊

Name giving gradually became a parental responsibility and, of course, remains so today. After quizzing hundreds of parents, US researcher Catherine Cameron found that parental name giving could get quite complicated. Parents have a number of different ways to name a baby. Most parents are what she calls 'relaxed namers'. They know that they will toss names around over several months until eventually one name emerges that they both agree on. However, sometimes the naming process becomes less relaxed, and the parents change from being 'allies' and 'debaters' to being 'scrappers' and 'warriors'.

One UK survey found that a third of couples completely disagreed about what name to give their baby, with many arguing throughout the nine-month pregnancy. At worst, parents never agree on a name, with one in four couples ending up either drawing names out of a hat or tossing a coin to decide. Some parents can be sore losers, so much so that it's not unusual for a parent to register a different name from the one originally agreed on. The matter might not even end when a name is registered. One mother told Catherine Cameron about how the father chose the child's first name and she chose the middle name. 'But we each use the one we like. Now, it seems even our families and friends are split over her name'. Even more extreme was where the parents couldn't agree on their daughter's name for almost two years, and the dispute had to be settled in court. I can see why Catherine Cameron says that 'sometimes the battle gets hot and heavy'.

Parents who are 'equal opportunity namers' have a system that they follow closely. For example, they may take it in turns, with the first baby named by one parent, the second by the other parent, and so on. It could be that the father names each son, and the mother names each daughter or, as in one of the earlier examples, the father may decide on a child's first name and the mother decide on the middle name. If a second child comes along, the parental roles are reversed, with the mother choosing the first name, and the father the middle name.

Catherine Cameron uses the term *solo naming* when only one parent decides on the baby's name. Sometimes this occurs after both parents agree that this is the best course of action. Usually the solo name giver is the mother, which may stem from girls being encouraged more than boys to play at being parents. Solo naming can also be the result of one parent unilaterally handing the decision to the partner, a situation that again is often the result of the father's lack of interest. At other times, solo naming is the result of one parent unilaterally taking over naming as an assumed right. A UK survey found that four in ten fathers had to back down and let their wives choose their baby's name. Not surprisingly, this can lead to frustration and disappointment.

Finally, there are what Catherine Cameron calls *little name givers*, the young brothers and sisters of the new baby. Some parents include their older children in a democratic process, such as voting on a list of favourite names. Several celebrities have given their children a naming role. Often, families of celebrities include half-brothers and half-sisters, and so having little name givers makes sense in terms of strengthening family ties. For example, when former Spice Girl Melanie Brown gave her 11-year-old daughter the task of naming her half-sister she chose the name Madison. However, younger children's choices can be less conventional. Australian singer-songwriter Kasey Chambers allowed her eight-year old step-son Talon and her four-year-old son Arlo to name their new sister. They chose *Poppin* because, according to journalist Siobhan Duck, 'the baby was always poppin' round like popcorn in Chambers' belly'. Kasey Chambers and her husband went along with this name, but I'm sure that many parents would think twice before agreeing to use such an eccentric name—which could, of course, lead to some family tension.

*

Some people decide to change their own name—to become their own name givers. For example, US rock musician Frank Zappa's oldest son is *Dweezil,* named, amazingly, after his mother's little toe. In fact, the nurse at the maternity hospital refused to register the name 'Dweezil' on the birth certificate. At first Zappa senior argued with her, but then he came to realise that the nurse would accept only conventional names. So eventually he rattled off a few names of people he knew—and named the baby Ian Donald Calvin Euclid Zappa. But the parents still called their son Dweezil, and he was five years old before he discovered that his real name wasn't Dweezil. The boy 'was very upset, and demanded that steps be taken to rectify this tragedy', which the Zappas duly did, legally changing his name to Dweezil. As father Frank pointed out, 'That may seem like an unusual kind of demand for a five-year-old, but Dweezil was a very unusual child' (and, no doubt, Zappa senior was a very unusual father).

Another unusual father is Dalton Conley, an American sociologist who gave his son the names Yo Augustus Eisner Alexander Weiser.

Three years later, the parents added the name Xing, and his 'rambunc-tious three-year-old' took the opportunity to give himself two extra names, Heyno and Knuckles. The first was because 'he had gotten so used to "Hey, no!" being yelled at him that he figured Heyno was his actual name'. Knuckles was the name of a family dog. Add both parents' surnames as a hyphenated family name, and the child's full name is Yo Xing Heyno Augustus Eisner Alexander Weiser Knuckles Jeremijenko-Conley—the longest name in New York City, his father proudly proclaimed.

Compared to Dweezil Zappa and Yo Jeremijenko-Conley, the American journalist and author Lionel Shriver changed her name late in life. As a child she was a bit of a tomboy, and hated the name Margaret Ann her parents had given her. When she was fifteen she legally changed her name to Lionel—presumably with the support of her parents. However, self-naming children are not just a modern phenomenon. In the mid-nineteenth century, Alexander Bell asked his father for an unusual eleventh birthday present—a middle name. He was unhappy that both his brothers had two given names while he had only one. At the time there was a lodger staying with the Bell family called Graham, whom the young Alexander greatly admired. Perhaps surprisingly, his father agreed to his unusual birthday request—and it's the name Alexander Graham Bell that we now associate with the invention of the telephone.

Nowadays, many adults in Britain change their name using a commercial *deed poll* company. One of the looniest name changes goes back to 1981 when John Lewis stood as a candidate for the Cambridge University Raving Loony Society at a parliamentary by-election. To demonstrate his looniness he changed his name by deed poll to *Tarquin Fin-tim-lin-bin-whin-bim-lim-bus-stop-F'tang-F'tang-Olé-Biscuitbarrel*. (The name comes from a Monty Python comedy sketch in which a character by that name wins an election for the Silly Party.) Over two hundred people voted for 'Mr Tarquin Biscuitbarrel', as the returning officer referred to him. As that was less than 0.4 per cent of the total votes cast, he wasn't as successful as his fictional namesake. Tarquin Biscuitbarrel then helped found the Monster Raving Loony Party, which is still contesting—and losing—elections.

Recently, it's become Britain's latest craze, with around 60,000 Britons changing their name by deed poll each year, the equivalent of five to ten per cent of all British births. (Many more will use the less formal—but still legal—method of simply making government agencies, banks and so on aware that they have changed their name.) The deed poll procedure is designed to be as quick and easy as possible. 'It took ten minutes online and £33 to change my name' reports journalist Brad Pitt, formerly 'plain old Matthew Rudd'. To help drum up further business, the deed poll company he used offers a discount for those who want to use the service again, which Brad Pitt did to change back to Matthew Rudd. Brad/Matthew points out that 'Now my wife can boast that she has spent the night with Brad Pitt.' It's the humorous examples like this one that make it into the media—such as when all ten staff at one Manchester pub changed their name to Wayne Rooney, the Manchester United and England soccer player; and when a British barmaid changed her name to include all the James Bond girls to become Miss Pussy Galore Honey Rider Solitaire Plenty O'Toole May Day Xenia Onatopp Holly Goodhead Tiffany Case Kissy Suzuki Mary Goodnight Jinx Johnson Octopussy Domino Moneypenny.

Of course, there are more serious reasons for a change of name. It can reflect a change in the personal circumstances of the holder, such as a move to another country. Traditionally international migrants have often tried to integrate more quickly into a new society by adopting a more mainstream name. Other examples include a change of gender or religious status. A recent high profile transgender name-changer is US WikiLeaks informant Bradley Manning who became Chelsea Manning. Another high profile example is Bruce Jenner, former husband of Kris Kardashian, stepfather of Kourtney, Kimberly and Khloé Kardashian, and father of Kendall and Kylie Jenner. In 2015, he became Caitlyn Jenner (after toying with, and rejecting, the family trademark *K* spelling, Kaitlyn). In terms of religion, Jorge Mario Bergoglio changed his name when he became Pope Francis, and Agnes Bojaxhiu became Sister

Teresa when she became a nun (and later became known internationally as Mother Teresa). But many name changes are based simply because some people don't like their existing name or, more generally, want to 're-invent' themselves—and a new name is symbolic of becoming a new person. (Chapter 12 takes up this story again.)

One final minor example of adults 'changing' their names relates not to the names themselves but to how they're written. There's a handful of celebrities who always write their names in lower case letters. Probably the best known is Canadian singer-songwriter Kathryn Dawn Lang, or *k.d. lang*, whose decision to use lower case letters honours one of her favourite poets, e.e. cummings. In part, of course, the lower case option may be simply a way of making her name stand out. On the other hand, the use of lower case lettering has been stoutly defended by US writer *danah boyd,* who sees her name as no more valuable than any other description of herself, and so not worth capitalising. She also believes that because everyone's name is their own, it's up to them to write it how they want. However, the use of lower case names has not caught on, and is not likely to, in Britain at least. One usually obliging UK deed poll company turned down my request to become *neil burdess,* saying in an email to me: 'We would not show your name as *neil burdess*. Even if we did, you will find you will not be able to get your documents and records changed to *neil burdess* since record holders have strict policy (as we do) on how names should appear on their documents and in their records i.e. in the traditional format'. So, Tarquin Biscuitbarrel is fine, but *tarquin biscuitbarrel* is not.

SIX

'A boy named Sue'

Gender and name giving

Social scientists often distinguish between *sex* and *gender*. Sex is a biological term—does a person have a male or female body? Gender is a social term—society expects males to behave in a masculine way, and females in a feminine way. Not surprisingly then, most of the names we give to boys usually come from a masculine pool of names, and those we give to girls from a feminine pool of names. Many parents-to-be who don't know the sex of their child draw up two sets of names to cover both eventualities. Of course, a name by itself doesn't have a gender. For example, unless you knew something about Japanese culture, you wouldn't know that *Ren* is a popular boys' name, and *Rin* is a popular girls' name. Similarly, it's only when you are familiar with English culture that you can interpret the gender of a name.

We are so used to the idea that there are boys' names and girls' names that it's easy to think this is how it's always been. However, you might recall from Chapter 3 that in the Middle Ages women often had what we now see as men's names. A common source of inspiration for parents was the names of saints, especially those found in the Bible, but there are many more male than female Biblical saints, and so it became an accepted practice to give girls the names of male saints. This was extended to include names in general. In the mid 1500s, Richard was in the top fifty names for *both* boys and girls. Other names commonly used for both boys and girls included Philip, Nicholas, Alexander, James, Gilbert, Aubrey, Reynold, Basil, Eustace, Giles, Edmund and Simon. However, when the Church authorities recorded names, they did so in Latin, and followed the rules of Latin grammar by writing the name with a feminine ending. So, Philip became *Philippa,* Nicholas became *Nicholaa,* and Alexander became *Alexandra.* Girls whose names were registered in this way were in fact baptized and called 'Philip', 'Nicholas' and 'Alexander'. It wasn't until much later that these written forms became regular girls' names as the custom developed that boys' names should be different from girls' names.

Occasionally, some longstanding male names become popular as female names. When this happens, the name becomes less popular as a boys' name. One example that goes back several centuries is the name Florence. In the Middle Ages, it was commonly given to boys, but gradually became exclusively a girl's name. Much more recently, Leslie, Kim, Evelyn, Beverly, Dana and Carol all became less used as boys' names once they became more used as girls' names. In the first half of the twentieth century, Leslie was primarily a boys' name, but when it became equally popular among girls in the middle of the century, its popularity as a boys' name declined rapidly, and Leslie eventually left the top 1000 boys' names in the 1990s.

Sociologists have never been afraid to ask difficult questions, and Harvard sociologist Stanley Lieberson has asked why this historical trend in names occurs. His answer is blunt: 'there are issues of contamination such that the advantaged have a greater incentive to avoid having their status confused with the disadvantaged'. For 'advantaged' read *males,* and for 'disadvantaged' read *females.* In other words, boys' names become 'contaminated' once they are used as girls' names, and so parents use them less as boys' names.

There's lot of anecdotal evidence that boys with 'contaminated' names can have a hard time. Most famously, the Johnny Cash song '*A boy named Sue*' tells of a life of ridicule and harassment because of the boy's name, and ends with the lines: '*Bill or George, any damn thing but Sue! I still hate that name!*' (Though to be strictly accurate, the real-life boy named Sue, Sue K. Hicks, who was named after his mother who died in childbirth, says that he was proud of his name—though perhaps more as an adult than a child.) In similar vein, Alexander McCall Smith, a favourite author of mine, has a character in one of his novels remembering a small boy from his schooldays whose middle name started with the letter B: 'When it was discovered that this was for Beverley, a name that is technically available for both boys and girls, his life had become a torment of derision.' As a result, he 'suddenly disappeared one day—driven out, no doubt, sent somewhere else where his name might not follow him.'

A real-world recent example comes from the *New York Times*. A four-year-old boy called Kelly was happy with his name until he went to preschool where there was also a girl called Kelly. After a day of teasing, he came home crying, and after that insisted on being called Kelvin. Not surprisingly, one US study found that when boys with names associated with girls move to middle school they become more disruptive than other boys in their class.

It won't be long before the US and British armed forces open all combat roles to women. In this context, the idea of boys' names being 'contaminated' when they are used by girls sounds somewhat old fashioned. Stanley Lieberson's research was done on naming trends in the twentieth century, and perhaps things are different now that the contamination he refers to no longer applies. However, I'm sure that Kelly/Kelvin and his mum would not agree, and the statistical evidence supports them. If you compare the top hundred boys' and girls' names in the US, you find that no name appears in both lists. Even if you extend the search to the top 200 names, there's still only a handful of names that appear in both lists (Avery, Hayden, Riley, Taylor). Unisex names are just as unpopular in Britain. No name appears on both top 100 lists, and there are only a handful in both top 200 lists (Beau, Frankie, Taylor). In contrast, the traditional distinction between boys' and girls' names is still going strong. The US top 200 names includes Adrian and Adriana, Alan and Alana, and Alex and Alexa—and so on through the alphabet. In Britain, Oliver is a top boys' name, and Olivia is a top girls' name.

What about the next few years? Two trends suggest that names might become less gender-specific in the next few decades. First, there's the tendency to use family names as given names. Avery, Cameron, Emerson, Hayden, Jordan, Parker, Peyton, Quinn, Riley and Taylor all appear in the top 500 boys' and girls' names in the US; Eden, Marley, Morgan and Taylor are on both British lists. Initially, at least, family names have no gender bias, and so are more likely to be used for both boys and girls. However, this often doesn't last. The name Madison came out of nowhere into the US top 1000 for girls in 1985; by the late 1990s it was in the top ten, where it has remained ever since, going as high as number two in 2001. In contrast, the name never caught on as a boys' name, and disappeared completely from the boys' top 1000 at the time when Madison was enjoying maximum popularity among girls. As is often the case, the movie industry has been cited as the reason why Madison suddenly became popular as a girl's name. Daryl Hannah plays a mermaid in the 1984 film *Splash*, and she adopts the name after seeing a street sign for Madison Avenue. 'But Madison isn't a name' explains a friend, trying to get her to see the difference between given names and family names. A later chapter looks in detail at the influence of celebrities on name giving.

The second possible influence on how names might become less gender specific in the next decade or two relates to the increasing use of *new* given names. A previous chapter showed that rare or unique names are increasingly common. For example, Oktober, Sunday, Havanna, Tennessee, Island, Alp, Mystery, Wing, Fenris and Rem are not names that immediately suggest a boy or girl. And yet … it's surprising that a seemingly completely gender-neutral name is given only to boys or only to girls. For example, the name *Abcde* was given to a hundred baby girls but no boys in the US recently. That intrepid Harvard sociologist, Stanley Lieberson, also has an explanation for this.

Although a name might be new, he says, it's likely to follow 'the cultural expectation' that boys' names and girls' names generally will *sound* different. In other words, there are unwritten 'rules' that parents follow, largely unconsciously, when deciding on appropriate names for their children. The lists below show the top 10 girls' and boys' names in the US:

Emma	Olivia	Sophia	Isabella	Ava	Mia	Emily	Abigail	Madison	Charlotte
Noah	Liam	Mason	Jacob	William	Ethan	Michael	Alexander	James	Daniel

There's an obvious gender difference in the number of names ending with an *a*-sound. The top six girls' names end with an *a*-sound. In contrast, only one of the boys' names (Noah) has this ending. Extending this beyond the top 10, nearly half of the top fifty, and two fifths of the top 100 most popular girls' names end with an *a*-sound. In contrast, only a handful of the top 100 boys' names end with an *a*-sound. Like Noah, all are Biblical names. Similarly, an *e*-sound ending accounts for nearly a third of the top 100 girls' names, but only a handful of the top 100 boys' names. Overall, 70 per cent of the top 100 girls' names end with either an *a*- or an *e*-sound compared to just ten per cent of the top hundred boys' names. So, naming only girls Abcde (pronounced *Ab-se-dee*) is not so surprising—it ends with an *e*-sound.

While girls' names usually end with a vowel sound, boys' names tend to end with a consonant. Currently, many of the most popular boys' names end with an *n*, including two of the top 10 boys' names (Mason, Ethan), compared to only one girls' name (Madison). In the top 50 names, there are nearly 20 boys' names ending in *n*, and only five girls' names. More than four in every 10 of the top 100 boys' names end with *n*, which is triple the number of girls' names.

Even though they aren't aware it's happening, parents choose different names for girls and boys partly because they sound different. The preferred *e*-sound for girls' names would explain why the family names Riley, Sydney, Mackenzie and Kennedy appear in the top hundred girls' names but not in the boys' list; and why the family names Mason, Logan, Jackson and Cameron appear in the top hundred boys' names but not in the girls' list. Even when parents try to come up with completely *new* names, they generally follow cultural expectations, with the sound of the name matching the gender of the child. For example, looking through the British and US official lists of rare names, I found that over half of the girls' names ended with an *a*-sound or *e*-sound (e.g. Jazzabella, Nigeria, Xienna, Wylee, Tawny). In contrast, only one in seven boys' names ended with an *a*- or *e*-sound—and three of these are traditional *girls'* names (Victoria, Wendy, Lily).

The above comments also apply to the most popular baby names in Britain. For example, the following list shows that no fewer than seven of the top ten girls' names end with an *a* compared to none of the boys' names.

Amelia	Olivia	Emily	Ava	Isla	Jessica	Poppy	Isabella	Sophie	Mia
Oliver	Jack	Harry	Jacob	Charlie	Thomas	Oscar	William	James	George

Most generally, a team of British scientists have concluded that name differences between men and women may well be the result of evolution. The thinking goes like this. As with many other species, male human bodies are on average larger than female bodies. As a result, overall, a man's voice sounds deeper than a woman's. In many societies, larger men are more sexually attractive to women, and smaller women are more sexually attractive to men. Wanting to maximise the chances of their genes being taken into future generations, without knowing it parents tend to give baby boys names with a deep, harsh sound (e.g. Thomas, Jack, Noah); while baby girls are more likely to be given names which sound higher and lighter (e.g. Emily, Lily, Mia). They tested the theory by looking at 15 *million* popular names given over a 10-year period in the UK, US and Australia. The results from a lot of complicated statistical analysis support the theory that name differences between men and women may well be the result of evolution encouraging parents to give names that will maximise their child's chances of finding a sexual partner, and thus making sure the parents' genes live on.

Parents are more conservative when naming boys or, to express it another way, parents are more adventurous when naming girls. The names from other cultures used by celebrity parents—Hiraani, Nahla, Suri—have all been given to their *daughters*. The same thing is true for celebrity parents using the wonders of nature as their naming inspiration—Peaches Honeyblossom, Bluebell, Willow, and so on. The children of celebrities are just the highly visible tip of an iceberg. For example, each year in Britain approximately the same number of girls and boys are born, yet the latest statistics show that there were 30 per cent more names registered for girls than boys—35,000 compared to 27,000. The extra 8000 girls' names show the extra effort made by parents to be *really* innovative when naming their daughters.

Let me illustrate the same idea from a slightly different angle—by looking at the top ten names given to boys and girls in Britain today and seeing how popular these names were one hundred years ago. Among boys, the traditional names Thomas, William, James and George are in both top ten lists. And there are also two pet names in today's list that appeared in more traditional form in the top ten names a century ago: Charlie and Charles; and Jack and John. In other words, over half of today's most popular boys' names were also popular a century ago. In contrast, *none* of today's top ten girls' names were as popular a century ago. In fact, only three of them were in the top *hundred* girls' names.

One explanation for these differences between boys and girls in naming is that for well over a century parents of girls have been more influenced by fashion in naming. One recent fashion is to give children an unusual name—ideally, a unique name. This has had the greatest impact on the parents of daughters, as shown by the much larger number of names given to girls than boys. In contrast, parents are more likely to continue the tradition of naming their son after a family member.

This difference between naming girls and boys often comes out most strongly in migrant families. For example, Hispanic migrants living in Los Angeles were more than twice as likely to give their daughters very English names (e.g. Jennifer, Kimberly) than to give their sons very English names (e.g. Kevin, Bryan). In contrast, one half of their sons had Spanish given names (e.g. Jose, Juan), but only one quarter of their daughters had Spanish names (e.g. Guadalupe, Maria). These name choices are partly explained by the fact that Hispanic mothers have the major role in naming girls, and Hispanic fathers have the major role in naming boys. Female migrants tend to be more positive about their new life in the US, and see their long-term future there. Giving their daughters English names is one way to help them assimilate more easily into mainstream US society. In contrast, their husbands are more likely to be nostalgic for their old life, and have plans to return home eventually. Giving their sons Spanish names is a reflection of this.

SEVEN

Kourtney, Kimberly and Khloé

Families and name giving

Given names, of course, are paired with family names. At the most basic level, avoiding clashes with the family's surname is one of the most important factors for most parents when choosing baby names. Problematic combinations are most likely to be accidental—what one baby name book calls the 'Justin Case syndrome'. Less obvious are given names that when shortened make unfortunate combinations with certain family names. For example, Donald Key is fine; Don Key less so. Edward Case and Benjamin Dover are two more when shortened to Ed Case and Ben Dover. I'm sure you can think of others.

Very occasionally, however, there are parents who go the other way, such as a couple with the family name Trees who named their daughter Merry Christmas, and their sons Douglas Fir and Jack Pine. Other examples include Cora Apple, Holly Berry, Pearly Gates, Phil Graves, Virginia Ham, Mince Pie, Belle Ringer and Annie Seed. The most famous historical example goes back to the nineteenth century when Texas governor Jim Hogg named his daughter *Ima*. (I'm pleased to say she went on to become one of the most respected women in Texan history.) Much more recently, Kim Kardashian and husband Kanye West named their first child, a daughter, *North* West. (Though the parents avoided rumoured given names such as South and Wild for their second child, instead calling him *Saint*.)

A similar caution about clashes between given and family names applies to the *initials* of a full name. So (to continue the Ima Hogg theme) Ian

72

Paul Grant might be a better choice than Paul Ian Grant. The initials of people's names have been looked at in detail by psychologists who studied death records in California. They found that among men especially, those with positive initials such as ACE, JOY, VIP and WIN on average lived longer than those with negative initials such as ASS, DIE, MAD and PIG. Among people in the negative initials group there were more deaths from causes that have 'obvious psychological components', such as suicides and accidents. However, readers called Paul Ian Grant, Angela Sophie Smith and so on should take heart from the fact that, as sometimes happens in academic research, when other researchers looked at the same death records they found no evidence that life expectancy is any different between the two groups.

Of most importance, of course, is the way that the same names keep occurring in families as names can serve to link different generations. In the US about six in ten babies are named after a relative, usually a parent or grandparent. In Britain, family influence is less, with just over one quarter of parents naming a baby after a family member. Names can link together the father's and mother's sides of a family, sometimes using family names as given names. Five of the dozen US presidents since 1945 have a middle name taken from their mother's maiden name: John *Fitzgerald* Kennedy (his mother was Rose Fitzgerald before she married), Lyndon *Baines* Johnson (Rebekah Baines), Richard *Milhous* Nixon (Hannah Milhous), Ronald *Wilson* Reagan (Nelle Wilson), and George Herbert *Walker* Bush (Dorothy Walker). Or parents can create a new name by combining names from two relatives, especially grandmothers (e.g. *Emma* from a combination of Emily and Mary). A third possibility is *cross-sex translations*, when a child of one sex is given a suitably changed name from a family member of the opposite sex. For example, a grand-daughter might be named Alana after her grandfather Alan or, less obviously, a grandson named Charles after his grandmother Caroline.

Royal families are particularly keen to use given names that link generations in order to highlight royal succession. This comes out clearly in the names given to a recent addition to the British royal family, Prince

George, who will be King George VII after the deaths of his great-grandmother, grandfather and father (so it won't be anytime soon). His three given names are George Alexander Louis. The fact that there have already been six kings called George firmly establishes his royal credentials; most recently, his royal grandfather has the name George as a middle name. Alexander and its feminine form, Alexandra, crops up a number of times in royal history, most recently as one of Elizabeth II's given names. Louis and its feminine form Louise also appear regularly in the royal family tree, including Prince George's father, great-uncle and great-aunt.

The first king to come to the British throne in the twentieth century was Edward VII, who was the oldest son of Queen Victoria and her beloved Prince Albert. All of Edward's three boys had the name Albert, and all three girls had the name Victoria. Edward's first-born son was named after *both* his royal grandfather (Albert) and grandmother (using a cross-sex translation: Victor ® Victoria). In fact, the child's grandmother and godmother, Queen Victoria, chose the names Albert and Victor.

However, Queen Victoria's wish for a 'King Albert' hasn't happened yet—and I suspect it's now very unlikely. Victoria's eldest son, Albert Edward, took his second name to become King Edward VII. He explained his choice as follows: 'I have resolved to be known by the name of Edward, which has been borne by six of My ancestors. In doing so I do not undervalue the name of Albert, which I inherit from My ever to be lamented, great and wise Father, who by universal consent, is I think deservedly known by the name of Albert the Good, and I desire that his name should stand alone.' (Or perhaps he simply didn't like the name Albert.) If he had used his first name, then the Edwardian era in Britain would have been known as the *Albertian* era—which somehow doesn't sound quite *British*.

One of George V's sons, Albert Frederick Arthur George, on succeeding to the throne in 1936 also decided against becoming Britain's first King Albert. Instead, he chose his last name to become

George VI, a regal name that he hoped would restore confidence in the British monarchy following the abdication of his brother. It was also a time of tension with Hitler's Nazi Germany, and the new king felt that people would see the title *King Albert* as too Germanic. This isn't surprising as the great-grandfather after whom he was named was originally a German prince, Prince Albert of Saxe-Coburg and Gotha.

The family trees of royalty of a rather different kind, members of the Beatles, show a similar pattern. John Lennon was named after his paternal grandfather, John ('Jack') Lennon, who was a talented musician. John was born at the height of the Second World War, and his mother gave him the middle name Winston, in honour of the war-time British Prime Minister, Winston Churchill. Lennon's first son is also named John, though is known by a middle name, Julian, to avoid confusion with his father.

Paul McCartney has always used his middle name instead of his first name, James, to distinguish him from his father and great-grandfather, both of whom were named James. It was McCartney's mother who decided that a middle name would be a useful way to identify her new son. Using your middle name rather than your first name may not be all that uncommon. Three of the last six British monarchs did this, as did five of the last ten British prime ministers, two of whom (Macmillan and Wilson), like Paul McCartney, had the same first name as their father. Paul McCartney maintained the family tradition, naming his son James Louis McCartney. Because his famous father is known as Paul, the younger McCartney was able to use his own first name, James. Other entertainers who go by their middle name include [Allen] Kelsey Grammer, [Christopher] Ashton Kutcher, [William] Brad Pitt, and [Laura Jean] Reese Witherspoon.

Ringo Starr is Richard Starkey's stage name. He was named after his father, and because neither father nor son had a middle name, the father was given the nickname 'Big Ritchie' when Ringo was born.

Ringo too named his first son Richard, but as a middle name, and so Ringo didn't take on his father's mantle and become Big Ritchie.

George Harrison is the only Beatle not named after either his father or grandfathers. This is not to say that the Harrison family didn't use given names to link generations. George was the family's third son, and his father Harold had already given his name to George's oldest brother. George is the only Beatle who didn't continue the tradition of passing names down to the next generation. He named his only son, *Dhani* after the sixth and seventh notes of the Indian music scale, *dha* and *ni*. (I suspect that neither Harold nor George had a sufficiently Eastern ring to it for the Harrisons to pair it with Dhani.)

Generally then, all the Beatles came from families that passed names on to the next generation. And despite the Beatles' reputation in the 1960s of being part of a counter-culture, all but one of them maintained this family naming tradition.

Of course, the clearest way of linking family members of two or more generations is to give them *exactly* the same name. The full name of actor Tom Cruise is Thomas Cruise Mapother IV, as his great-grandfather, grandfather and father were also Thomas Cruise Mapother. *Junior* (*Jr.*) and *Senior* (*Sr.*) are other possible 'generational titles'. These titles are much more common in the US than the UK. Four of the twelve US presidents in office since 1945 have had a generational title: Gerald Rudolph Ford, Jr., James Earl Carter, Jr., William Jefferson Blythe III, and Barack Hussein Obama II. You may be scratching your head at 'President Blythe'. In fact, I'm cheating a bit as he's much better known as President Bill Clinton. At birth he was named after his natural father, William Jefferson Blythe, Jr., who died before Bill was born. Bill adopted his stepfather's family name, Clinton, when he was a teenager so that he would have the same last name as his much-loved younger half-brother. If he hadn't changed his name, the 42nd president of the United States would have been 'President Blythe'. (Or would William Jefferson's career have been different if he'd been called Blythe rather than Clinton?) In contrast, none of the British prime ministers since

1900 have had a generational title—though Alec Douglas-Home *gave up* his hereditary title of Lord Home in order to become prime minister and sit in the House of Commons.

In some families, given names show some sort of pattern within the same generation. One of the most high profile examples at the moment are the Kardashian sisters, Kourtney, Kimberly and Khloé (not forgetting half-sisters Kendall and Kylie). Their mother, Kris, explains how she loved the name Courtney, but wanted it to be 'really different and amazing and unique', and so changed the name to start with a K because 'I loved the letter *K*'. (Perhaps that's one reason why she married Robert Kardashian.) The Padilha family goes two better, with seven sisters all with names starting with *J*: Jocely, Jonice, Janea, Joyce, Juracy, Jussara and Judeseia. They run the *J. Sisters* salon in Manhattan, which is famous for popularising the Brazilian body wax in the United States. Not so high profile, perhaps, but still stars of their own reality TV show, are the Duggar family, which includes nineteen children (at the moment). There are ten boys and nine girls, all with names starting with the letter *J*: Joshua, Jana, John-David, Jill, Jessa, Jinger, Joseph, Josiah, Joy-Anna, Jedidiah, Jeremiah, Jason, James, Justin, Jackson, Johannah, Jennifer, Jordyn-Grace and Josie.

In fact, the Kardashians, Padilhas and Duggars are all following an ancient English naming custom. Before the Norman Conquest of England in 1066, the Anglo-Saxon population didn't use family names. In order to show family connections, parents often named their children using the same letter of the alphabet. For example, Merewalh, a ruler in seventh century Mercia in western England, had six children, three sons (Merchelm, Mildfrith, Merefin) and three daughters (Milburh, Mildred, Mildgyth). Amazingly, all three daughters became saints—a feat the Kardashian sisters are unlikely to equal.

Patterning like this helps keep a family together and sets it apart from other families. And once the pattern has been set, it becomes difficult to break as later children may feel left out if they don't fit the pattern. Clearly, Kris Jenner (formerly Kris Kardashian) thought this, explaining that she needed to 'commit to another *K* name' for her fourth daughter, Kendall. If she didn't, Kris was afraid that her new daughter 'wouldn't feel like she was a part of the rest of the family'. This was particularly important as the new daughter was a *half*-sister to Kourtney, Kimberly and Khloé, their mother having divorced and re-married.

There are other possible systems of patterning in the names of children. For example, one family named their children by going through the alphabet (Alexis, Bartholomew, Claudius Daniel, Ernest Francis, and so on to Xyzella). The Cable family used their children's given names to spell out the family name (Charles, Alan, Bruce, Lowell, Edwin). But generally, of course, most couples don't have enough children to do this sort of thing.

There's also the hidden influence of parents *avoiding* naming children after relatives. One problem with naming children after grandparents is that everyone has two grandfathers and two grandmothers—and if parents use the name of only one of them, the other can get upset at being left out. One of the best-known stories of parents avoiding family tensions like this concerns US President Harry S. Truman, whose parents came up with an ingenious way of honouring both his grandfathers. They gave young Harry the middle 'name' *S* after his paternal grandfather, Anderson Shipp Truman, *and* his maternal grandfather, Solomon Young. The initial stood for nothing, so neither grandfather would feel left out. Another traditional Scottish naming custom applied when both grandfathers had the *same* name. Rather than simply making sure that one son was given his grandfathers' name, the parents also gave a second son the same name to honour both grandparents.

Giving children the distinctive names of family members can also pose problems if the name recipient develops a hearty dislike for their namesake. A very clear example of this occurs in the recent autobiography of British comedian John Cleese—or John Marwood Cleese to give him his full name (though he wouldn't thank you for using it). His first name comes from his paternal grandfather, who he describes as having 'a kind and gentle air'. (So far, so good.) His middle name comes from his maternal grandfather, Marwood Cross, whom Cleese describes as a bully, a coward, a poison-pen letter writer, and a cheat—and this in an autobiography that is almost always generous to the people he describes. The comedian ends his description of his namesake saying: 'I'd like to apologise publicly for the fact that some of his genes are present in my body. They will be hunted down when the technology is available.' Clearly, John Cleese is *not* happy with his parents' choice of middle name. I suspect that problems like this are not uncommon—but you rarely see them expressed publicly in such unambiguous terms.

EIGHT

Moshe, Mohammad and Kobe

Ethnicity and name giving

Your ethnic group is made up of people who share the same culture as yourself, in particular your language and religion. As everyone has a culture, everyone is also part of an ethnic group. However, the term *ethnic* is most often applied to a cultural group who form a minority of the population, and especially when the cultural differences are highlighted by racial differences.

The names that members of some ethnic groups give their children may well reflect their cultural background, particularly when the political climate allows minority groups to highlight rather than hide their ethnicity. Prejudice against particular ethnic groups can vary over time. When it is very strong it can lead to group members trying to downplay their ethnicity, in part by changing their personal names to ones more like those of the majority culture. Prejudice and name changing has long been a part of Jewish history, going back 3,000 years to the time of Moses. Coming a bit closer to the present day, the chapter on stage names shows that anti-Jewish sentiment was strong in the US during the Great Depression of the late 1920s and 1930s. As a result, movie studios routinely changed the names of their Jewish actors. So, Bernard Schwartz became Tony Curtis, and Issur Danielovitch had the stage name Kirk Douglas.

However, Jewish actors today, such as Jesse Eisenberg, Jerry Seinfeld and David Krumholtz, see no need to change their names, and they represent the tip of an iceberg. More generally, there has been a marked increase in the popularity of traditional Jewish names such as Moshe, Chana and Chaya since the 1970s. As the proportion of Jews in the US has decreased during this period, the increased popularity of these names is likely to be because of their greater use by American Jews. In New York, the city with the world's largest Jewish population, official statistics show that Moshe is now in the top ten of the most popular white boys' names, and Chana and Chaya are in the girls' top ten list.

These changes have happened over a period of decades. However, changes in the use of ethnic names can also occur more quickly. Following the attacks in the US by the Islamist militant group al-Qaeda on September 11th, 2001, the wave of anti-Islam feeling in the US led to many Muslims coming into the Civil Court clerk's office in New York to adopt Anglo-American names. This anti-Muslim feeing was not confined to New York. Throughout the US after 9/11 there was a drop in the number of births registered in that most recognisable of Muslim names, Muhammad. It took nearly a decade for the popularity of the name to reach its pre-9/11 level.

Muhammad is believed by Muslims to be a prophet of God, and is generally considered to be the founder of Islam. Throughout the Muslim world, it's popular for parents to name their sons after him in the hope that they will be like him. The Prophet's name was originally written in Arabic script and so for English readers it had to be changed (or *transliterated*) into English alphabetic characters. The spelling Muhammad is one common transliteration, but there are many others. In the US, the most common variations are Mohamed, Mohammed and Mohammad. But even when all four spellings are added together, the name just makes it into the top 200 most popular names in the US.

In contrast, in Britain three spellings (Muhammad, Mohammed, Mohammad) *each* make it into the top 100 boys' names, and when these are combined with the other sixteen alternative spellings, it's the most common name for boys born recently in Britain. Its popularity is partly because two of the largest ethnic groups in the UK are from Pakistan and Bangladesh, countries where over 90 per cent of people are Muslims. Muslim parents of girls also honour their Prophet by using the name of his most beloved wife, Aisha—though again there are several alternative spellings (e.g. Aishah, Aaisha, Aaishah). However, only Aisha makes it into the British top 100 girls' names.

*

There are over forty million African Americans, who make up about one in seven of the US population. Most of their ancestors were brought from West Africa as slaves, the slave trade going on for 200 years until the mid-1800s. Almost all of the original culture of these African slaves was lost, including their personal names. Even after slavery was fully abolished in the US in 1865, for the next hundred years or so African Americans continued to be treated very much as second-class citizens, and it's only in the last few decades that the social status of African Americans has markedly improved.

This mini-history is relevant here because the changing fortunes of African Americans over time have been reflected by changes in their personal names. As slaves, they didn't have the right to name themselves. At first, slave owners gave slaves names that were simple and easy to shout. Jack, Tom, Harry, Bet, Mary and Jane were the six most common names of slaves in the eighteenth century. In fact, there was a marked overlap between the names given to slaves and to farm animals, reflecting the attitude of most slave owners that, like farm animals, slaves were regarded as property. Later, slave owners began to use classical, literary and noble names, such as Nero, Venus, Cordelia, Caesar and Duke—perhaps showing a grim sense of humour.

Freed slaves adopted names that offered more dignity, though still reflecting an English tradition. Ironic names such as Caesar were dropped by freed slaves, and shortened names such as Will and Nan were often replaced by more dignified full names such as William and Nancy. But freed slaves generally used given names that were favoured by whites, resulting in only modest naming differences between black and white Americans at the start of the twentieth century.

Although this part of the book focuses on given names, I think it's useful here to continue the story of African American names by also looking at family names. Slave owners didn't bother giving their slaves family names. Slaves were encouraged to have children as they expanded the workforce, but parents and children were often split up and sold to different owners—'negroes will be sold separately or together as desired' concludes a typical advertisement for a mother and her two young children. The only reason a slave needed a second name was when a slave owner needed to identify a slave as his own. The obvious way to do this was for a slave owner to use his own surname. For example, if the slave was called John and the slave owner's family name was Hatcher, then the name *Hatcher's John* or more simply *John Hatcher* might be used. The term *family name* clearly meant something different in the context of slavery.

However, with the abolition of slavery in the US in the 1860s, freed slaves needed a family name. Booker T. Washington (1856-1915) was a freed slave who for many years was very influential in US society. In his autobiography, he points out that 'a feeling got among the coloured people that it was far from proper for them to bear the surname of their former owners, and a great many of them took other surnames. This was one of the first signs of freedom.' He describes his first day at school when he heard the roll being called, and realised that all the other children had at least two names. But not him: 'From the time when I could remember anything, I had been called simply *Booker*. Before going to school it had never occurred to me that it was needful or appropriate to have an additional name.' Thinking on his feet, the young boy gave himself the family name of the first US president, and became Booker Washington. There were many more similar stories, resulting in Washington now being the 'blackest name' in America, with African Americans making up 90 per cent of families named Washington.

Although they make up only 13 per cent of the US population, African Americans form the majority of Americans with eight other surnames. They include two other presidential names, Jefferson (the 2nd 'blackest' name) and Jackson (5th). However, like most large US landowners born in the eighteenth century, Washington, Jefferson and Jackson were all slave owners. Washington did specify in his will that all his slaves should be freed—but only after the death of his widow. Other popular African American surnames are Booker (3rd), I assume in recognition of Booker T. Washington; and Banks (4th), perhaps after a highly successful general appointed by Lincoln during the American Civil War.

Although Abraham Lincoln was the US president when slavery was abolished, his surname is no more widespread among African Americans than the US white population. At first glance, this seems odd— surely former slaves would be keen to honour the man who was most influential in ending slavery? However, in the years immediately after the Civil War many of the plantation owners continued to be extremely powerful figures, meaning that there was a clear advantage for freed slaves to use the local landowners' family names. On the other hand, if freed slaves named themselves after Lincoln, they would very likely have antagonised many of the large plantation owners—who would have seen them as troublemakers and not employed them.

However, during the course of the twentieth century the myth developed that the majority of African American family names originated when slave owners gave their own surnames to their slaves. Groups such as the Nation of Islam (or Black Muslims) fostered this idea. They advocated setting up a separate African American nation, and one immediate way of symbolising this separateness was to get rid of the family names they associated with the slave-owning past. This was done initially by substituting the initial X for their original family name. For example, the Nation of Islam's most charismatic figure was Malcolm X, formerly Malcolm Little, who explained his change of name as follows: 'The Muslim's 'X' symbolized the true African family name that he never could know. For me, my 'X' replaced the white slavemaster name of 'Little' which some blue-eyed devil named Little had imposed upon my paternal forebears.'

Perhaps a quarter of African slaves were Muslim, and the Nation of Islam used this pre-slavery tradition to emphasise their break with the white, Christian majority in American society. Although Malcolm X is best known by that name, like many Nation of Islam members he later adopted a Muslim name, Malik El Shabazz. However, by far the best-known Nation of Islam recruit today is boxing legend Muhammad Ali. His original name was Cassius Marcellus Clay, Jr., named after a nine-teenth century politician who was a prominent anti-slavery crusader. When he joined the Nation of Islam in 1964, he was initially renamed Cassius X, and then quickly given his Muslim name, Muhammad Ali. Journalist Mike Marqusee explains the importance of this name change in the context of the politics of the time: 'This was a black man signalling by his name change, not a desire to ingratiate himself with mainstream America, but a comprehensive rejection of it.' (Muhammad Ali later left the Nation of Islam and joined an orthodox Islamic group.)

More generally, the 1960s were a time of intensified African American 'Black Power' protests, with marches, riots and an emphasis on a distinctive black culture. Personal names became part of the trend to emphasise this cultural distinctiveness. At the start of the 1960s, the given names used by black and white Americans were very similar, but then a major shift took place, especially among African Americans in racially separate neighbourhoods. By the early 1970s, African American babies living in these areas were given names that were many times more popular among black than white parents. This was particularly true of girls where, on average, each name was twenty times more popular among African American girls than white girls.

However, relatively few African Americans followed Muhammad Ali's lead by converting to Islam and adopting a Muslim name. There were a few high profile converts, such as Kareem Abdul-Jabbar, possibly the greatest basketball player of all time. He changed his name from

Hello, My Name Is...

Ferdinand Lewis Alcindor, Jr., Alcindor being the family name of an eighteenth century slave owner. Generally, only about one per cent of African Americans are Muslim, but many more African Americans have drawn on their African heritage and given Muslim names to their children. Official figures show that among African Americans in New York City, about twenty of the hundred most popular girls' names are Islamic, such as Aaliyah, Sanaa and Fatima. And ten of the hundred most popular boys' names are Islamic, such as Mohamed, Nasir and Malik. In contrast, none of these Islamic names were in the top 100 for white girls or boys.

Religion isn't the only factor explaining the marked change in African American names in the last few decades. In fact, it's not even the most influential one. More important has been the use of unique or very rare names by African Americans. For example, there were eleven African American players on the men's US basketball squad at the 2012 Olympics. They included Kobe Bryant, who may well have been the only Kobe born in the US in 1978; and LeBron James, who was one of only five babies named LeBron born in the US in 1984. The nine African American players on the women's basketball squad included three players with possibly unique given names—Seimone, Swintayla and Asjha.

One Californian study found that well over one in four African American girls born each year had a unique name. Among white girls only one in twenty had a unique name. The percentages for boys are lower, but unique names were still much more frequent among African Americans. The difference between the two racial groups is still clear when you also include names that are very rare—those shared by only five babies or less in any year. Not far off half of African American girls had unique or very rare names, compared to one in ten of white girls. Among boys, over one in four African Americans had unique or very rare names compared to just one in twenty white boys.

In some cases, the uniqueness or rarity of an African American name is because of an unusual spelling of a more common name—as with US Olympic basketball player Seimone Augustus. The number of different spellings of the same name is incredible. One baby name book lists over *seventy* different spellings of Abigail, a popular name for African American girls. Another spelling option is to add punctuation—a capital letter, accent, or apostrophe—inside a name. To continue the basketball theme, examples include LeBron, LaMarcus, MarShon, Amar'e and E'Twaun. As that indefatigable name researcher Stanley Lieberson points out, the vast majority of unique African American given names are 'because they are invented or are adaptions from existing words not initially used as first names, for example, a geographical name, a surname, or a commercial product'. An excellent example of this is the name Kobe, which is the name of a city in Japan. The story goes that Kobe Bryant's parents chose the name after seeing Kobe beef on a restaurant menu.

NINE

Benedict, Jemima and Arabella

Class and name giving

The rich and powerful have been trendsetters in all sorts of ways throughout history. Most obviously, poorer members of society have long copied the clothes of the rich. In the 1500s, this was so widespread that Queen Elizabeth I introduced laws which decreed that only peers and knights could wear purple clothes, silk scarves and long pointed shoes. Everyone else could be fined or imprisoned for wearing these clothes. These laws have long gone—too many people kept ignoring them. But the idea of passing yourself off as being richer and more important than you actually are still applies—just look at the street vendors in most big cities selling fake purses and bags labelled *Louis Vuitton* and *Gucci* (or is that 'Louise Vuiton' and 'Guci'?).

Even though you don't have to *buy* them, exactly the same idea applies to personal names. Sometimes, the taking on of the names of the rich and powerful by those lower down the pecking order is clearly a good move. Recall that after the Norman Conquest of Anglo-Saxon England in 1066, there was a dramatic change in naming habits. Within 150 years, Anglo-Saxon names like Ethelred, Godwin, Edith and Mildred had almost died out, to be replaced by Norman names. There were two very good reasons for these changes—life and liberty. Many of the more prominent Anglo-Saxons, those who had not fled or been sold into slavery overseas, attempted to show loyalty to the new king by giving Norman names to their children. And what better way to show

88

loyalty than to name their children after the new Norman king and queen, William and Matilda? However, it's difficult to extend this life and liberty argument to the landless peasants, who later also adopted Norman names. It's more likely that they were simply copying their social superiors—to become more like them in what historian David Morris calls a *trickledown* effect.

Here's another example of this trickledown naming effect. The use of middle names came from aristocratic naming customs in Italy, where given names came to be seen as a sign of prosperity—the more names, the more prosperous the name-holder. By the 1600s some Italian nobles had ten or more names; one nobleman in Rome had twenty-five. In Britain, members of the royal family were among the early adopters of middle names. For example, at the start of the seventeenth century King James VI and I had two given names, Charles James. The tradition has been maintained by the British royal family, the prize for the most given names going to Edward VIII, who had seven—Edward Albert Christian George Andrew Patrick David (his last four names include the patron saints of England, Scotland, Ireland and Wales).

Historically, the tradition of giving children a middle name grew among the rich and powerful in the US in the eighteenth and nineteenth centuries. None of the three presidents born in the first half of the eighteenth century (Washington, Adams, Jefferson) had a middle name; but by the second half of the century about a third had a middle name. This increased to about half among those born in the first half of the nineteenth century, and in the second half of the century all but one president (Theodore Roosevelt) had a middle name. *All* the US presidents born in the twentieth century have had middle names. Americans much lower down the social pecking order quickly followed their presidents' lead, so that by 1917, when American men were drafted to fight in World War I, the US Army assumed that every draftee had a middle name—and if he didn't the Army simply added a name or initial into his record.

Even the custom of using an initial for a middle name spread through all levels of US society. For example, in his autobiography, Booker T.

Washington mentions that following the abolition of slavery in the 1860s, it was not unusual for former slaves to add a middle initial 'standing for no name, it being simply a part of what the coloured man proudly called his *entitles*'. (In case you're wondering, the 'T' in Booker T. Washington stood for *Taliaferro*, the name he later discovered his mother had given him soon after he was born. It's the surname of a prominent, wealthy family in the area where he grew up, and so may give an indication of the identity of Booker T. Washington's father. However, his autobiography doesn't give any details.)

In Britain, the use of middle names took considerably more time to trickle down to working class families, but by the mid-twentieth century the practice was commonplace. You may recall that two of the four members of the Beatles had middle names (John Winston Lennon and James Paul McCartney). Thinking about the Beatles led me to wonder how common middle names were among some of their contemporaries. I looked at the original names of members of another half dozen of the biggest British groups from the 1960s. Three quarters had at least one middle name, including Sir Michael Philip Jagger (better known as Mick Jagger of the Rolling Stones) and Peter Dennis Blandford Townshend (Pete Townshend of The Who). Looking at British bands formed in the 1990s and later, virtually all band members have middle names, such as Chris [Anthony John] Martin of Coldplay and Harry [Edward] Styles of One Direction. Admittedly, it's a completely unscientific survey, but the results do give an indication of the increasingly widespread use of middle names for mainly working class boys born in Britain from the 1940s onwards.

Another American naming custom is to add the title 'Junior', 'II' or 'III' after a son's name if it is exactly the same as his father's or grandfather's. Rich US families who wanted to highlight the continuity of their owner-ship of land or business started using generational titles in the nineteenth century. However, it wasn't long before families lower down the social pecking order began to copy the practice, first the professional class, then the white working class, and finally the black population. This, in turn, led to generational titles becoming less popular among the elite, so that today they are rarely seen. This decline among the elite has been mirrored by a similar decline in the population generally.

Another historical example of how social status has influenced name giving concerns godparents. For several centuries godparents were responsible for giving names—their own names usually—at baptisms. For much of its history, English society was divided into several distinct bands: royalty at the top, then peers, gentry, yeomen, artisans, husbandmen and, at the bottom, labourers. There were also divisions within each social group. One way to improve a family's social standing was to have someone of a higher social standing act as a godparent. The father of the future Queen Victoria was the fourth son of the king, but Victoria's godparents were even higher up the social ladder. They were the future King George IV and the Russian Emperor Alexander I. Similarly, many members of the peerage were named after the reigning monarch, who acted as a godparent. The same handing down of names from one social level to the next went on at all levels of society. British historian Will Coster describes how 'names could move down through the social structure, until they reached a point at which they would have ceased to be reused... New names were most likely to enter towards the top of society, working their way down, and occasionally being dropped.'

A final historical example of how the rich and powerful have influenced name giving concerns the use of family names as given names. This practice began around the time of Shakespeare in the sixteenth century, often in an attempt by a member of the British peerage to persuade a rich relative to remember the child in a will. It wasn't long before using family names as given names was taken up more widely. In fact, during Shakespeare's lifetime William Camden lamented that 'Surnames of honourable and worshipfull families are given now to mean mens children for Christian names'. (It was originally published in 1605, when spelling and punctuation were more flexible than today.)

Presumably, the hope of these 'mean men' (yeomen, artisans and labourers) was that if, for example, they called their son Percy he would gain prestige from having the same name as the Percy family, who had been Earls of Northumberland for hundreds of years. I suspect that the several hundred American parents who recently named their son Beckham were hoping that he would have some of the glamour of soccer player David Beckham (or is that baseball player Gordon Beckham?). What's clear is that the prestige status of the Beckham family name, like the Percy family name before it, will be lost in the not-too-distant future, and Beckham will become simply another given name.

There is a widely held view that name giving today is strongly influenced by celebrities. This is certainly true to some degree, and is most obvious when a name is initially unique to a celebrity. Kobe Bryant may well have been the only boy named Kobe born in the US in 1978. However, in 1997, his first year in the NBA, Bryant won a high-profile basketball competition—and the name Kobe shot into the US top 1000 list of names. It has remained there ever since.

Fluctuations in the popularity of the name over time gives further evidence that the name's popularity is based on Kobe Bryant. The dip in popularity coincides with his arrest for rape in 2003. The case never went to trial, and a later civil case was settled out of court, but Bryant's reputation was badly tarnished. At best he was seen as an adulterer, and at worst as a rapist. His endorsement contracts were cancelled and sales of Bryant merchandise plummeted. It's reasonable to suppose that many parents who might otherwise have named their sons Kobe now chose another name. His reputation has since recovered to some degree, with Bryant being named 'NBA Player of the Decade' in 2009. But the popularity of the name hasn't returned to its earlier high level. As he's now retired after a less-than-stellar final season, it's likely that the recent decline in popularity of the name Kobe will continue.

British actress Keira Knightley also illustrates the importance of celebrities on name giving. You may recall that her given name was misspelled when her mother registered her birth. The more standard spelling is *Kiera*, which is a feminine form of Kieran. In 2001, Kiera was three times more popular than Keira in Britain, though despite the popularity of Celtic names at the time even Kiera wasn't in the top 100 list. Ms Knightley's film career took off in 2002 with *Bend It Like Beckham,* and the next five years saw her appearing in several major movies, including three in the *Pirates of the Caribbean* series, *Love Actually, Pride and Prejudice* and *Atonement*. It's very likely that she was the inspiration for the rapid rise in popularity of 'Keira'. It rocketed into the British top 100 names in 2004, rapidly overtaking the more established spelling. By 2007, at the height of its popularity (and, perhaps, Knightley's) there were three times as many babies named Keira than Kiera. More recently, Knightley's film output has gone down—and so has the popularity of her given name, which left the top 100 in 2013.

However, it's easy to overplay the role of celebrities in name giving. For example, one of the most popular names in Britain recently is Harry. The British press linked the result to the growing influence of Prince Harry. The difficulty is that there's often a well-known figure that can be linked to a popular name. The Harry Potter books were published between 1997 and 2007, and may have influenced some parents. Most recently, Harry Styles from the boy band One Direction could also have had an impact. But, more likely, a name has a certain trajectory over time—in Harry's case, ever upwards in Britain for the last decade, from being the eleventh most popular boys' name in 2002, to fifth in 2006 and then the most popular name in 2011. The fact that there are celebrities with the same name at the same time may be largely coincidental.

There is some evidence to suggest that this is the case. If the higher media profile of Prince Harry led to the popularity of his name, surely there would be similar results for his high-profile peers. One of the big events of 2011 in Britain was the marriage of Prince Harry's older brother, Prince William, to Kate Middleton. You would expect that the names William and Kate would have become more popular in their wedding year. But in fact the opposite occurred. The name William dropped three places to tenth, and the name Kate fell 57 places to a lowly 267th. Similarly, following Kate Middleton giving birth to Prince George in mid-2013, one headline trumpeted: 'George makes a comeback as parents copy Wills and Kate'. Its popularity did increase from 10th in the year the Prince was born to 7th the following year—but a more meaningful measure is that only 118 more babies were named George in 2014 compared to 2013.

Here's a US example. In the US, the popularity of the name Jacob has been associated with Jacob Black, a character from the *Twilight* series of books and movies, which began in 2005. However, Jacob was already the most popular boy's name in the US when the first book appeared, and had been for several years before that. It's been in the top 20 names since 1990. Thus, it's just as likely that *Twilight* author Stephenie Meyer chose the name Jacob for one of her main characters because it was already the most popular boys' name at the time she was writing; and as Jacob had been in the top 20 names since 1990, it would be the name of many of her young adult readers.

Harvard sociologist Stanley Lieberson has done detailed historical research on the influence of celebrities on given names. Looking at movie stars, he concludes that 'The vast majority of prominent star names scarcely affect naming practices'. In fact, in the mid twentieth century, when movie actors routinely used stage names, the trend was often for actors to 'ride the curve' and adopt a name that was already popular— Marilyn Monroe (originally Norma Jeane Mortenson) is a good example. When a movie actor has an uncommon name, there's usually only a 'minor subsequent increase' in the name's popularity. Claudette, Greta, Lana, Ingrid, Raquel, Bing, Charlton, Elvis, Humphrey and Rock never became really popular despite the fact that they were the given names of major stars such as Greta Garbo and Rock Hudson. Of all the stars Stanley Lieberson studied, only three clearly generated increases in the popularity of their given names—Jennifer Jones, Marlene Dietrich and Gary Cooper.

Certainly, Stanley Lieberson would not be surprised to learn that while Kobe Bryant is a modern-day Gary Cooper, another basketball super-star, LeBron James, has had minimal impact on name giving. James has won numerous honours since his rookie year in 2004, including several Most Valuable Player awards. Despite this, less than a hundred couples each year in the US have named their child LeBron, and the name has never appeared in the top 1000 names. It might be argued that many white parents might not want to give their child an African American name like LeBron, but equally you could turn this around and argue that LeBron should have become a popular name among the thirteen per cent of parents who are African American. But it didn't.

Here are a couple of very different examples that also suggest name giving is only marginally influenced by what's going on in the world at the time. Neil Armstrong enjoyed huge celebrity status when millions of people watched him making history as the first man to walk on the moon, in July 1969. Even now, many people can recall his famous first words, 'That's one small step for [a] man, one giant leap for mankind'. Streets, schools and other public buildings were named after him; there was even a song recorded as a tribute to him. And yet ... In terms of name giving, the first man on the moon had minimal impact on the popularity of the name Neil in the land of his birth; for fifty years it enjoyed moderate popularity, though never breaking into the top hundred names. However, since the 1980s it has gone into steep, possibly terminal, decline. The details are slightly different in Britain, but the impact of astronaut Neil Armstrong seems just as small. The name entered the British top 100 names in the 1930s, and climbed as high as 22nd in 1964. However, the 1969 moon landing didn't boost its popularity further, as it was still ranked 22nd in 1974, after which it nose-dived to outside the top 200 in 1996, and it's been downhill ever since.

A very different example is the name *Adolph*, which with a slightly different spelling was the given name of Adolf Hitler, the Nazi leader whose actions resulted in the horrors of World War II. Despite Hitler being the most infamous figure of the twentieth century, the popularity of the name Adolph in the US was only briefly affected by its link to Hitler. The name was in a steady decline in the 1920s and 1930s. It declined more rapidly in the war years, but then actually increased slightly in popularity after the war, before resuming its previous steady decline, and eventually dropping out of the top 1000 in the 1970s. Hitler's impact on the name Adolph was little different from Armstrong's impact on the name Neil. Both names had a certain trajectory, which the in/famous holders of the names changed only briefly.

So, the evidence seems to suggest that often celebrities have only a minor impact on name giving. Much more influential are families living nearby in more affluent neighbourhoods where the houses and cars are bigger and better. For many people, these are things that show success in life, and the names these parents give their children reflect that success. Many poorer parents believe that they can give their children a better chance of success in life by giving them names that are popular in the richer suburbs. One Californian study by Steven Levitt and Stephen Dubner shows that there is a clear pattern of name giving. Once a name catches on among high-income, highly educated parents, it starts working its way down the socioeconomic ladder. However, 'as a high-end name is adopted en masse, high-end parents begin to abandon it. Eventually, it is considered so common that even lower-end parents may not want it, whereby it falls out of the rotation entirely'. (Just as happened in Britain several centuries ago.)

The authors of this 2005 Californian study were so sure that their explanation is true that they predicted that some of the names given by high status parents at the time of their research 'are bound to become tomorrow's mainstream names'. Their predictions were remarkably accurate. Altogether, two dozen of their high status names increased in popularity compared to only a handful that decreased. The most successful predictions were Liam, which since the book's publication shot up in popularity nationally from 131st to 2nd, and Ava, which went from 132nd to 5th.

Let me end with a couple of predictions of my own, one about name giving in Britain, the other about the US. In Britain, the births of children of the most influential people are traditionally announced in *The Times* newspaper. There are differences between *The Times* lists and the national lists of popular boys' and girls' names. For example, recently there were two boys' names and three girls' names in *The Times*' top twenty that didn't make it into the top 150 British list. The boys' names were Wilfred and Benedict; and the girls' names were Arabella, Elodie and Jemima. If there is a social trickle-down effect in name giving, then these names are likely to be become more popular in Britain in the next few years.

Here's a final prediction based on the idea that high status parents are name giving trendsetters. A recent US study found that high status parents were more likely to call their children by both their first *and* middle names, even when the two were not hyphenated. Examples include Abby Grace, Lauren Taylor, James Robert, and John Walker. If history repeats itself, then this is likely to become generally popular in the next several years in the US. We'll have to wait and see how accurate this prediction will be, though history is on my side. In early eighteenth century England, the daughters of high status parents had double names—but they fell out of fashion after becoming stereotyped as names of serving-girls.

TEN

Ayden, Jayden and Zayden

Fashion and name giving

The final chapter in this part of *'Hello, My Name Is ...'* focuses on something that's important but a bit fuzzy. For want of a better term, I'll call it *fashion*. Of course, the term is most closely associated with clothes, but there are fashions in everything to do with culture, alphabetically from architecture to zoos, and that includes name giving. Basically, most of the chapter looks at how name giving has become much more fluid, with certain names enjoying popularity for a limited time.

It hasn't always been like this. In thirteenth century England over half of all men were named Henry, John, Richard, Robert or William. By the fourteenth century nearly *two thirds* of all men had one of these five names. This tendency for name-givers to select from a very small stock of names continued for several more centuries. Even in the late 1700s, the names William, John and Thomas accounted for over half of all male baptisms; and Elizabeth, Mary and Anne accounted for over half of all female baptisms. However, from the nineteenth century onwards, there was a consistent decline in the importance of the most popular names.

Most recently in Britain, the top three boys' names (Oliver, Jack, Harry) were given to only five per cent of boys; and the top three girls' names (Amelia, Olivia, Isla) were given to only four per cent of girls. In the US, the trend away from the most popular names has been even more marked, with less than three per cent of boys given the top three names

(Noah, Liam, Mason), and just over three per cent of girls given the top three names (Emma, Olivia, Sophia). Despite the most popular names no longer being all that popular, the majority of parents who gave these most popular names to their children later wished they had chosen a less popular name.

So, for several hundred years until the 1800s, name giving was relatively fixed, the custom being to name children after godparents and parents. After this time, name giving became much more fluid, with certain names enjoying popularity for only a limited time. How can we explain this change in name giving, from fixed to fluid—or from custom to fashion? That indefatigable Harvard sociologist Stanley Lieberson believes that the answer lies in the Industrial Revolution, which got underway in Britain at the end of the eighteenth century. It brought about a massive increase in the proportion of the population living in towns and cities as people in the countryside flocked to them for work. This in turn had a major impact on virtually all aspects of life, including name giving.

First, the Industrial Revolution weakened the traditional influence of the extended family as contact between family members declined. Previously, most people worked alongside each other on the family farm each day, but when the younger generations moved to the cities for work this close contact became a thing of the past. Traditionally, the younger generation learnt their work skills and general outlook on life from the older genera-tions, who as a result were given a place of honour in family life. This was symbolised by the names of the older family members being given to the youngest generation at baptism. The new social order brought about by industrialisation led to a change in the way younger people saw the older generations, whose rural work skills and traditions were no longer relevant to their city-based offspring. Consequently, the position of honour traditionally held by older people declined, and the given names associated with the elderly became less attractive to new parents.

Secondly, the migration of villagers to large towns and cities during the Industrial Revolution weakened the traditional influence of the wider village community, in particular that of the church and parish priest.

Previously, the parish church was not only the place where each child was baptised, but also where the birth was recorded in the parish register. However, this traditional system couldn't cope with the population upheavals brought about by industrialisation. As a result, a system of civil registration of births was begun in Britain in the 1830s, which led to a weakening of the influence of the church on name giving.

Thirdly, the growth of towns and cities during the Industrial Revolution speeded up the development of education. This was important because as more and more people began reading newspapers and books, they came across a wider variety of names than there were among people they knew personally. For example, Charles Dickens, one of the most widely read nineteenth century novelists, created nearly a thousand named characters. As a result, new parents became familiar with many more possible names to give their children.

Chapter 4 points out that one of the first fashions to emerge in the nineteenth century was to use the names of flowers, trees and so on as given names for girls. This was a fashion that Charles Dickens probably helped foster as his novels include characters named Daisy, Flora, Rose and Rosa. In fact, the use of flowers as girls' names, Rose and Lily in particular, goes back several centuries, though it was only at the end of the nineteenth century that botanical names started to become very fashionable. Names included Daffodil, Daisy, Fern, Flora, Gloxinia, Hazel, Heather, Hyacinth, Iris, Ivy, Jasmine, Lavender, Lily, Marigold, May, Myrtle, Olive, Pansy, Poppy, Primrose, Rosa, Rose, Viola and Violet.

As with all fashions, the very popularity of botanical names also sowed the seeds of their downfall. Names like Lily and Hazel became old-fashioned, and new parents dropped them in favour of more fashionable names. The popularity of three botanical names, Daisy, Lily and Hazel, went steadily down in the US during the twentieth century, Lily and Hazel dropping out of the top 1000 names for several years.

However, in the last few decades the popularity of several botanical names has soared again. In the US, Lily is now in the top thirty names, and when you add the alternative spellings (e.g. Lilly, Lillie) it's a top twenty name. This resurgence in popularity has been even stronger in Britain, where Poppy, Lily and Daisy are all top thirty names. If you add all the alternative spellings of Lily, it's the second most popular girls' name in Britain. This is partly because the stigma of being 'old fashioned' lessened with the deaths of the older generations of women named Lily, Hazel and so on. In time, these botanical names were re-discovered by a new generation of parents for whom the names were again fresh, modern and fashionable.

Another fashion in name giving that has developed in the last few decades is for parents to give their children names that are unique or very rare. You may recall that this trend can be traced back to the 1960s when many African American parents began giving their children names that emphasised their cultural distinctiveness. Since then, the practice has become widespread. It's easy to give examples of unique or rare names as showbusiness celebrities often seem to use them. My favourite goes back to the 1960s when rock musician Frank Zappa and his wife Gail named their four children *Moon Unit, Dweezil, Ahmet Emuukha Rodan* and *Diva Thin Muffin Pigeen*.

It's more difficult to get hard data to back up the claim that giving unique or rare names is the current fashion. This is because the government authorities that collect birth data don't publicly release information that can identify individuals—and by definition a unique name identifies an individual. The US Social Security Administration releases information on names given to at least five boys or girls during the year; and the British Office for National Statistics publishes names given to at least three boys or girls.

Even though there aren't lists of rare names, it's possible to work out how significant they are. Currently in Britain, published figures show that there are 120 names that have been given to thousands of babies (e.g. Amelia, Archie), 700 names that have given to hundreds of babies (e.g. Amy, Andrew), 4000 names that have given to dozens of babies (e.g. Amanda, Anton), and nearly 9,000 names that have been given to a handful of babies (e.g. Augusta, Aziz). So, a total of nearly 14,000 names have been given to at least three children. But in total, British parents registered about 63,000 different names, meaning that nearly 50,000 names have been given to only two children or a single child—approximately four out of every five names.

Another thing we can do is look at the other side of the coin—at the most popular names. For much of the twentieth century, nine in every ten babies in the US were given one of the top 1000 names. But that proportion began falling in the 1960s for girls, and a bit later for boys. Most recently, only two-thirds of girls and four-fifths of boys have names from the top 1000 list. It's likely that as the number of babies with very popular names gets smaller, the number of babies with very rare names gets larger.

Another approach is to drill down deeper into the published US statistics—to *all* the names registered to five or more boys or girls in any one year. What's crystal clear is that parents are using a lot more given names than before. The number of all published given names in the US almost *tripled* over the last half century. Today, about 20,000 different names are registered for girls, and around 15,000 names for boys (parents are more adventurous with their daughters' names). My first thought was that this whopping increase in the number of names had something to do with an increase in the number of births. But, in fact, the number of births in the US in the early 1960s was about the same as half a century later.

How can we explain this fashion for unique and rare names? We know that African American parents in the 1960s and 1970s used them to emphasise their cultural distinctiveness from mainstream white America, but clearly this won't do as a more general explanation. One possible answer has to do with the development of a consumer culture over the last half-century that has led to an ever-increasing choice of goods and services. The message from advertisers is that we choose what sort of person we want to be by careful selection of what's on offer. Social scientists call this *individualization*. One aspect of individualization is our personal name.

Some people become self-namers, changing their name by deed poll often because they want to 're-invent' themselves. But these are just a small minority. In contrast, *all* parents can 'individualize' each of their children by giving a name that makes them stand out in a crowd. You don't do this by choosing a name already taken by many other parents. Ideally, you need something new—a trend that inevitably means an ever-increasing number of given names. I'm sure it's no coincidence that this increase in the number of given names matches the increase in the number of registered names for biscuits, breakfast cereals and so on.

This process of individualization has been bolstered by the fact that these days most parents-to-be have access to a huge amount of information about names. For example, my search on Amazon.com for 'baby name books' resulted in nearly 30,000 hits. The Web also has many sites selling products and distributing information, including baby names, to prospective parents. Government authorities have also obliged by making available online the wealth of information on names held on birth and other registries. Most importantly, in 1997 the US Social Security Administration opened up its huge database of names that includes virtually all US citizens, and goes back over one hundred years. So, at one time parents might have hit on what they thought was a unique name, calling their daughter *Unique* because they personally knew no one else with that name. Today, the US government database tells them that, nationwide, hundreds of other parents have had the same idea—resulting in the registration of similar but rarer names such as Amunique, Eunique, Imunique, Omunique, Uniqua, Younique and Yunique. And these are just the published alternatives in one year.

The final example of the influence of fashion on name giving is about how the preferred sounds of names change over time, both in the short-term and long-term. A team of researchers made a surprising discovery about the unpredictability of short-term fashions in names. Hurricanes have long been identified by personal names, with various meteorological institutions drawing up lists of names for the next several years. Katrina, Sandy and Ike were the most destructive hurricanes in US history. Of course, the more destructive a hurricane, the more its name appeared in the news media; and the greater the number of times a hurricane was mentioned on TV, newspapers and so on, the greater the number of babies born at the time who were given the name. For example, following Hurricane Katrina, the name Katrina and other names that began with a hard *K* sound such as Katie and Carl showed almost a ten per cent increase in popularity. Clearly, short-term fashions like this are generally unpredictable.

Of more importance are the longer-term fashions about the preferred sounds of names. The chapter on gender and name giving points out that these days there are big differences in the final sounds of boys' and girls' names. Girls' names that end with an *a*-sound were popular back in the 1930s, but have become even more so recently, with around two fifths of the top hundred girls' names ending with *a*. The trend is even more pronounced when you look at the top ten names, with Emma, Olivia, Sophia, Isabella, Ava and Mia holding the top six spots today in the US. The popularity is as strong in Britain, with seven of the top ten names today ending with an *a*-sound, including Amelia in top spot and Olivia next. In contrast, boys' names tend not to end with an *a*-sound. In fact, there are only six names ending with an *a*-sound in the US top hundred list, all of them Old Testament names such as Noah and Elijah.

Another major group of girls' names are those ending with an *e*-sound. Again, they were popular in the 1930s, including the top three names, Mary, Betty and Dorothy. They have become even more so recently, with nearly one third of the top hundred girls' names ending with an *e*-sound. However, they are less dominant among the most popular names, with only one, Emily, in the top ten. A similar pattern occurs in Britain with 29 names ending with an *e*-sound in the top 100; three of these (Emily, Poppy, Sophie) are in the top ten. Among boys in the US, there has been a marked decline in names ending with an *e*-sound. This is because of the decline in popularity of the short or pet forms of many traditional names. In the 1930s and 1970s, the majority of the boys' names ending with an *e*-sound were pet names like Billy, Bobby and Larry. Today, none of these short forms made the top hundred; in fact the most popular pet name, Charlie, just makes it into the top 250. Surprisingly, things are very different in Britain where there are a dozen pet names in the top hundred, including Harry and Charlie in the top ten.

A third group of names are those ending with an *n*-sound. In the 1930s, these names were the dominant group for US girls, with nearly one third of the top hundred ending with an *n*-sound including two (Joan, Helen) in the top ten. The decline in these names is in part the result of the decline of several traditional names, including Joan, Helen, Jean and Anne. In fact, only three of the 1930s list, Evelyn, Lillian and Katherine, make it into today's top hundred. If it weren't for the take up of family names and place names such as Madison, Addison and Brooklyn, the names ending with an *n*-sound would have been left almost entirely to the boys. The popularity of these boys' names has doubled since the 1970s, with forty of the hundred most popular boys' names now ending with an *n*-sound, nearly half of which were originally family names like Mason, Logan and Jackson. More traditional *n*-ending names that are in the top hundred today include the Biblical names Benjamin, John and Nathan.

So, even though they're not necessarily aware it's happening, parents choose names partly on what *sounds* fashionable. But every fashion comes to an end as it begins to be seen as overused. Stanley Lieberson suggests that the limit to the popularity of a sound is about forty per cent of leading names—which just happens to be the percentage of names ending with an *n*-sound currently being given to boys. One newspaper article I read recently had the heading 'Aydin, Jaden and Zayden: newborn names all sound the same'. The author, Laura Wattenberg, ends by saying that 'In our rush to bless our children with uniqueness, we've created a generation that sounds more alike than ever'. Articles like this are likely to sound the death knell for this fashion. In fact, I'm willing to make two predictions. The first is that the current fashion for ending boys' names with an *n*-sound will be replaced by a new fashion in the not-too-distant future. The second prediction (which I'm not as sure about) is that the fashion for girls' names ending with an *a*-sound will become less popular in the next few years, perhaps losing out to more names ending with an *e*-sound. We'll have to wait and see.

PART THREE...

The story of family names

ELEVEN

Tom the Goatherd, and Dick son of Harry

Before inherited family names

For most of the several centuries of Anglo-Saxon rule, England didn't exist as a single country. Instead, it was divided into separate earldoms, such as Wessex and Mercia. The best-known Anglo-Saxon ruler is Alfred the Great—the king who burnt the cakes. He declared himself 'King of the Anglo Saxons' in the late ninth century, but it was his much less well-known grandson, Ethelstan, who united all of England in the mid-tenth century. Vikings from Denmark also regularly invaded England, and in the half-century before the Norman Conquest in 1066, it was not unusual for the king of Denmark also to be the king of England. (Alfred was in hiding from the all-conquering Vikings when he burnt the cakes.) One reason why the Anglo-Saxons were defeated by a Norman army in the south of England in October 1066 was that in September 1066 they had fought and won a major battle against a Danish army in the north of England. So, before 1066 naming customs in England were a mixture of those from Anglo-Saxon and Danish cultures. After 1066, Norman naming customs were added to the mix.

In Anglo-Saxon times, a family relationship was shown through given names. One option was to use part of each parent's name for a child. For example, Wulfstan, Bishop of Worcester, took the first part of his name from his mother, Wulfgifu, and the second from his father, Ethelstan. Another Anglo-Saxon naming custom was to give children names that started with the same letter of the alphabet as one of their parents. An

Old English version of the name Alfred is *Elfred* (it means 'elf counsel'). His son Edward then became king, followed by Edward's sons, Ethelstan, Edmund and Eadred. Edmund's sons, Eadwig and Edgar then became king, followed by Edgar's sons, Edward and Ethelred. Finally, Ethelred's sons, Edmund and Edward, became king. The alphabetical thread in the line of succession is hard to miss.

Often, a nickname was added next to a king's name to identify him more precisely. This nickname is usually called a *by-name*—a term I'll use from now on. I particularly like Ethelstan *the Glorious,* and Edmund *the Magnificent.* Edmund the Magnificent's great-grandson, also called Edmund, was given the by-name *Ironside* because of his courage in resisting the Danes. The name that always intrigued me as a schoolboy was Ethelred *the Unready.* I was disappointed to learn that it was all a mistake, and that 'Unready' is simply a mistranslation of an Old English word meaning 'badly advised'. One of Ethelred's sons was Edward *the Confessor,* his by-name indicating that he had lived a holy life—in fact, he's the only English king to be made a saint. Identifying women with a by-name was even more important as the number of female names was smaller. For example, the wife of Edward the Confessor was Edith of Wessex. And Edward's successor, Harold Godwinson had both a wife and a mistress named Edith—Edith of Mercia, and Edith the Fair. (It made life easier for him, I suppose.)

Although some kings of England before 1066 used by-names, others used the *patronymic* naming system. You might recall that it involves adding a father's given name as part of the name of each of his children. It was the naming system traditionally used by the Danish invaders. The son of Harald Gormsson was Sweyn Haraldsson; and Sweyn's son was Canute Sweynsson. England's last Anglo-Saxon king, Harold, also had a patronymic, being named Harold Godwinson after his father Godwin, who lived for a time in Denmark and had a Danish wife. Incidentally, Harald Gormsson is better known by his by-name, Harald *Bluetooth.* Today's Bluetooth technology is named after him—though it's not clear why Harald had this by-name.

These are the names of kings, but it's always tricky extending comments about kings to the rest of the population. Some by-names may have been coined by historians years after the king's death—this certainly seems to be the case with Ethelred the Unready. However, it's likely that both by-names and patronymics were used by at least some members of the English elite in the period before the Norman Conquest. Of course, neither by-names nor patronymics were family names in the sense of linking several generations of one family. You can't tell from their names that Harald Gormsson is the grandfather of Canute Sweynsson; or that Ethelred the Unready is the father of Edward the Confessor, but they show that the custom of adding another name to a given name had already begun in England before the Norman Conquest.

We know the names of only a few of the nobles who accompanied William across the English Channel from Normandy to Hastings. In fact, historians have identified only about two dozen nobles as definitely part of the invading army. They are sometimes called the 'Companions of the Conqueror'. Three companions had only a given name, such as Vitalis. Two had a given name followed by a family name, such as Walter Giffard. All the rest had a given name followed by a by-name: some described the companion's father, such as Roger, son of Turold; others described his place of residence, such as Hugh de Montfort ('Hugh of Montfort'); and the rest described his social position, such as Odo, Bishop of Bayeux.

It seems reasonable to assume that the names of the Companions of the Conqueror were not too different from the rest of the new Norman rulers in England. As by-names were already in use at the highest social level in England before 1066, you'd expect those remaining Anglo-Saxon nobles not killed, imprisoned, or sold into slavery, would quickly adopt by-names like their Norman masters. You might then expect a trickle-down effect as the poorer sections of the English population copied the naming customs of the rich.

Fortunately, we can check these expectations against official documents of the time. In 1086, William sent out officials to record exactly who owned what in his new kingdom, so that he could tax them. Their records were collected in what was dubbed the *Domesday Book*. This is an old English spelling of Doomsday, the Day of Judgement in the Bible because, like the Day of Judgement, entry into the Domesday Book couldn't be avoided. Altogether, fifteen per cent of tenants are recorded by more than just a given name. But, as expected, the percentage increases as you go up the social ladder. Forty per cent of middle-ranking under-tenants had a second name, and at the highest social level seventy per cent of the mainly Norman tenants-in-chief had more than just a given name. Half a century later, another official list showed that 95 per cent of people who paid taxes to the king had a given name followed by a second name—a remarkable change compared to only fifteen per cent less than fifty years earlier. Clearly, second names had become the norm by the mid-twelfth century among those rich enough to pay tax, but what about the names of poorer people?

One study of the village of Warboys in East Anglia found that near the end of the 1100s almost no villager had a second name but, just half a century later, in 1251, the custom of using only given names had almost died out, with only a handful of villagers listed simply as Beatrix, Lucas and so on. About one-third had what were clearly by-names, such as 'Thomas, son of Henry' and 'Richard the Goatherd'. The rest had what we would now see as standard names, such as Simon Bonde and Matilda Pyntel—though it's more likely that at this time they were non-inherited by-names rather than inherited surnames. Similar changes in naming customs took place at all levels of society but, as often happened, poorer people later copied the rich. These East Anglian villagers were about a century behind the nobles in terms of adopting second names.

It's difficult for us today to fully appreciate the significance of the introduction of by-names in the period after the Norman Conquest. This is because we're so used to thinking of a personal name as having at least two parts. It seems 'natural' to us to add another name to a given name but, of course, that's just because we've been brought up thinking this way. To appreciate just how big a step it would have been to add a by-name, we need to think of a possible major change to our current naming practices. Perhaps a few high-profile newly married couples might decide to replace both their pre-marriage surnames with a completely new one. This would be entirely voluntary, just as adding a by-name was voluntary. I would expect that there would be little chance of this becoming the norm, and being done by everyone within a few generations. So, how can the spread of by-names within a few generations be explained? In truth, explanations are largely speculation as no written accounts have survived from the period. However, the following seem important.

In terms of social status, a major factor was likely to have been the need for landholders to be clearly identified with their land so that if there were any legal disputes about ownership, the family could link their land with their name. In the unsettled period following the Norman Conquest, the followers of King William who had been granted English land were anxious to make sure that their families hung onto it. This comes through clearly in the Domesday Book, which shows that many Normans holding land in England had adopted by-names based on their new estates. For example, Robert *de Stafford* was a major landowner in Staffordshire, and Robert *de Hastings* owned land at Hastings in Sussex. As government administration became more document-based rather than relying on word-of-mouth, it became clear to all landowners that they needed to link the family name and family land on these documents.

As well as social status, two other factors influenced the speed at which people adopted by-names. The first was settlement size. People in big towns added by-names before those in small towns; and people in small towns changed before those in the countryside. The most obvious explanation is that each Tom, Dick and Harry wanted to distinguish himself from every other Tom, Dick and Harry. The larger the town, the greater the chance the inhabitants would be involved with the legal, financial and other aspects of government. As a result, it became increasingly important for both individuals and government officials that everyone be clearly identified. This is well illustrated by what Cecil Ewen calls the 'grave confusion' that often came from the duplication of names, 'resulting in miscarriage of justice'. For many years, when someone was declared an outlaw, everyone with the same name in the county was 'liable to lose liberty and goods, and to suffer not only the discomforts and dangers to health which abounded in medieval gaols, but a very real likelihood of being overtaken by death before the mistake was discovered and rectified'. Clearly, this was a big incentive for people to avoid having their names confused with anyone else's!

As well as social status and settlement size, a third factor influencing the spread of by-names was distance from London. People in London and southern England adopted by-names before those in northern England. The Scots and Welsh were the last to change. To explain this, you need to bear in mind that the Norman success at the Battle of Hastings did not mean that they then controlled all of England. Generally, the further from London, the less control King William had. In fact, one of the most horrific acts of English history was the *harrying of the North*, when in the winter of 1069-70 William decided to crush the rebellious northern region. His troops laid waste to large tracts of the north of England, burning crops, slaughtering herds, destroying tools, and salting the soil to make it useless for farming. Whole villages were razed to the ground, and over 100,000 people were either killed by Norman troops, or died later of hunger. A measure of the destruction is that 16 years later, at the time of the Domesday Book, much of the north of England was still described as 'wasted'. It's not surprising then that the non-Norman populations in the far-flung parts of England and across the borders of Wales and Scotland were reluctant to take up Norman customs.

Early examples of by-names, such as those held by many of the Companions of the Conqueror, are clearly single-generation names, such as William, son of Richard. At the other end of the social spectrum is Richard the Goatherd, one of the peasants from the village of Warboys. However, everyday speech often resulted in by-names being shortened to forms that are much more like today's surnames. For example, William, son of Richard may have been shortened to William Richardson, and Richard the Goatherd may have become Richard Goates. So, many of the Warboys villagers' names, such as Simon Bonde and Matilda Pyntel, could have been either by-names or recently created surnames, and the only way to distinguish between them would be to have a list of several generations from the same family to see whether the name was inherited.

Unfortunately, only the rich appear on most early documents, as they were the ones of most interest to the king's tax collectors.

Genealogists, who are interested in family history, have a particular dislike of by-names as they can lead them completely up the wrong path. For example, recall that many landowners in the Domesday Book were named after their English estates. But the estate name went with estate ownership, and so if, say, Robert de Stafford sold his estate to someone from a different family, then the new owner (let's call him Thomas) would be named Thomas *de Stafford,* even though he had no family connection with the former owner. In addition, Robert de Stafford would have to change his by-name to reflect the fact that he no longer owned the Stafford estate.

The need to highlight land ownership also resulted in all but the eldest son and heir of an estate taking on different by-names. For example, after the Norman Conquest, one Cheshire landholder had several sons, grandsons and great-grandsons who used a dozen different by-names. They included *de Malpasse, Egerton, de Cotgrave* and *de Overton,* all of which are references to where they lived; *le Clerke,* referring to a son's literary abilities; *Little* and *Gogh,* references to the one grandson's stature and another's red hair; and *Goodman* and *Richardson,* referring to one great-grandson's personal qualities and another great-grandson's father's name.

As well as by-names varying between generations, the *same* person could be known by different names by different people, as the following example from the thirteenth-century illustrates. Oliver owned land in two places, at Stilton and at Opton. In Stilton, he was known as *Oliver de Stilton*; in Opton he was known (not surprisingly) as *Oliver de Opton.* In addition, he was known generally for his scholarly abilities— a distinguishing feature at a time when only clerics (i.e. clergymen) could read and write. As a result, he was also known as *Oliver Clericus.* So the same man was recorded by three by-names (de Stilton, de Opton and Clericus) in five documents in less than a decade.

Having a number of by-names was probably most common among poorer people in the centuries after the Norman Conquest. Imagine a redheaded young man called Tom who lived by the bridge in the village of Norton. A blacksmith like his father, Dick, he was one of several Toms in the neighbourhood, and to identify him more clearly he was known by a variety of by-names: 'Tom by the Bridge' by people who knew the layout of the village well; 'Tom of Norton' by people from further afield; 'Tom the blacksmith' by his customers; 'Tom the redhead' by people who knew him by sight; and 'Tom, son of Dick' by those who knew his family. Because the full by-names are a bit of a mouthful, they were probably shortened to Tom Bridge, Tom Norton, Tom Smith, Tom Red and Tom Dickson. Tom's own son, Harry, might have had his own by-names: Harry Green if he lived by the village green; Harry Norton or Harry Smith, if he took over his father's blacksmith's shop in Norton; Harry Longman if he was well-known for his height (or lack of it); or Harry Tomson, after his father, Tom.

This fictional account of Tom, his son Dick and grandson Harry illustrates the various types of by-names that were introduced in the period after the Norman Conquest. There are four basic types: parental, occupational, geographical and personal. *Parental by-names* were based on the given name of the father or, much less commonly, the given name of the mother. *Occupational by-names*, not surprisingly, described what individuals did for a living. *Geographical by-names* referred to either a person's birthplace, or some natural or man-made landscape features close to where they lived. *Personal by-names* described people's appearance or behaviour.

Parental by-names came from the given name of a person's father or mother. They are sometimes referred to as *patronyms* or *matronyms*. The idea was long established in those areas of England where there was a strong Viking influence, with their use of the patronymic naming system. Recall, for example, that Harald Gormsson's son was Sweyn Haraldsson, and Sweyn's son was Canute Sweynsson. The idea also came across the English Channel in 1066, with several of the Companions of the Conqueror being referred to as 'son of' an important father.

The simplest way for ordinary people to adopt a parental by-name was to add a parent's given name after their own. Tom, son of Richard might be known simply as Tom *Richard*. Or, especially in the south of England, they added an *s* to the parental name, and so Tom, son of Richard, was Tom *Richards*. Further north, perhaps showing the greater Viking influence, Tom, son of Richard, was more likely to be Tom *Richardson*. These weren't the only ways to create a parental by-name in England. An equivalent to 'son of' is the Anglo-Norman word *fitz*. For example, one of the Companions of the Conqueror was William *fitz Osbern*, meaning 'William, son of Osbern'. William's son, Roger *fitz William*, inherited his father's extensive English estates—but came to a sticky end after he rashly conspired against King William. Two other possible ways to show a paternal relationship are the suffixes *–kin* and *-cock*, as in Wilkin and Wilcock, both referring to the son of William.

Parental by-names in the Celtic areas of the British Isles were rather different. In Wales, the father-son link was shown by the word *map* ('son of'), which over time was shortened to *ap* (or *ab* before a vowel). Often, people could cite several generations, such as *David ap Thomas ap William ap Dafydd* ... and so on, a bit like the lists of 'begats' in the Bible, but going in the opposite direction. In Gaelic-speaking Ireland and western Scotland, *Mc* or *Mac* was often added to a given name. The prefix is usually translated as 'son of', but the name after the Mc/Mac prefix was usually that of a clan rather than a family. In the ever-changing, violent local politics of many Gaelic areas, having the same clan name as that of the local chieftain might literally have meant the difference between life and death. Another well-known Gaelic prefix is Ó, which has been anglicised to O'. It means 'grandson of', and was used in Ireland earlier than *Mc* or *Mac*. However, this prefix too was more to do with where you lived rather than whom you were related to, as everyone living in the same locality used the same the name regardless of whether or not they were from the same family.

Anglo-Saxon, Danish and Norman given names were all in use in England in the decades following the Norman Conquest. Although many pre-Conquest given names were quickly replaced by Norman ones after 1066, many survived long enough to be incorporated into parental by-names. Examples of Anglo-Saxon given names used as by-names include *Ælfred,* which survived in the parental by-names Alfred and Averay, *Brun* (Brown) and *Cniht* (Knight). Some Old English names were unchanged in spelling, such as Flint, Hand, Swift and Swan. Because of the more limited influence of the Danish invaders, there were fewer Scandinavian given names used as by-names. They included *Asgautr,* which survived as Osgood, *Bondi* (Bond) and *Koli* (Cole).

As well as the popular Norman given names, such as William, Robert and Richard, there were other given names that are more familiar now as surnames, such as Baldwin, Everard and Eustace. In addition, there were the shortened or 'pet' forms of many popular Norman names, such as Tom, Dick and Harry. Sometimes, we no longer recognise the pet form as, for example, with the name Hick, a pet form of Richard. As with Dick, Hick resulted from the inability of the Anglo-Saxons to get their tongues around the R sound at the start of the Norman name Richard. Short forms of given names were also made into new parental names such as Thomson, Dickson, Hickson and Harris. And as all these by-names came into being when there were no spelling rules, multiple possible spellings usually developed for most names, such as Dickason, Dickson, Dickinson, Dickison, Dixon and Dixson.

Although I've used the label *parental* by-names, so far I've mentioned only fathers. That's because for many centuries western societies have been patriarchal, with men playing the dominant role in society. Nevertheless, there were some parental names derived from the mother—perhaps the result of the father dying young, and the children being brought up by their mother. The by-names occasionally came directly from female given names, such as Hanna. More often, the by-names came from pet names rather than the more formal given names, such as Sissons from Sissy, one of the pet names for Cecilia. Some by-names were formed by adding an *s* to the mother's pet name, such as Ibbs, from the pet name Ibby, which was short for Isabel. Others had a *son* ending, such as Anson, meaning son of Ann. And occasionally the by-name ended in *kin* or *cock,* as in Babcock—son of Babs, the short form of Barbara. Most surprising is the name Hannibal, which came from the given name

118

Amabilia, meaning 'lovable'; similarly, the now rare names Maggitt, Maggett and Maggott all derive from pet names for Margaret.

One thing is sure. None of the by-names based on mothers' given names ever became very common. Only one is now in the top 100 US and UK surnames—Bell, which comes from one of the pet names for Isabel, but this is only part of the story. The following explanations have also contributed to the current popularity of Bell: (i) it described someone who made or rang church bells; (ii) it described someone who lived in or close to either a church tower or an inn named after church bells; and (iii) it described the personal appearance of a man, the nickname *Bel* coming from the Old French word meaning handsome. In other words, my neat division of by-names into parental, occupational, geographical and personal categories is often not that neat. Nevertheless, the categories are still useful when describing the range of by-names, as long as we bear in mind that there is often a lot of overlap between categories. The second group of by-names are those describing a person's occupation, such as a bell-maker.

Occupational by-names described what individuals did for a living. In the eleventh and twelfth centuries, when by-names began to be widely used, smiths were incredibly important as everyone depended on their metal-working skills for farming implements and weapons for hunting and fighting. Because smiths were held in high esteem, the occupational by-name was one that fathers were particularly keen to pass on to their sons. One result is that Smith is today's most common surname. There were many types of smith, including whitesmiths, blacksmiths, greensmiths, coppersmiths, goldsmiths, silversmiths, arrowsmiths and knifesmiths. Some became by-names themselves; others took on different forms; and many were truncated over time to just Smith.

Another common by-name was Wright, a wright being someone who worked with wood. Wrights were not quite as important as smiths, having a smaller military role, and the occupational by-name was not as widely used. Another reason why Wright was less common than Smith is that the Anglo-Saxon term 'wright' was often replaced by the Norman word *carpenter,* especially in the south of England where the Norman influence was strongest. As with smiths, there were many different types of wright, such as cartwrights, housewrights, ploughwrights, shipwrights, timberwrights, wagonwrights, wheelwrights, boatwrights, wainwrights and arkwrights. Some of these specialisations became by-names such as Wainwright and Arkwright. Wainwrights made *wains,* or large agricultural wagons, like the one in Constable's famous painting 'The Hay Wain'. Arkwrights weren't mediaeval Noahs. The arks they made were chests, like the biblical Ark of the Covenant.

As well as Smith, Wright and Carpenter, there were many other obvious occupational by-names: Archer, Baker, Brewer, Butcher, Butler, Carter, Clark, Cook, Draper, Dyer, Farmer, Forester, Gardiner, Glover, Mason, Merchant, Miller, Parson, Potter, Saddler, Shepherd, Taylor, Tyler, Weaver ... and so on—the list is a long one. But when you include those family names that most people today would not recognise as starting life as occupational by-names, the list is even longer.

In the thousand years or so since occupational by-names began, many once-important jobs have died out. For example, in medieval times everyone knew that Tom Fletcher made arrows; that Dick Frobisher 'furbished' or polished armour; and that Harry Jagger was in charge of pack-horses. The name Walker in part has an occupational origin, walkers being cloth-workers who walked on raw cloth in a large tub to clean and thicken it. In some parts of England, walkers were also known as *fullers, tuckers* or *bowkers,* and so these too became occupational by-names. Incredibly, the cloth industry alone gave rise to no fewer than 165 different occupational by-names; and the metal trades generated over a hundred different by-names.

Incidentally, it's interesting to speculate what occupational by-names we might have if they were being introduced today. For example, we now don't have many smiths, but we do have a lot of engineers. The term came into general use after most British surnames were fixed; but in India, where surnames were adopted much later, Engineer is a common family name. Cricket fans may recall Indian test cricketer Farokh Engineer, whose family name originated in the late nineteenth century when his great-grandfather became a professional engineer. As with smiths, there are many types of engineer, such as aeronautical engineers and biomolecular engineers. However, no biomolecular engineer would use this full job title as an occupational by-name (*Ben the Molecular Engineer*), preferring perhaps the snappier *Tom Bioeng*, *Tom Beng* or simply *Tom Be*. Other modern occupations lend themselves more readily to being shortened—for example, Tom the chief executive officer could be *Tom Ceo*, and Tom the information technology manager might be *Tom Itman*. I suspect that there would be quite a lot of by-names ending with *man*.

I'll mention just one more historical occupational by-name, Hall. It has two possible origins. In terms of an occupation, it referred to someone who was employed at a large house, or hall. It could also refer to someone who lived near to a hall, or possibly came from a village called Hall—and this leads me neatly onto geographical by-names, which are of two types. First, *topographical* by-names described natural or man-made landscape features close to where a person lived. Second, *locational* by-names referred to the name of a person's farm, village, town, region or country.

Topographical names were the most common geographical by-names because they often described some fairly widespread man-made or natural feature on the landscape. Commonly occurring by-names based on natural features included Brook, Wood, Hill and Moore. And common by-names based on man-made features include Hall, Green, Mills and Bridge—not to mention the numerous names derived from each of them, such as Bridgeman, Bridgewater and Bridgewood.

Many other surnames would not be generally recognised today as coming from topographical by-names. This is because over the last thousand years, many terms have become obsolete or, at best, confined to very limited areas. For example, the fairly common surname Shaw started life as a topographical by-name. A shaw was a small wood, and the by-name indicated that the holder lived close by. Similarly, the name

Moss originally referred to a bog; Clough to a steep-sided ravine; Edge to a ridge with a sharp crest; Riding to a clearing; Holme to an island; Beer to a grove of trees; and Yeo to a brook.

In contrast to topographical by-names, locational by-names were usually quite rare. This was because they tended to come from fairly small places rather than large ones. After all, being one of many thousands of people called 'London' living in the British capital wouldn't be very useful for identification purposes. The few locational by-names that became more common, such as Ashby, Kirkby, Burton and Norton, did so because there were several places in Britain with these names.

Some place-names were brought across with William the Conqueror in 1066. Brett, Britten and Britain are all derived from Brittany, one of William's closest allies being the Count of Brittany. Similarly, Percy is the family name of the Dukes of Northumberland. It comes from the village of Percy-en-Auge in Normandy. The first part of the place-name survived in part because of the status of the family, and also because it was easy for the native English to pronounce. Other Norman names were not so lucky. The surname Dabney comes from the Norman place-name Aubigny; Dangerfield comes from Aungerville; and Menzies comes from Mesnières.

The idea of a by-name saying something about where a migrant came from is not confined to the Norman invaders. A migrant family's place of origin could well be their most distinguishing feature in their new home, and so be reflected in a new by-name. For example, early Welsh migrants to England often had by-names such as Welsh, Walsh and Wallace that identified them as from Wales. Similarly, English migrants to Wales were known by the Welsh word *sais*, meaning 'Saxon', and this developed into the by-name Sayce. In Scotland, the name Inglis was given to English settlers and, of course, the name Scott refers to migrants from Scotland though, having said that, it's a bit surprising that the name should be most common in Scotland, the one place where it wouldn't be much help to identify the holder. Similarly, the name English and England are both common in England. One explanation is that the names are historical throwbacks to when the cultural geography of Britain was rather more complicated than today. In the eleventh century the Danes occupied large parts of Britain, and in Cornwall the population spoke a Celtic language similar to that of Wales. In such areas, the Cornish and Danish majority might have identified Anglo-Saxons with by-names such as English and England.

*

Personal by-names usually described people's appearance or behaviour. They were what we now call nicknames. For example, the only Companions of the Conqueror who had hereditary surnames in 1066 were Walter Giffard and William Malet. (We know this because their children were named Giffard and Malet before the Norman invasion.) Giffard was a Norman nickname for someone with chubby cheeks; and Malet was a Norman nickname for a fearsome warrior.

So, Giffard is an early example of a surname based on a by-name that described the holder's appearance. Nicknames like Chubby Cheeks are still widely used, of course, but modern nicknames can't begin to compete with the range of nicknames used in medieval England. Hair was one characteristic often used to describe someone. For example, people with brown hair had the by-names Brown, Burnett or Sorrell. People with black hair had the by-names Black, Blake or Dunn. Those with blond hair were called White, Blundell or Blunt. Grey hair, of course could result in the by-names Grey or Gray. Red hair led to the personal by-names Read, Reed, Fox or Todd (the last two referring to the red fox), and white haired people sometimes had the by-name Snow. It wasn't only hair colour. Curly-haired people were called Crippen, Cripps or Crisp. People with beautiful hair were Fairfax, and people with no hair often had the by-name Ballard, Callow, Cave or Nott.

Other physical features also led to by-names. Good-looking people might have the name Fairchild, Bell, Belcher or Bellamy, the last three based on the French word *belle* or 'beautiful'. On the other hand, if you had a crooked or bent nose, you might have the by-name Cameron, from the Gaelic *cam* meaning 'bent', and *sron*, meaning 'nose'. Similar Scottish names include Campbell meaning 'crooked mouth', and Kennedy, meaning 'ugly head'. If you had a small head, you might be called Smollett. And by-names weren't confined to the head. Short people (not surprisingly) were called Short, or sometimes Pettit or Base—Bassett if they were *really* short. People who were stooped had the by-name Crump or Bossey. Long, Lang and Grant described tall people (or, ironically, very short people). Someone with crooked legs was called Cruikshank, and someone with a clubfoot was Puddifoot. And so on…

The second type of personal by-name generally described a person's behaviour. So, for example, William Malet's by-name meant fearsome warrior—though he's not recorded as actually fighting at the Battle of Hastings, he was badly defeated by the Danes at York, and was killed trying to defeat the legendary Hereward the Wake (whose by-name means 'awake' or 'watchful'). Malet is one of many nicknames that described how the holder was tough, bold, brave, valiant, strong and courageous. Others were Hardy, Keen, Moody, Prowse, Rank, Snell and Turnbull.

This last example, Turnbull, suggested that someone was so strong that he could 'turn a bull'. A bull was used because it was seen as the very epitome of strength. Many other animals were seen as having real or imagined characteristics, and nicknames were often developed from them. Legend has it that one of the pre-Norman kings of England, Harold Harefoot, was given the by-name because he ran as fast as a hare. The animal's name later became a common by-name. Here are a few more examples. I mentioned the names Fox and Todd earlier in connection with redheads. But these names can also refer to the fox's speed and cunning. The name Doggett was a reference to the dog-like characteristics of faithfulness and friendliness displayed by bearers of the name. Similarly, Lamb denoted meekness, Colt a lively, frisky person, Peacock a vain person, and Stallion a notorious womanizer.

Stallion wasn't the only by-name that referred to sexual behaviour. For example, Toplady, Tiplady and Pullen all were names for philanderers.

Even the hallowed name Shakespeare might be a sexual reference, along the same lines as Wagstaff and Longstaff, the 'spears' and 'staffs' that were shaken or wagged being anatomical ones. This explanation might seem a bit far-fetched, but as Percy Reaney points out, 'the language of the time was much less inhibited than that of today and much that we regard as indecent or obscene was to them normal and natural.' Two of the more polite examples are Prikehard and Gildanbollok. (So, the by-name Gildanbollok pre-dates David Beckham's nickname 'Golden Balls' by about one thousand years.)

✳

Over time these non-inherited by-names were replaced by the inherited surnames we use today. Not surprisingly perhaps, most men chose to base their families' surnames on their father's name. As the list below shows, eight of today's top ten British surnames are based on parental by-names.

| Smith | Jones | Williams | Brown | Taylor | Davies | Wilson | Evans | Thomas | Johnson |

Most are self-evident, such as Williams and Wilson, both of which mean son of William. Only two need explanation: Jones is from the given name John (or Jon); and Brown may come from a now unused Old English given name, *Brun*. The name Brown also shows again that my categories of by-names are not watertight, as the surname could also be come from a personal by-name for someone with a brown complexion or hair, or someone who always wore brown clothing, such as a monk. The two remaining surnames, Smith and Taylor, are of course from occupational by-names.

Smith is today's most common surname. In fact, about one in every hundred families is called Smith. This might not seem very much, but you need to bear in mind that there are hundreds of thousands—possibly millions—of family names. In fact, there are many more family names than given names. This is a bit surprising considering that parents have an open choice of given names for their children, but are much more restricted by tradition for their children's family names. It's difficult to say exactly how many family names there are. For example, the US Census Bureau counted over six million, but then found that four million names occurred only once. Now, I'm sure there are a number of people whose family names are literally on their last legs (theirs)—but surely not as many as this at any one time. Instead, it's likely that the six million different surnames are more a reflection of how clearly people filled in their Census returns, and how carefully they were added to the database.

TWELVE

William Shakspere and Mick Jagger

Life and death of family names

Traditionally, family names have been inherited through the men in a family, so that a son's surname is the same as his father's and his father's father. As a result, genealogists can trace a family tree back in time. More importantly, a lawyer can identify lines of inheritance from one generation to the next. This, of course, is different from the system of by-names, where a son's by-name was likely to be different from his father's and grandfather's.

We can think of inherited family names as having a birth, a life, and possibly a death. The birth, or starting point, of each British surname is usually shrouded in the mists of time. It occurred many centuries ago when a father first gave his by-name to his children as a family name. In England, this began after the Norman Conquest in 1066, and continued for several centuries. However, not all surnames did equally well. Some prospered, and are now found across Britain and in former British colonies throughout the world. Some were less successful, and are still found mainly where they first appeared. And some went into a terminal decline, disappearing with the marriage, migration or death of the last holder of the name.

The spread of inherited family names was very much like the spread of non-inherited by-names that went before them, with an uneven take-up after the Norman Conquest. Geographically, it was the region around

London in south-east England that first adopted by-names. The practice then spread north and west, with Scotland and Wales adopting them last. People in towns adopted by-names before people in the country-side, and as with so many customs, members of the social elite were the first to use them, with the practice trickling down to those at the very bottom of the social ladder.

Exactly the same comments describe the take-up of inherited family names, the only major difference being that it occurred later. The 'Companions of the Conqueror', the Norman nobles who came over with William in 1066, are a useful starting point when plotting the historical take-up of surnames. Nearly all of these two dozen Companions had by-names; only two had surnames. But big land-holders quickly realised the value in having a clear connection through an inherited family name, and by the middle of the thirteenth century most great landholding families were using hereditary surnames. By the end of the thirteenth century, surnames were common among the London elite.

So, in less than 150 years surnames became firmly established among the most influential people in the country. The trickledown effect then began, and it took another 150 years for surnames to be widely used by all members of English society. It's pretty certain that most people in England had a surname by the early fifteenth century. The last group in England to adopt family names were landless labourers in the north— the social and geographical opposite of the London elite. After another century, surnames were so entrenched that in 1538 Henry VIII was able to legislate for parents to provide the parish priest with their surnames when registering a child's birth.

This is not to say that family names have always been used in exactly the same way as they are today. You may recall that one feature of by-names was that they were not set in stone, so someone could have a number of different by-names. This long-established custom did not suddenly disappear with the change to surnames. It gave rise to the use of *aliases* to link different surnames. Today, the word is generally limited to criminals who adopt different names to avoid the long arm of the law, but in the past it indicated simply that someone was known by more than one name.

One of the most prominent examples of an alias comes from the Cromwell family tree. In the seventeenth century, Oliver Cromwell became the English 'Lord Protector', or head of state, following the execution of King Charles I. The Cromwell surname was not a long-established one in his family tree. His Welsh great-great-grandfather was born Morgan *ap* William ('Morgan son of William') in accordance with the traditional Welsh naming system. Later, he adopted an English-style surname and became Morgan Williams. His son, Richard Williams, married the sister of Thomas Cromwell, who was a great favourite of Henry VIII (that's Thomas, not his sister—though she may have been as well). The king 'recommended' to Richard Williams that, as his surname had been adopted only recently, he might instead use the name Cromwell, in honour of his brother-in-law.

As only fools and the foolhardy ignored what King Henry 'recommended', Richard Williams became Richard *Williams alias Cromwell*, a name that he passed on to his son, Oliver's grandfather, Henry *Williams alias Cromwell*. It was only with the next generation, Oliver's father, that the alias was dropped. So, had it not been for the recommendation of King Henry VIII, England's Lord Protector would have been Oliver Williams, not Oliver Cromwell.

This example is very unusual in that it was triggered by the recommendation of a king. Much more common was the use of an alias to denote stepchildren or illegitimate children. British historian David Hey tells us that in 1573 a Sheffield parish registered a baptism as follows: 'Anna Fyrthe alias Stead, child of Alice Fyrthe, supposed father Nicholas Steade'. Aliases were also used to preserve a woman's maiden name in her children—especially an heiress. In the seventeenth century, the unusually named Fisher Dilke married heiress Sybil Wentworth and had a son, Fisher *Dilke alias Wentworth*. Another generation on, the grandson was known by the compound surname *Dilke Wentworth*. Another use of the alias tag had to do with a much more general issue in the early days of surnames—names officially recorded with different spellings. Sometimes, if confusion arose, family members would draw attention to the alternative spellings using an alias—for example, *Brownhill alias Brownell*, and *Mirfield alias Murfin*.

In general, a few hundred years ago people paid little attention to how names were spelled. I wonder, for example, if you noticed something in the previous paragraph that a proof-reader would pounce on—that the parish register has two spellings of the same name, *Stead* (the child's alias) and *Steade* (the child's supposed father). Probably the most extreme example can be seen on a tombstone in Ireland, where the family name of the father, mother and children is shown variously as *McEneaney*, *McAneany*, *McAneny*, *McEnaney* and *McEneany*. This lack of concern about the spelling even shows in the spelling of the family name of William Shakespeare (1564-1616). In his famous will—the one in which he leaves his wife his 'second-best bed'—he signs his name in two ways, *Shakspeare* and *Shakspere* (hence the spelling in the title of this chapter). Four more of his signatures survive, all with different spellings, and none of them is the same as the one we regard today as the 'correct' spelling. We can't accuse the greatest writer in the English language of being a really bad speller. He was simply following the custom of the time.

In Shakespeare's time, seventy per cent of men and ninety per cent of women in England couldn't even sign their names. This is important because parents were compelled by law to register the birth of each child with the parish priest. The priest was often from a different social class, and from a different part of the country, with a different local dialect. Not surprisingly, there were times when he had difficulty understanding the names of his parishioners. The end result was that the official records showed a variety of unusual spellings of the same surname. A good example of this lack of understanding between resident and official comes from the 1851 Scottish Census, where one Ayrshire resident appears under the surname *Araphady*. Scottish gene- alogist David Webster comments that this is 'not a surname that I can fit to anything recognisable, unless I imagine a broad southern Irish pronunciation of O'Rafferty heard by an Ayrshire ear unaccustomed to such accents'.

However, the fact that surnames were incorrectly recorded on parish registers didn't make any difference to the people concerned as most parents couldn't read, and so couldn't identify the spelling errors. And as William Shakspeare/Shakspere shows, even among those who could read, there was little importance attached to the exact spelling of names. The end-result, however, is that there's now a huge variety or spellings for what at one time would have been the same name. And because now we *do* put importance on the exact spelling, even names that clearly go together— such as Smith, Smyth, Smythe and Smithe—are treated as different surnames.

*

Despite the best efforts of Rolling Stones' front-man, father of seven Mick Jagger, it looks as if he is one of a dying breed—the number of people named Jagger has gone down in the last hundred years or so. In contrast, Keith Richards, his song-writing partner, is one of growing band with that family name. Similar stories apply to the other members of the group. Bill Wyman is in the same boat as Jagger, and Charlie Watts and Ronnie Wood line up with Richards. You might want to check on the progress of your family name and that of your partner or close friends over the same period by going to the Public Profiler website (gbnames.publicprofiler.org). You may find that there are different trends in the number of people with these names over the last hundred years.

Why do some family names flourish and others fade? A family name is traditionally handed down from father to son. Clearly then, the best chance for a family name to prosper is to have a large number of sons, each having several sons of his own. Of course, a man may have no children, or have only daughters. In these circumstances, the family name has much less chance of survival. Experts believe that very many English surnames originated with a single family, the surname often coming from the name of the family farm. Consequently, it's very likely that over time many surnames have died out.

What ordinary mortals call *chance,* statisticians call *probability.* Once they have the data for such things as marriage rates, average family size and infant mortality levels, statisticians can model what might happen in the real world, and so predict the probable rate of growth or decline of surnames over time. In these statistical models, chance is taken into account by the computer equivalent of tossing coins or throwing dice.

Why some family names prosper while others do not can be put down partly to chance or, more scientifically, to genetic differences, but there are also more tangible explanations. Even today, how rich or poor a family is can make a big difference to the likelihood of children surviving into adulthood. In the past, a family's level of income was even more important as there was less social support for the very poor. So, the food a family was able to buy, beg or steal had a major impact not only on whether a woman became pregnant but also on whether the child survived to become an adult and a parent.

As well as food, the other major influence was housing. Both the house and its neighbourhood were important. Poor people who lived in the countryside often had a less deadly environment than those in large towns and cities, where damp, crowded, squalid living conditions plus a lack of piped water and sewage led to high infant mortality rates. During epidemics these conditions went from bad to worse.

Undoubtedly, the worst epidemic was the Black Death that occurred in Europe in the mid-fourteenth century, and returned many times over the next two centuries. The Black Death epidemic of the 1340s is particularly important as far as names are concerned. First, the death toll was enormous, with up to *one half* of the total population of England dying. Not surprisingly, poor people living in the biggest towns—especially London—were most badly hit as they lived in overcrowded and poorly ventilated houses on narrow streets flowing with human sewage and animal blood from local abattoirs. The existing cemeteries were soon filled and many new ones had to be consecrated.

Secondly, the Black Death struck at the time when surnames were beginning to take over from by-names. With such a large proportion of the population dying, it meant that many surnames were also lost. In fact, it may be that there were more surnames in England before the Black Death than there are today, despite the fact that the population then was only one tenth what it is now. Interesting examples of medieval family names that didn't survive include Scytheward, Sitadown, Squell and Scarehare.

Cataclysmic events such as the Black Death are not essential for surnames to come to the end of their life cycle. Although the twentieth century had more than its fair share of disasters, none came anywhere close to the Black Death in terms of its impact on British population levels. However, a comparison of surnames listed in official records in 1881 and 1998 found something quite remarkable. A total of 130,000 family names appear on both lists. In other words, 130,000 family names survived from 1881 to 1998. But a larger number, a whopping *140,000*, appeared on the earlier list but not the later one. In other words, 140,000 surnames became extinct in Britain in just over a century. Another way to measure this loss is to average it out over time—about a hundred surnames disappearing every month for more than a century. Some of the family names that disappeared include Hatman, Rummage, Southwark and Chips, so it really was 'Goodbye Mr Chips'. (Though to be pedantic, the surname of the teacher in the book is not Chips but *Chipping*, a name that is still hanging on in Britain with a couple of hundred people with that name.)

One major event of the twentieth century that *did* have an impact on the lifespan of some family names was World War I (1914-1918). The British death toll was nearly one million, or about two per cent of the entire population, and because it was mainly young men who died, the effect on family names was larger. Locally, the impact was sometimes huge because of the way men were recruited into the armed forces before conscription began. The British Secretary of State for War Lord Kitchener (who appeared on the iconic 'Your Country Needs YOU' recruitment poster) authorized the creation of *pals' battalions*, made up of men who were friends and neighbours. At first, the idea seemed to be a good one, because it improved morale. But when some battalions suffered mass casualties, it meant that some villages lost a generation of young men. Worst hit was the town of Accrington in Lancashire. Of 720 Pals, 584 were killed, wounded or missing in the Battle for the Somme. Even in the twentieth century, some family names were still very localised, and so the wiping out of a pals' battalion could result in the death of these local names. However, this was the reason for only a small percentage of the 140,000 extinct names.

Much more significant is the fact that many surnames that became extinct by 1998 were nearing the end of their life cycle in 1881 when nearly 100,000 names were held only by women. Many of these surnames would have become extinct when, in the late nineteenth and early twentieth centuries, the women who bore them either married and changed their surname, or died.

Not all surname extinctions are quite as final as this. Fifty thousand of the names that became extinct in Britain between 1881 and 1998 were still in use at the end of the twentieth century in the US and elsewhere. It's likely that at least some of these 50,000 names became extinct in Britain because the last people to bear the name left the country as part of the great international European migration in the nineteenth and early twentieth centuries. During this period, over ten million people left Britain to settle in North America, Australia and elsewhere. In one year alone, 1890, nearly one in every hundred people in Britain left to live abroad.

The dying out of a branch of a family tree because of the lack of a son to carry on the family name has occurred countless times. However, particularly in eighteenth and nineteenth century England, wealthy people used a number of strategies to protect their family name and wealth. For example, an eighteenth century English politician who was born Thomas Brodnax changed his name to Thomas May and then to Thomas Knight. He made these name changes in order to inherit first the May estate, and later the Knight estate, both of which had no natural male heirs. The estates were willed to Thomas provided he changed his family name. Later in the eighteenth century, his son, also called Thomas Knight, had a chance brush with fame. He and his wife were rich but childless. In contrast, the Reverend George Austen was poor but had seven children—one of whom was Britain's best-loved novelist, Jane Austen. One of Jane's brothers, Edward, was sent to live with the Knights to become the son they never had. In order to inherit the Knights' estates, Edward Austen had to change his surname to Knight.

On the death of the Reverend Austen, his wife and daughters Jane and Cassandra had to move out of the vicarage. Edward provided his mother and sisters with a house in the village of Chawton. Largely free of financial worries, Jane wrote all her novels there. So it might not be too much of an exaggeration to say that some of the most admired books in English literature are the consequence of Edward's change of family name. Such adoption arrangements were fairly commonplace at the time. As well as her brother, one of Jane's uncles was also adopted by rich, childless relatives, and changed his family name.

However, as the nineteenth century progressed, demands for a total surname change declined. Sometimes, it was enough that the beneficiaries add a name to their own, thus potentially leading to the end of two existing names and the creation of a new double-barrelled surname. Prominent British historian Hugh *Trevor-Roper* owed his double-barrelled name to a nineteenth century will. His ancestor, the impressively named Cadwallader Blayney Roper, added the surname Trevor as required under the will of his cousin, whose maiden name was Mary Jane Trevor. His name then became the even more impressive Cadwallader Blayney Trevor-Roper.

Names could get really complex when a man who already had a double-barrelled name was required by the terms of a will to add a second double-barrelled name. Examples given by David McKie include the Earl of Buckinghamshire, Sidney Carr Hobart-Hampden who became Sidney Carr *Hobart-Hampden-Mercer-Henderson* to comply with the will of George Mercer-Henderson. Probably the ultimate in multi-barrelled names occurred when the 3rd Duke of Buckingham and Chandos became Richard Plantagenet Campbell *Temple-Nugent-Brydges-Chandos-Grenville*. (His friends probably called him 'Buckingham'; his closest friends possibly called him 'Bucks'.)

You may recall that in the sixteenth century having more than one given name was a sign of prosperity. Similarly, in the nineteenth century, having more than one family name began to be a mark of high status. Of course, you don't really need either wealth or a title to have a double-barrelled name. As early as 1852, the satirist William Makepeace Thackeray was lampooning the practice in his *Book of Snobs:* 'He *double-barrelled* his name, (as many poor Snobs do) and instead of T. Sniffle, as formerly, came out, in a porcelain card, as Rev. T. D'Arcy Sniffle.' Ironically, Thackeray used always his middle name, and so gave the impression of having a double-barrelled surname—William Makepeace Thackeray.

So, historically money and social status were often why men changed their name. More recently, new names often symbolise major lifestyle changes, such as a change of religion. Most famously, African American boxer Cassius Clay took the name Muhammad Ali when he converted to Islam in the turbulent 1960s. A name change can also reflect a sex change, such as when Richard Raskind became Renée Richards following sex reassignment surgery. She became the focus of much media attention when she was initially banned from playing as a woman in the US Open Tennis Championships.

Perhaps the most serious reason for a name change is when it's literally a matter of life or death. Examples here include the 20,000 or so witnesses and family members who have been protected by the US Marshalls Service as part of the Witness Protection Program. Not surprisingly, the names used by people in this program rarely come to light. One of the few exceptions is Gary Thomas Rowe who was in Witness Protection for over thirty years after testifying against Ku Klux Klansmen in a murder trial. His Witness Protection name was Thomas Neal Moore, though of course his identity was made public only after his death.

A surname that was once ordinary and uncontroversial can change dramatically when someone with that name becomes notorious. Undoubtedly the clearest example is the surname *Hitler*. Before Adolf Hitler's rise to power in the 1930s in Germany there were two-dozen families with that name in the New York telephone book. Ironically, many of them were descendants of Jewish refugees who had left Europe following earlier Jewish persecution. Not surprisingly, by the end of World War II the name had disappeared from the phone book. There still aren't any people named Hitler in the New York White Pages. In fact, throughout the entire US, there are still only a couple of dozen telephone entries for people named Hitler, including a handful named Adolf Hitler.

Anti-German sentiment in Britain during World War I led to one of the most high profile changes of surname. In 1917, the German air force began bombing London using long-range aircraft known as Gothas. At the time, the British royal family had the surname *Saxe-Coburg and Gotha*, the name coming from Queen Victoria's husband, the German-born Prince Albert. The year 1917 was also when the Russian emperor, Nicholas II, a cousin of the British king, was overthrown, raising fears among all European royals that they might be next. As a consequence, in July 1917 George V issued a proclamation declaring that from then on 'Our House and Family shall be styled and known as the House and Family of Windsor'. The choice of Windsor was probably made to help cement the idea of the long history of the royal family in Britain, with Windsor Castle being used as a royal residence since the twelfth century.

More generally, the close relatives of convicted criminals often feel that their names have been tainted by the negative publicity resulting from the crime. The bigger the crime, the greater the publicity; and the greater the publicity the more intense the public reaction against the criminal. In terms of white-collar crime, there's none bigger than what came to be known as the 'Madoff investment scandal'. Bernie Madoff, a Wall Street investment banker, admitted to defrauding his investors of over $50 *billion* (that's $50,000,000,000!), and he was sentenced to 150 years in prison. The Madoff name became toxic, and close relatives who knew nothing about the fraud became concerned for their safety. For example, Madoff's younger son and his wife changed their now-poisonous surname, and Madoff's wife started using her maiden name because she might be assaulted if people found out who she was.

On the other hand, a name change can allow someone to be linked with a highly respected public figure. Early in his career Dale Carnegie, the author of *How To Win Friends and Influence People,* changed his surname from Carnagey to Carnegie. At the time, Andrew Carnegie was one of the world's most successful businessmen and biggest philanthropists. According to his biographers Giles Kemp and Edward Claflin, Dale never claimed any family relationship to Andrew, but realised that it made good business sense for people to make that link. Talking about his change of name, Dale Carnegie commented that 'It was against my principles of showmanship to leave it the way it was'. After all, he *was* an expert at influencing people.

Many changes are based simply on the fact that some people don't like their existing name or, more generally, because they want to have a complete make-over—and a new name is symbolic of becoming a new person. A good example is Bill Wyman, former bass guitarist with the Rolling Stones. His original name was Bill Perks, and he grew up in the London working-class suburb of Penge. Bill hated both his name and his birthplace, believing that Perks and Penge 'both reeked of failure'. When he was in his late 20s, he legally changed his name from Perks to Wyman, the surname of his best friend when he was in the Army. The result was dramatic. Bill Wyman confided to journalist Simon Hattenstone that 'It completely changed my life. I felt confident, I was proud of the name.'

By just looking at the two names, Perks and Wyman, we can't understand Bill Wyman's dislike for his old surname and enthusiasm for his new surname. But sometimes we can more easily put ourselves into other people's shoes. For example, embarrassment is certainly the most likely explanation for the marked decline over the last 120 years of a number of names. In 1915, British comedian John Cleese's father Reg changed his surname from Cheese to Cleese because he 'was fed up with being teased that he was a fermented curd'. It's likely that Reg Cheese wasn't alone in changing his name. The chances of meeting someone called Cheese fell by a third between 1881 and 1998. However, John Cleese regretted his father's decision to change his surname: 'I always preferred "Cheese" to "Cleese", which is, quite simply, not a proper name'. One of his most famous *Monty Python* sketches is the 'Cheese shop'.

Of course, there are other surnames that have a much greater potential for embarrassment—such as Looney, Smellie, Daft (and Dafter), Balls, Bottom and Cock. Variations on the last two names are also in rapid decline. They include Shufflebottom, Longbottom, Handcock, Wilcocks, Cockshott, Cockcroft, Bulcock and Glasscock. Today, probably the best-known name change of this type concerns movie stars Joaquin and River Phoenix, who were originally called Bottom. In an early interview, members of the family explained that, following a major change of life-style, they had changed the family name to Phoenix—but refused to say what their former name was.

In many instances, these names originally had quite different meanings to now. For example, *Bottom* referred to a valley bottom. *Cock* was a cockerel (or rooster), and was often used to describe the way in which young men strutted around like a cockerel. The word eventually came to refer to young men in general. In fact, *cock* or *cox* was often added to a given name to refer to a man's son; for example, the surnames Wilcocks and Wilcox referred to the son of William. However, schoolboys rarely appreciate history, and it looks as if a lot of couples changed to less embarrassing surnames. Or perhaps men with embarrassing surnames had more difficulty finding women who would marry them...

Recently, it's become Britain's latest craze, with around 60,000 Britons changing their name by deed poll each year, the equivalent of 5 to 10 per cent of all British births. (Many more will use the less formal—but still legal—method of simply making government agencies, banks and so on aware that they have changed their name.) The deed poll procedure is designed to be as quick and easy as possible. 'It took ten minutes online and £33 to change my name' reports journalist Brad Pitt, formerly 'plain old Matthew Rudd'. To help drum up further business, the deed poll company he used offers a discount for those who want to use the service again, which Brad Pitt did to change back to Matthew Rudd. Brad/Matthew points out that 'Now my wife can boast that she has spent the night with Brad Pitt.' It's the humorous examples like this one that make it into the media. For example, you may recall that all ten staff at one Manchester pub changed their name to Wayne Rooney.

The last word (literally) in frivolous name changes is the fellow who changed his surname to *Zzzyzzx* in order to become the last entry in the telephone book. The move from printed to electronic phone books may well have taken something away from his 'achievement'.

*

To end this chapter, I want to look at American Indians (or Native Americans), whose personal names have a very different history from those described so far. Like English by-names, traditional American Indian names were based on such things as character traits, physical appearance, physical prowess, clothing and war. They include *Iron Heart, Cherry Eye, Fast Horse, Blue Blanket* and *Running Shield*. Some names had three or even four words, such as *Owns Many Horses* and *Kills And Comes Back*.

The traditional naming system used by many tribes is clearly illustrated by probably the most famous American Indian, Sitting Bull. Originally, it was his father who was called Sitting Bull. Because his young son did things slowly and carefully, his father named him *Slow*. However, after Slow displayed spectacular courage in battle, his father paid him the ultimate compliment and gave his son his own name, Sitting Bull. The name described the huge male buffalo who was afraid of nothing, fighting to the death if need be. Sometimes it would sit down to fight to the death. From then on his father took the name Jumping Bull.

The American Indian custom of individuals changing their names at critical points throughout their lives ended early in the twentieth century when the US government decreed that the father's name should be the family name, and that it should be written as one word. This meant that what was in effect a by-name of a father suddenly became the family's surname. There are still some US surnames that clearly have American Indian origins, such Buffalohead, Fasthorse, Runningbear, Ironcloud, Ironhawk, Thundercloud, Thunderhawk and Wolfkill. More confronting are the surnames Fourkiller, Sixkiller and Whitekiller. (Though names can often be misleading—for example, Sixkiller may come from a German word *Sechsheller*, meaning someone from the village of Sechshelden.) Most of these names are held by no more than a couple of hundred people.

American Indian surnames are rare, in part because the population was decimated during European colonisation, and partly because those who remained were divided among many different tribes, each with its own language and names. Later, intermarriage between American Indians and white Americans usually resulted in Indian surnames being lost. This was because the subordinate social status of American Indians meant that it was much more likely that white men married American Indian women, rather than vice-versa. Charles Curtis, the 31st US Vice President, had a father with British ancestry and a mother whose parents and grandparents were largely American Indian.

The rarity of American Indian surnames is also the result of US government social policy. In the late nineteenth century, the Bureau of Indian Affairs started boarding schools in which the children were forced to abandon their American Indian identities. They had to adopt mainstream dress and hairstyles, attend Christian church, speak only English, and use new Americanized names, perhaps figures from US or British history, or even from a random list of names written on a blackboard. There was a similar name change whenever a child with an American Indian name was admitted to a government-run hospital. A less assimilationist policy came about only gradually during the course of the twentieth century.

It's also likely that many American Indians, like immigrants from Europe and elsewhere, voluntarily changed their traditional surnames to simpler, more familiar ones, particularly as they increasingly came into contact with mainstream US society. In a period when US citizens were shortening Davies to Davis, it's not surprising that many American Indians with surnames that were decidedly *not* simple and familiar opted to change them. I wonder, for example, just how many American Indian families named Ironhawk decided over the years to simplify their name to Irons or Hawk.

So, it's not surprising that the *Dictionary of American Family Names* concludes that 'many if not most American Indians have adopted English or Spanish surnames'. This comes through clearly if you look at a list of prominent American Indians from the last few decades. Choosing randomly, I found Charles Curtis, the US Vice-President mentioned earlier; Charles Bender, a member of the National Baseball Hall of Fame; John Herrington, a NASA astronaut; and Jaime Luis Gómez, a member of the hip hop group, the Black Eyed Peas. One final example will show my age, I'm sure. It concerns the actor Jay Silverheels, who played the loyal side-kick Tonto in the *Lone Ranger* TV series. I discovered that, although he was the son of a Mohawk chief, Jay Silverheels was his stage name. His real name was Harold J. Smith.

THIRTEEN

Catherine Zeta Jones and Andy Murray

Family names in Wales and Scotland

In both Wales and Scotland the move to inherited surnames came later than in England. Traditionally in Wales, as in other Gaelic regions of Britain, knowing your lineage was very important—knowing the name of your father, your grandfather, your great-grandfather, and even further back. The Welsh word for 'son of' is *map* or *mab* (like *mac* in Scotland and Ireland). And just as *mac* is often abbreviated to *mc*, in Wales *map* and *mab* are abbreviated to *ap* or *ab*. So, the name *David ap William* means 'David son of William'; and *Hugh ab Owen* means 'Hugh son of Owen' (*ab* usually goes before a vowel). According to Welsh scholar Hywel Wyn Owen, families could often recite their lineage back over several generations—though rarely the twelve generations included in the name of one sixteenth century Welshman: *David ap William ap David Lloyd ap Thomas ap Dafydd ap Gwilym ap Dafydd Ieuan ap Howel al Cynfrig ap Iorwerth Fychan ap Iorwerth ap Grono ap Tegerin.* It's even more impressive to say that Tegerin, the last named ancestor, was David's great-great-great-great-great-great-great-great-great-great-grandfather. Many of us these days have difficulty going back further than our grandparents.

As in England, members of the Welsh aristocracy were the first to see the political value of adopting English social customs, including the use of surnames. In the fifteenth century, Oliver Cromwell's paternal great-great-grandfather was a Welshman whose birth name was Morgan *ap*

William ('Morgan son of William'). He became the first in his family to adopt the English practice of surnames, and changed his name to Morgan Williams. The old naming system was linked to traditional Welsh land inheritance laws. When Henry VIII replaced them with English inheritance laws in the sixteenth century, it became even more important for wealthy Welsh families to safeguard their wealth by replacing their traditional Welsh names with English-style surnames.

Once the wealthy began using surnames, the practice then spread through the rest of the population, though it took many generations before everyone in Wales had a surname. For example, an official report from the mid-*nineteenth* century noted that in Wales surnames 'can scarcely be said to be adopted among the lower classes in the wilder districts, where, as the marriage registers show, the Christian name of the father still frequently becomes the patronymic of the son'. The language in official reports then was somewhat more direct than it is now.

Although inherited surnames did eventually replace by-names in Wales, the Welsh pattern of names was rather different from that across the border in England. For example, in Wales the traditional importance of a person's lineage was reflected in an even greater emphasis on surnames derived from a father's given name (the *patronymic* in the quote above). In fact, all the current top 10 Welsh surnames are based on fathers' given names:

| Jones | Williams | Davies | Evans | Thomas | Roberts | Lewis | Hughes | Morgan | Griffiths |

The top surname is not surprising, Jones being the name most clearly associated with Wales. In fact, you have more than a one in twenty chance of being right when guessing that someone from Wales is called Jones. Compare this to the one in a hundred chance of correctly guessing that someone from England is called Smith. Famous Welsh Joneses include actress Catherine Zeta Jones, comedian Griff Rhys Jones, Monty Python's Terry Jones, and singer Sir Tom Jones. Not surprisingly, at the time of writing the First Minister in the Welsh Assembly is also called Jones—it probably helps your electoral chances when you have the same surname as five per cent of your constituents. Jones means *son of Jon,* from the old spelling of the given name John. Another top ten name, Evans, means son of Iefan, which is a Welsh form of John. And a top twenty name, Jenkins, comes from a pet form of John with the addition of *kin*, meaning 'son'. Welsh movie star Richard Burton was originally Richard Jenkins. Trivia buffs will know that he married Elizabeth Taylor twice.

As well as Jones, other top ten Welsh surnames based on Norman given names are Williams, Thomas and Roberts. These, of course, are now names that we see as essentially 'Welsh' names. One quarter of players in the current Welsh rugby union squad, the national sport of Wales, are called Jones, Williams or Roberts. Historically, the player who has represented his country most often is Stephen *Jones*, and the player who has scored most tries is Shane *Williams*. As well as rugby, the Welsh are renowned for their love of music and poetry, and probably the best-known Welsh poet is Dylan *Thomas*, the inspiration for Bob Dylan's stage name.

The other top ten Welsh surnames all originally come from traditional Welsh given names. As well as Evans from Iefan, there's Davies from *Dafydd*, Lewis from *Llywelyn*, Hughes from *Hywel*, Griffiths from *Grufydd*, and Morgan from *Morcant*, an ancient Welsh given name. A few Welsh surnames retain traces of the earlier *ap* and *ab* system of naming, such as Upjohn which came from *ap John*, or 'son of John'. Much more common is when only the *p* or *b* has been integrated with the given name. For example, *ab Owen* became Bowen, *ab Evan* became Bevan, *ap Henry* became Penry, and *ap Huw* became Pugh.

Unlike in England, there are few Welsh surnames based on a person's occupation or where they lived. Even the usually dominant Smiths don't make it into the top ten surnames in Wales. And only a handful of surnames based on a person's appearance or behaviour are common in Wales. They include Lloyd and Gwynn, which originally described hair colouring; Bach, which referred to the person's small stature; and Vaughan, which was used when a father and son had the same given name.

Unfortunately, the pool of *given* names used in Wales was also quite small in the period when most Welsh surnames were created. By

145

the sixteenth century, many traditional Welsh given names, such as Cadell and Cynfyn, had been largely abandoned, and the number of Norman names that were introduced to replace them, such as John and William, was fairly small. In addition, making surnames from the short or pet forms of given names was much less common in Wales than in England.

The end result was that a very small pool of surnames developed in Wales. Add this to the equally small pool of popular given names, and the result was that Welsh personal names often didn't clearly distinguish someone from their neighbours. One solution was to add a by-name to the not-so-distinctive surname, a back-to-the-future option. Some were based on the person's occupation, such as the postman *Lloyd the Post;* or, less obviously, the schoolteacher *Evans the School;* or, least obviously, the undertaker *Evans Above.* Sometimes, the definite article was left out, so that *Jones the Draper* became simply *Jones Drapes.* Or it could be a geographical reference, such as adding a farm name to distinguish the Morgan Williams who lives on the east side of the valley from the Morgan Williams living on the west side.

Sometimes, the expanded name could be quite poetic, such as *Mostyn the Grove* and *Williams Holly Dingle.* And some Welsh by-names highlighted a well-known quality of the holder, such as *Hopkins Schopenhauer,* a coalminer well known for studying philosophers such as Schopenhauer; and *Jones First Corinthians,* a bus driver whose knowledge of the Bible was restricted to the First Epistle to the Corinthians.

Another long-established naming practice is for Welsh people to make use of their middle name, and become known by their full name. A current example is the Welsh-born actress Catherine Zeta Jones. Her family name is Jones, but even at school she realised that she was one of several girls named 'Catherine Jones', and so began to use her middle name Zeta (a grandmother's given name) as if it were part of her surname. Nowadays, you'll often come across references to

Catherine *Zeta-Jones*—notice the hyphen making a double-barrelled surname.

A rather more heavyweight example is David Lloyd George, who was British prime minister during most of the First World War. He was the son of William George and Elizabeth Lloyd, and is still the only British PM from Wales. In Wales, George is a common surname and David is a very common given name. In order to stand out in a crowd (always useful for an ambitious politician) David Lloyd George used his full name, so that *Lloyd George* in effect became his surname. He never hyphenated it, but when he was given a peerage he became Earl *Lloyd-George* (with a hyphen).

✲

If you were asked to give some typical Scottish surnames, there's a good chance that you'd come up with some starting with *Mac* or *Mc*—MacDonald, McGregor, Macmillan, and so on. There are certainly a lot of them in Scotland—an incredible 40,000, or about one in eight of all Scottish surnames. They range alphabetically from McAbee to MacZewnie, and take in such interesting names as McClammy, McCool, McSporran and MacVanish.

And yet, as the following list shows, the top 20 most frequently occurring Scottish surnames include only one *Mac* name, MacDonald.

Smith	Brown	Wilson	Campbell	Stewart	Thomson	Robertson	Anderson	MacDonald	Scott
Reid	Murray	Taylor	Clark	Ross	Watson	Morrison	Patterson	Young	Mitchell

Once again, it's the all-conquering Smiths who top the list. Second is Brown and third is Wilson, which are also top ten surnames in England. A fourth top ten name is Robertson, which is a variation of Roberts, another top ten British surname. And a fifth, Thomson, is a variation of a top twenty English surname, Thompson. (*Tintin* fans will be reminded of the two incompetent detectives, Thomson and Thompson.) In other words, although they have some distinctive features, Scottish surnames bear a lot of similarities to those south of the border.

Malcolm III was king of Scotland when William of Normandy conquered England in 1066. (He's the Malcolm who appears in Shakespeare's *Macbeth*.) However, the Highlands were not under his direct control, and even the Lowlands were unruly. When Malcolm's daughter Matilda married one of William's sons, the future King Henry I, Malcolm saw an opportunity to replace many of the unruly local chieftains. It led in the twelfth century to members of the Norman aristocracy being granted land in lowland Scotland. These new settlers brought new surnames into Scotland, such as Bruce and Menzies. As happened in England, once the aristocracy adopted family names, the custom began trickling down through the rest of society.

The same types of surnames began to appear in Scotland over the next few centuries as they did earlier in England. Once again, they include surnames based on a father's given name, surnames based on occupations, surnames based on geographical names, and surnames based on personal characteristics of appearance or behaviour.

Paternal surnames, based on a father's given name, make up half of the Scottish top twenty list: Wilson, Thomson, Robertson, Anderson, MacDonald, Watson, Morrison, Paterson, Young and Mitchell. Of course, the most distinctive Scottish surname is MacDonald, and I'll start by looking at it and other *Mac* names. Like kilts and bagpipes, surnames beginning with *Mac* or *Mc* are now a defining characteristic of 'Scottishness', though such surnames are also common in Ireland, where Gaelic is the traditional language.

The surname MacDonald literally means 'the son of Donald'. Strictly speaking, there's no difference between *Mac* and *Mc*. According to George Black, a leading expert on Scottish surnames, *Mac* has been 'wrongly contracted' to *Mc* and *M'*. It may be that the contraction to *Mc* has occurred less in Scotland than in Ireland. For example, according to one large surname dictionary, almost half of *Mac* surnames but only one fifth of *Mc* names clearly originated in Scotland. In contrast, almost half the *Mc* surnames but only one fifth of *Mac* names clearly originated in Ireland. Experts are unsure about which side of the Irish Sea the remaining *Mac* and *Mc* names originated, which is not surprising given the complex comings and goings of people between the two countries. Certainly, *Mac*Donald is the only *Mac/Mc* name in the Scottish top twenty, while *Mc*Carthy is the only *Mac/Mc* name in the Irish top twenty. Of course, the most widespread Irish names start with *O'*, the prefix meaning 'grandson of'. But in Scotland family names starting with *O'* are very rare.

I mentioned earlier that about one in eight Scottish family names begins either with *Mac* or *Mc*. The fact that there are so many of them goes a long way to explain why only MacDonald is in the Scottish top twenty names, and just five others (McDonald, Mackenzie, Mackay, McLean, and MacLeod) are in the top fifty surnames. Of course, if there is no difference between *Mac* and *Mc* names, it makes sense to combine each *Mac/Mc* pair, such as *Mac*Donald and *Mc*Donald. When you do this, the combined name shoots up to second place in the Scottish surname list, and it's joined in the top twenty by another combined name, MacKenzie/McKenzie.

In the late Middle Ages, Gaelic was the dominant language in Scotland. However, its influence gradually waned and by the eighteenth century it was spoken mainly in the Highlands and Islands of north and west Scotland. It was in this area, well away from the government in Edinburgh, that the Scottish clans had most influence. The word 'clan' is a Gaelic word meaning 'family', and the head of the largest landowning family in the area was the clan chief.

One of the ways of symbolising the power of the clan was to have everyone living in its territory take the clan name as their own. So, the name was not a family name in the usual sense. For example, inhabitants of a village may have had the same clan name, but were not necessarily blood relatives. Territorial disputes often led to clan warfare, and as a result land passed from the control of one clan to another. The local population affected by these local political changes would often adopt the name of the new clan chief in an attempt to keep their life and liberty. At other times, local people were bribed into adopting a clan name.

It was common throughout England and in the lowland areas of Scotland for workers on a landowner's estate to adopt the surname of their master. But the clan system in the Scottish Highlands made the process much less voluntary. The use of the clan name didn't serve to distinguish a family from its neighbours. In fact, it did the opposite: the name was a unifying symbol of clan membership. One way around the resulting problem of identification was to add an alias—for example, Roderick MacLennan *alias Watson*. Alternatively, as happened in Wales, a by-name or nickname was added after the surname. Called *to-names* in Scotland, they often described the person's appearance or manner, such as *Biggelugs* (Big Ears), *Carrot* (red-headed) and *Toothie*.

The *Mac* names we are familiar with today are not how they were originally written in Gaelic. For example, MacDonald comes from the Gaelic name *MacDhòmhnuill*, and MacKenzie comes from *MacCoinnich*. The gradual replacement of Gaelic names with ones that English-speakers could more easily say and spell reflects in part the gradual replacement of Gaelic with the English language in Scotland. In particular, after the Highland uprising in support of Bonnie Prince Charlie ended in defeat at the Battle of Culloden in 1746, the government prohibited all aspects of Highland culture, including the Gaelic language. This speeded up the trend to anglicise Gaelic names.

Later in the eighteenth and early nineteenth centuries, the local land-owners enclosed large areas of the Highlands for sheep farming, and most of the local Gaelic population were forced to move off their traditional land. These 'clearances' led to a rapid fall in the population of many areas as people migrated to lowland Scotland, England and overseas. Like many migrants before and since, the Highland Scots attempted to integrate into their new environment by adopting names that the local population could handle more easily. Those who migrated to lowland Scotland had the additional problem of the long-standing animosity between Highlanders and Lowlanders. They used a variety of ways to anglicise their names.

Most commonly, they attempted to spell the sound of the Gaelic name using the English spelling system. Of course, you need to know how the original Gaelic name is pronounced in order to see the connection, but I understand, for example, that MacKenzie sounds reasonably close to *MacCoinnich*.

Another way used to anglicise Gaelic surnames was to translate the meaning of the original into English. *MacNider* means 'son of the weaver', and so was translated into Weaver. For some surnames, it was an easy matter to replace the *Mac* at the start of the name with *son* at the end—such as MacDonald being anglicised to Donaldson.

A third option was simply to choose a new name almost at random. For example, in 1792 Neil M'Leay left one of the western islands to find work in a cotton mill near Glasgow. (*M'* is another short form of Mac.) Like others in his clan, he changed his name from M'Leay to Livingstone, though there isn't any obvious connection in the meaning of these two names. His grandson, David Livingstone, became a famous explorer in Africa. In one of life's little curiosities, he's now best known from Henry Morton Stanley's ironic greeting after tracking down the explorer—the only European for hundreds of miles around—saying: "Dr Livingstone, I presume?" Had it not been for his grandfather's change of name, the phrase would have been, "Dr M'Leay, I presume?" (Though, of course, if Livingstone's grandfather had not gone to Glasgow, then the M'Leay family history would almost certainly have been very different...)

Generally, the geographical origins of most *Mac* surnames is still apparent in the present-day distribution of surnames. *Mac* surnames make it into the top ten in only a handful of Scottish local government areas. They are located almost entirely in the Highlands and Islands, particularly in two council areas: in the Outer Hebrides, where they make up six of the top ten surnames (MacLeod, MacDonald, MacKenzie, MacKay, MacLean and MacIver); and in the Highland local government area around Inverness, where they make up four of the top ten surnames (MacDonald, MacKenzie, MacKay and MacLeod).

Apart from MacDonald, Anderson is the only other top twenty paternal surname with a reasonably distinctive Scottish flavour. It occurs throughout Britain, but its stronghold is in Scotland, hence its 8th position in the Scottish list, but 38th on the British list. Originally, it showed its origins more clearly, being *Andrewson*. Andrew has long been the patron saint of Scotland, and the Scottish national flag is the St Andrew's Cross. So, it's not surprising that many patriotic Scots proudly displayed their nationality by adopting the name of the patron saint as the family name.

What about the other paternal surnames in the top twenty Scottish surnames? Wilson is the most common one in Scotland, and it's also in the English top ten surnames. And the other two in the top ten, Thomson and Robertson, are variations of two English top ten names, Thompson and Roberts. Other paternal surnames in the Scottish top twenty include Morrison, which comes from the given name Maurice; Paterson from Patrick; Mitchell from Michael; and Watson from Walter. One peculiar Scottish trait applies to surnames created from shortened forms of given names, which often end in *ie* rather than the more general *kin*. For example, Walter was often shortened to Wat. The 'son of Wat' in Scotland often had the surname Wattie, whereas south of the border it was more likely to be Watkins. Another example is the 'son of Dick', which in Scotland gave rise to Dickie rather than Dickens.

The final paternal surname in the top twenty is Young. It's much more common in Scotland than elsewhere in Britain. The by-name Young was given when the son had the same name as his father. For example, if both were named Robert, then in Middle English the son might be known as Robert *le Yunge*. So, the name is the equivalent of Vaughan in Wales.

There are only four occupational surnames in the Scottish top 20: Smith, Stewart, Taylor and Clark. Stewart is the only one that is essentially Scottish. It has a long history in Scotland, going back to the twelfth century when the Scottish king appointed Walter Fitz-Alan as High Steward of Scotland, his right-hand man. The position became hereditary, and Walter Fitz-Alan was succeeded as High Steward by his son, Alan Fitz-Walter. By-names were still in use at this time. It was his son, another Walter, who was the first in the family to have a surname. Not surprisingly, the High Steward chose the family name Steward, which in time became corrupted to Stewart.

In the fourteenth century, the 7th High Steward of Scotland, Robert Stewart, became King Robert II of Scotland, and Stewart then became the name of the royal house of Scotland. Mary, Queen of Scots, changed the spelling from Stewart to *Stuart* in the sixteenth century to make it easier for French speakers to pronounce correctly. However, it came too late to have much impact on Scottish surnames. So, off the top of my head I can think of no Scottish *Stuarts*, but four Scottish *Stewarts*—entertainer Rod Stewart, racing driver Jackie Stewart, soccer player Michael Stewart, and Andy Stewart, composer of the comic song 'Donald Where's Your Troosers?' (I'm showing my age here!)

Given this highest of high profiles in Scottish history, it's not surprising that Stewart became a popular Scottish surname. The numerous royal descendants founded other branches of the family throughout Scotland, and many of their servants also adopted the surname, wanting some of the prestige that went with it. Outside the top twenty names, other typically Scottish occupational surnames include Lamont (lawmaker), Lorimer (harness maker), Naismith (cutler), Napier (linen maker) and Sillars (silversmith). These common Scottish names are all quite rare in England.

The most famous Scottish geographical name is Burns, made famous by Scotland's much-loved poet, Robbie Burns (of 'Auld Lang Syne' fame). In Scotland, a *burn* is a stream, and originally someone with that name would have lived by a burn. Burns is not in the top twenty Scottish surnames, but three other geographical surnames are—Scott, Murray and Ross. All have a Scottish flavour.

Some by-names referred to a person's country of birth— for example, Welsh and Walsh identified Welsh migrants in England. Using this logic, it's not immediately clear why the name Scott should occur most often in Scotland itself—the one place where it wouldn't help identify the holder. One explanation is that the name was used to describe Gaelic speakers living in non-Gaelic-speaking areas of Scotland.

A similar surname is Wallace, a top fifty Scottish surname made famous by a thirteenth century patriot, William Wallace, who fought against the English in the Wars of Scottish Independence. He has been immortalised in print and film, such as the movie *Braveheart*. The name comes from the Old English word *waelisc*, meaning 'foreign', and was applied to people of the old kingdom of Strathclyde in southwest Scotland, whose ancestors were ancient Britons. Those who survived into the medieval period with some of their original culture intact were regarded as foreign by the Scots majority, hence the surname Wallace.

Scotland's favourite tennis player is Glasgow-born Andy Murray—the only Scot to win an open men's singles championship at Wimbledon (so far!). His popularity in Scotland is helped, of course, by the fact that his given name is the same as the Scottish patron saint, and his family name is also one that's particularly Scottish. Murray comes from the place name Moray, as in Moray Firth, the large bite that the North Sea has taken out of northeast Scotland. Tradition has it that the name originated in the twelfth century when a Flemish settler was given land there by the Scottish king and told to adopt a surname from a local place name. The family prospered, often through well-chosen marriages, and their landholdings increased, taking the surname across Scotland.

However, Murray is not just a geographical surname. In Ireland it's a paternal name coming from the Gaelic name *Mac Giolla Mhuire*, meaning descendant of the servant of the Virgin Mary. Not surprisingly, Murray is also a top twenty surname in Ireland, traditionally a strong

Catholic area. It's likely then that some of today's Scottish Murrays are the descendants of Irish settlers who came over to Scotland to find work during the nineteenth century. Famous Scots with an Irish heritage include Arthur Conan Doyle, the creator of Sherlock Holmes, movie actor Sean Connery, and comedian Billy Connolly.

Perhaps the most Scottish of geographical surnames is Ross, which although in the top twenty of Scottish surnames, doesn't make it even into the top hundred British surnames. A map of its distribution still shows a concentration of the name around the ancient earldom of Ross in the far north of Scotland, and then a steady fall in frequency as you move into southern Scotland, and then northern England. The name is rare in southern England.

Not all well-known Scottish geographical surnames are home-grown. For example, the family name Bruce owes its high profile to Robert the Bruce who, following the defeat of the English in the Wars of Scottish Independence, went on to become King Robert I. The first Robert *de Brus* was probably from either Brix or Le Brus in Normandy, and came over with William the Conqueror. The royal Bruce line quickly died out, but its several offshoots became major landowners, and the name multiplied as thousands of workers on the Bruce estates also took the same name. A similar example is the geographical surname Menzies. Widespread in Scotland, it's virtually unknown south of the border. This surname can also be traced back to Normandy, to the district of Mesnières, where the family were local landholders. They were one of the Norman aristocratic families granted land by royal decree, and went on to become an influential Scottish family in the central Highlands.

There are three surnames in the Scottish top twenty based on personal characteristics of appearance or behaviour: Brown, Reid and Campbell. If you leave out the *Mac* names, then Campbell is probably the most Scottish of surnames. Legend has it that the name originated in the thirteenth century with an individual whose by-name came from the Gaelic word *cambeul*, meaning 'crooked mouth'. Clan Campbell figures large in Scottish history. During the Wars of Scottish Independence, the Campbells fought on the winning side of the Scottish king, Robert the Bruce. They were richly rewarded, with grants of lands, titles and good marriages, including that of the king's sister to the clan leader, Neil Campbell. They went on to be a powerful force, owning over one million acres of land by the nineteenth century.

Cameron is less common than Campbell, but still a top fifty Scottish name. It too is from a Gaelic phrase, *cam-shròn*, which is usually translated as 'hooked nose'. Apparently, a hooked nose was a distinguishing feature of old Clan Cameron families—though it's doubtful whether the nose of the British Prime Minister David Cameron (who has a Scottish heritage) could be described in this way. Still, it could have been worse. Another surname which comes from a Gaelic nickname is Kennedy, which means 'ugly headed' or, if you're being kind, 'grim headed'.

*

I've mentioned the often-turbulent history of Scotland a number of times, with fighting between Scottish clans, and between the Scots and English. It was the first of these that led to two clan names being banned by a despairing Scottish King James VI and I, who was trying to rule a country that one historian describes as being 'in a constant ferment of clan feuds and border raids, punctuated with massacres, burnings, robberies and hangings'.

One of the most unruly clans was the MacGregors, who had long-standing conflicts with the Campbells, MacLarens, Drummonds and Colquhouns. In 1603 the MacGregors routed the Colquhouns in battle, and slaughtered a group of clerical students who had turned up to watch. (These were obviously interesting times, though I'm sure the MacGregor version of events is somewhat different.) At this point, King James lost patience and issued an edict proclaiming that the name MacGregor was *altogidder abolished*. Those who renounced the name MacGregor adopted other surnames such as Stewart, Grant and Dougall, but many men refused to give up their clan name, and fled into the countryside. Those who were captured alive were executed. But many died trying to avoid being captured, as there was a government reward for each MacGregor head brought in. The women and children were sold as slaves in America.

Although the political climate changed, and the ban was lifted briefly in the mid-seventeenth century, it was reintroduced several years later, meaning that the MacGregors' most famous son, Rob Roy MacGregor (1671-1734) was forced to give up his birth name. For political purposes, he chose to use his mother's name, Campbell, despite the deep-seated animosity between the two clans. The ban on the name MacGregor was not finally abolished until the late eighteenth century. Since then, it has made a comeback, being a top 100 Scottish surname (as *Mc*Gregor) for at least the last century.

The Ruthven clan doesn't have a famous son like Rob Roy MacGregor, though one son did win a Victoria Cross and went on to become Governor-General of Australia, but the story of the banning of their clan name is very similar to that of the MacGregors. In the sixteenth century, one of the clan, William Ruthven, played a major part in kidnapping the teenage King James VI and I, and took control of the government of Scotland. Of course, it didn't end happily. When the king was eventually freed, William Ruthven was beheaded for treason. King James obviously had a long memory, because twenty years later, his men killed two of William's sons, John and Alexander Ruthven. The official story was that they too were trying to kidnap the king. They were then posthumously condemned for treason, their bodies were hanged, drawn and quartered, with their heads displayed in Edinburgh, and their arms and legs displayed in Perth. For good measure, the king decreed 'that the surname of Ruthven shall now and in all tyme cumming be extinguischit and aboleissit for euir'. However, the Ruthven story does eventually have a happy ending. James's successor, Charles I, didn't have such personal memories of Clan Ruthven, and he rescinded the ban on the use of the surname.

FOURTEEN

Elvis ~~Bressler~~ ~~Preslar~~ Presley

Migration and family names

In one of the classic BBC TV comedies, *To the Manor Born,* the main female character, the aristocratic Audrey fforbes-Hamilton, has to sell her beloved manor house to cover her debts. (The *ff* isn't a misprint; this was how a medieval scribe wrote a capital *F,* showing that the surname is an old one.) The buyer is Richard DeVere, the owner of a chain of supermarkets. His surname, which harks back to the Norman Conquest, suggests that he comes from a long-established English family—a suggestion he is happy to go along with. However, it turns out that Richard DeVere is not quite who he says he is. Eventually, he tells Audrey that he is a migrant from Czechoslovakia, and that his birth name was Bedrich Polouvicka. Of course, after many false starts, the couple fall in love and marry ... However, like much good comedy, *To the Manor Born* is grounded in reality as many migrants do their utmost to fit into their new country, often taking on a new name.

Large-scale migration leads to major changes in naming patterns. We've already seen how the Norman invaders changed Anglo-Saxon names. Migration to Britain didn't stop with the Normans. For example, Flemings from what is now Belgium migrated to Britain not long after the Norman Conquest. At first they were encouraged to come, but by the mid-twelfth century they were seen as competitors for local jobs. In those less genteel times, things could get really rough, with mobs in London hunting down possible Flemish migrants. Anyone whose English accent

158

sounded foreign was likely to be attacked and possibly murdered. Not surprisingly, Flemish migrants were keen to fit in, and quickly took local personal names to help them do this. However, individual Flemish families in smaller places would often be given the locational by-name *Fleming*, which over time developed into an inherited surname.

While the driving force behind the migration of Flemings to Britain was economic prosperity, what pushed the Huguenots out of France was religious persecution. They were Protestants in a predominantly Catholic country, and tension between the two groups developed into civil war in the mid-1500s. Many Huguenots fled from France to more welcoming Protestant countries, such as England. The migration lasted well into the eighteenth century. Indeed, the migration was on such a large scale that a new word was coined to describe them, *refugees*. The number of Huguenot refugees in relation to the national population size was so large that most English people today will have some Huguenot blood in their veins.

At first, Huguenot refugees were hopeful that conditions in France would improve, and they would then be able to go back. As a result, they tended to keep their own names. But many did not return, and what were once Huguenot surnames, such as Bosanquet, Courtauld and Garrick, are now seen as English names. However, conditions in France deteriorated in the seventeenth century, and it became obvious to Huguenot migrants that they would not be returning to France. As a result, the Huguenots proved very willing to become English, including taking on an English name. For example, the French surname Andrieu became the English surname Andrews; Boulanger, the French word for baker, became Baker; de la Croix became Cross; and so on.

There have been many other arrivals in Britain since the Flemish migrants and the Huguenot refugees. People from South Asia began to arrive in the seventeenth century. In the eighteenth century, thousands of West Africans were brought as part of the slave trade. The eighteenth century also saw the arrival of many refugees from parts of Germany that had been invaded by French forces. One of the most famous fictional characters in English literature was the son of a German immigrant called *Kreutznaer*, who after settling in England changed his surname to Crusoe. His wife came from 'a very good Family' named Robinson, and of course their son was Robinson Crusoe.

In the nineteenth century, many Jews who were being persecuted in Russia came to Britain; and in the twentieth century, persecution of Jews in Nazi Germany resulted in more Jewish arrivals. After World War II, there were also many refugees from Soviet-controlled Eastern Europe. The years after World War II also saw many people from Commonwealth countries, especially those in South Asia and the Caribbean, come to work in Britain. Most recently, there have been migrants from Eastern European countries such as Poland as the expansion of the European Community has freed up movement of people. Today, almost one in ten people in Britain were born overseas.

Like the Flemings and Huguenots, these more recent migrants from overseas have had an impact on naming patterns in Britain, in particular migrants from the Indian sub-continent who are most likely to keep their original name. In fact, there are now eight names with an Asian origin in the top hundred British surnames: Patel, Begum, Khan, Singh, Hussain, Ali, Ahmed and Kaur. There are several possible reasons behind this.

First, a change from an Indian sub-continental name to a traditional British name is less likely to be accepted either by the general public or by the migrant's own community. Secondly, many Asian family names like Patel and Begum are easy to say and spell, and so the general public is comfortable using them. Thirdly, Asian migrants are sometimes keen to keep their family names because they say something about the social status of the family in the home country. Particularly in South Asia, family names vary according to *caste*, the traditional status group. The most common South Asian surname in Britain is the Indian name Patel. Traditionally, it is an official title showing that the person is a village headman. Similarly, the family names Begum and Khan are ones that most Pakistani migrants would be reluctant to give up. Begum is the used by women of high social status; and Khan originally meant ruler or nobleman (as in Genghis Khan), and is now a title for a Muslim property owner. Begum and Khan are the second and third most common Asian surnames in Britain.

Asian family names can also have religious significance. Singh and Kaur were at one time mandatory names for Sikh men and women, the names being laid down in the seventeenth century. And the Arabic names Hussain, Ali and Ahmed are all closely associated with Islam: historically, Hussain and Ali were close relatives of the Prophet Muhammad; and Ahmed is an alternative name for Muhammad.

✳

However, by far the largest international movement of people has been to the US, particularly at the end of the nineteenth century and the start of the twentieth century. Around this time, one in five people in the US were born elsewhere, almost all of them in Europe. The American *melting pot* describes how US migrants were willing to lose at least part of their original culture to become integrated into American culture. The adoption of a more Americanized personal name was part of this. The practice was also what the existing American population expected of migrants from other cultures.

There are lots of anecdotes about how immigration officials at reception centres, most famously Ellis Island off New York, mangled the names of many of the migrants they processed—such as the Italian who said his name was *Mastroianni* but was recorded as *Mr Yanni;* or the Swedish family called *Ness* who thought they were being given a name when the immigration official called out *Next!* Sadly, it turns out that most of these stories are not true. The truth is that before 1924, immigrants arrived with their names given on a passenger list drawn up before the ship sailed from Europe; and from 1924, immigrants had to have visas complete with their full name. So, the naming role of immigration officials was confined to those early migrants who didn't have a surname when they landed in the US. For the vast majority who did, the Americanization of their European family name came *after* they had landed, possibly in the following one or two generations.

Not surprisingly, poorer migrants have always been the ones most willing to jump into the American melting pot. For example, in the earliest days of European immigration to America Dutch settlers were among the first to experience the pressures of cultural change. Some of the wealthier strongly resisted, and as a result their family names and family fortunes survive, but their poorer kinsfolk couldn't resist the cultural pressures, and so for example most of the *Kuipers* became *Coopers,* and the *Haerlens* became *Harlands*.

Some migrants, of course, were more than happy to leave their past—and their name—behind, to start their lives afresh in their new country. In 1859 Ola Månsson abandoned his family in his native Sweden without answering questions about a financial scandal. He settled in rural Minnesota with his mistress and child, and changed his name to August Lindbergh. In 1927 his grandson, Charles Lindbergh, for a while became the most famous person in the world following his single-handed flight across the North Atlantic. In fact, he was so famous and adored that the government of his home state considered changing its name from Minnesota to *Lindberghia*. If his grandfather had kept his original surname, the state government might have looked more favourably on the name *Mansonia*.

The nineteenth and early twentieth centuries were characterised by a general trend in the US to simplify the language, and so make American English different from (and better than) British English. It was during this time that dictionary guru Noah Webster was pushing for simplified, phonetic spelling of ordinary English words such as *plow* rather than *plough*. When it came to place names, the federal government's Board on Geographic Names was busy making spelling more phonetic so, for example, *Greensborough* became *Greensboro*. There was no federal government Board on Personal Names, but the general culture of the times encouraged similar changes.

There's no doubt that in a period less restricted by written records, there were a lot of changes to migrants' names. An article written in 1932, at the end of nearly a century of mass migration, provides a close-hand account of what had been happening to surnames in the United States. The conclusion reached was that many of the name changes were based on the idea that Americans should have a name that was both simple and familiar.

Even traditional English names were not immune from this trend to make names as simple and familiar as possible. For example, the surname Davies, which today is a top 10 name in Britain, in the US was usually shortened to Davis, with the result that today Davis is a US top ten surname, while Davies just scrapes into the US top thousand. But, of course, the longer and less familiar the name, the more likely it was to be shortened. For example, the Polish name Mikolajezyk often became Mikos, and the Greek name Pappadimitracoupoulos, not surprisingly, became Pappas or Papas.

Many of the personal names from northwest Europe have a common source, and so it wasn't difficult for many migrants from there to find a familiar English surname. Johnson is the second most common surname in the US, having incorporated the Scottish Johnston, the Irish Johnstone, the Swedish Johansson, and the Dutch and Danish Jansen. This didn't happen to anything like the same extent in Britain, with the result that Johnson is a less common surname there. Similarly, Miller is in the US top ten because it has incorporated several European variants such as Müller, Millar and Mueller. In Britain, where such large-scale incorporation didn't occur, Miller isn't in the top fifty surnames.

More generally, simplifying the original spelling while keeping at least some of the original pronunciation has long been a practice for people migrating to another culture. Well-known American figures whose family name illustrates this include General William Custer (of 'Last Stand' fame) whose great grandfather was called Kösters; William Cody (better known as Buffalo Bill) whose family was originally called Kothe; General John Pershing (a US Army commander with a tank and missile named after him) whose ancestors were named Pfoersching;

Herbert Hoover (the 31st US President) whose great-great-great grandfather was called Huber; and, last but *certainly* not least, there's Elvis Presley (the 'King of Rock and Roll') whose ancestors (as the chapter title suggests) changed their surname from Bressler to Preslar and then to Presley.

Another way that US migrants Americanized their family names was to find an English translation of what their surname meant. This was common among those with occupational family names. As happened in sixteenth century England among Huguenot migrants, French-speaking migrants to the US often changed their surname from Boulanger, the French word for baker, to Baker—as did many Bäckers from Germany, and Bakkers from the Netherlands. Similarly Zimmermann, the German word for a carpenter, was replaced by the surname Carpenter. Using the same logic, Bauer became Farmer, Schneider became Taylor, and Gerber became Tanner. Non-occupational examples include the Scandinavian Nyhus, German Neuhas and, less obviously, the Hungarian Újházi, all of which became Newhouse. And, least obviously, Irish settlers named MacConchoille often changed to Woods, the Gaelic name meaning 'son of the Hound of the Wood'.

You may have noticed that there are a lot of German names mentioned so far. There are two main reasons for this. First, immigration to the US from what is now Germany has been so large over several centuries that people claiming German ancestry now make up the largest ancestral group in the US—nearly fifty million Americans.

Secondly, there was considerable anti-German feeling among the US population in the two world wars, with thousands of German Americans being interned. During the First World War, war hysteria resulted in violence for many German Americans. One way for German Americans to show their loyalty to the US and, at the same time, hide their German origins was to Americanize their names, just as street names and business names were Americanized. In fact, purging the language of any German 'contamination' went so far that sauerkraut was re-named *liberty cabbage* and, believe it or not, German measles became *liberty measles.* Not surprisingly, the surname Hitler, which had been a fairly common name in the US before the rise of Nazi Germany, disappeared from the telephone directory by the time war broke out in Europe in 1939. Ironically, most Americans named Hitler were Jews who in the nineteenth and early twentieth centuries had migrated to the US to escape persecution by central European governments.

There's an intriguing story about one US migrant called Hitler who didn't change his surname, at least not at first. Patrick William ('Willy') Hitler was the British-born nephew of the Nazi leader. Although hard to believe, the story was that he travelled from Britain to Germany in the 1930s, and persuaded his uncle to find him several jobs, none of which he stayed at for long. He tried to blackmail Uncle Adolf into getting him more highly paid work by threatening to circulate a rumour that one of Adolf Hitler's grandmothers was Jewish. Realising that he might have gone too far, Willy left Germany in a hurry. He ended up eventually in the US, where he tried to enlist in the US Navy under his own name. When his application was turned down, he wrote an open letter to the US President asking for his support. He eventually did join the US Navy after being vetted by the FBI. After the war, he changed his surname from Hitler to Stuart-Houston. Strangely, this surname was very similar to that of an anti-Semitic author, Houston Stewart Chamberlain who was popular with the Nazis. Even more curious was that he gave his oldest son the names Alexander Adolf.

Jewish migrants are another group who have experienced general hostility in the US. For example, in the first half of the twentieth century, anti-Semitism led many Jews in the US to change their family names. In the early years of Hollywood, Jewish actors found it impossible to get on unless they had a non-Jewish stage name. So, David Kaminsky became Danny Kaye, Bernard Schwartz became Tony Curtis, and Jerome Levitch became Jerry Lewis.

Jewish migrants were generally less attached to their family names than other groups. In part, this was because they had not had their surnames long. Historically, Jews used patronymics, such as *David ben Joseph*

(David, son of Joseph) or *Miriam bat Aaron* (Miriam, daughter of Aaron). Jews had been compelled to adopt surnames by many European governments who wanted a better system for keeping their Jewish population under surveillance. Government officials punished anyone who resisted, perhaps by not paying the expected bribe, by giving them ridiculous surnames such as *Gimpel* ('dunce').

Not surprisingly, many Jewish immigrants willingly took on standard American surnames to get rid of their recently adopted European surnames. Sometimes, they took similar-sounding names, such as when a Russian Jewish immigrant called Moishe Gershowitz changed his name to Morris Gershwin. He passed this family name on to his two sons, George and Ira Gershwin, creators of some of the most memorable songs of the twentieth century. Sometimes, Jewish migrants shortened their surnames, so Davidovich became Davis, and Goldberg became Gold. They also translated their surnames into English, so Gruenfeld became Greenfield. Often they chose completely new surnames, such as Cooper, Gordon and King, to mark the end of their old life in Europe, and the start of their new life in the US.

On the other hand, there have always been many migrant families who resisted the pressures to Americanize their family names. This was easier to do when migrants came in such numbers that they became the dominant ethnic group in a city neighbourhood. For example, after 1890 there was large-scale US immigration from the south of Italy, with many coming over with friends and neighbours from their home village. Consequently, they formed tight-knit communities in US cities, maintaining their own culture, including speaking Italian. As a result, you see many famous Americans with Italian names.

While browsing the Baseball Hall of Fame (I had time on my hands...) I noticed two very famous players with Italian names. First, there's Giuseppe (Joe) DiMaggio, whose marriage to Marilyn Monroe, though it only lasted only 274 days, pretty much guarantees that his name will be famous regardless of his baseball status. Second, there's Lorenzo (Yogi) Berra, whose nickname related to yoga, not bears—in fact, he sued the cartoon company for naming Yogi Bear after him. But Italian names like DiMaggio and Berra make up just some of the many ethnic surnames of players in the Hall of Fame, whose careers go back to the 1860s. A quick count showed that well over one third of players have ethnic names—alphabetically, all the way from Roberto Alomar to Carl Yastrzemski.

Today, the cultural climate has changed, and the pressure on migrants to Americanize their names is nothing like as strong as it was. Oscar winners Dustin Hoffman and Richard Dreyfus both kept their original Jewish names. One of my favourite TV shows is the US comedy *Big Bang Theory*. It has four main American characters: Sheldon Cooper, Penny X (we don't know her surname), Leonard Hofstadter and Howard Wolowitz. These characters are played respectively by Jim Parsons, Kaley Cuoco, Johnny Galeki and Simon Helberg, but I suspect that most viewers don't really notice the mixture of English, German, Polish, Italian and Jewish surnames among the characters and cast.

Today, rather than *melting pot*, terms such as *salad bowl* or *kaleidoscope* are often used to suggest that migrants are now much more likely to retain many aspects of their home culture, including their names. The rest of the chapter looks at two of the most significant groups of migrants in the US salad bowl of the twenty-first century, Hispanic Americans and Asian Americans.

Population changes over the last few decades in the US may well have led to a reduction in pressure on migrants to adopt more American surnames to help them blend into mainstream US culture. Over the last half-century or so, the descendants of migrants from Europe, the drivers of mainstream culture, have declined as a proportion of the total US population. Just after World War II, they made up nearly nine in ten of the total population; they now comprise less than two-thirds; and the US Census Bureau forecasts that they will make up less than half the total US population by the middle of this century.

One of the main reasons for this decline has been the increase in *Hispanic* migrants from Latin America whose first language is Spanish. Just after

World War II, these migrants formed a negligible proportion of the total US population; now, they comprise one in six; and by the middle of the century it's likely that one on four Americans will be Hispanic. Because of this large-scale migration, two Spanish surnames, Garcia and Rodriguez, are in the top ten of US surnames, and one in five of the top hundred surnames are Spanish. The chances are that these numbers will increase as the US Hispanic population increases because history shows that most Hispanic migrants keep their Spanish surnames. One reason for this is that mainstream America has long seen Hispanic surnames such as Garcia, Martinez, Lopez, Perez, Gomez and Diaz to be both simple and familiar.

Another reason is that the scale of Hispanic migration to the US has meant that the areas where they form the majority of the population has expanded from the neighbourhood level up to city level. In the not-too-distant future, they will form the majority in some states. Hispanics make up almost one half of the total population of Los Angeles, the second biggest city in the US. At the state level, Spanish speakers make up almost half of the population of New Mexico, and over one third of the population of California and Texas. As a result, many government documents and services in these states are bilingual. Consequently, the practical importance of integrating into mainstream US society has lessened, including the need to master English and adopt American surnames.

Migrants from Asia also have family names that are simple for most Americans to say and spell. The top 500 US surnames include Indian names Patel and Singh, Chinese names Wong and Wang, Korean names Kim and Park, and Vietnamese names Nguyen and Pham. In that list, only Nguyen might cause some pronunciation and spelling problems. *Really* short Asian surnames include Li, Lu and Wu from China; Yu and Ho from Korea; and Le, Ly, Vu and Vo from Vietnam.

Although most Asian surnames are simple to say and spell, they are still unfamiliar to many Americans. This is because Asian migrants currently make up just one in twenty of the US population. However, this is likely to change with migration from Asia growing as quickly as that from Latin America. Asian surnames like Nguyen, Kim and Wong are most often found on the Pacific coastline, the region of North America closest to Asia. For example, Asian migrants and their descendants make up about one in seven of the population of Los Angeles and Seattle. Across the Canadian border, forty per cent of the population of the city of Vancouver are of Asian descent.

FIFTEEN

Mr Tom Dixon & Mrs Tom Dixon

Marriage and family names

I live in a part of Australia that wasn't settled by Europeans until the 1830s. The main town in the district, Warrnambool, dates back to the 1840s. Today, by the beach there's a memorial plaque for one of the early European settlers that reads: 'Granny's Grave. In memory of Mrs James Raddlestone, the first white woman buried in Warrnambool. Died 1848. Erected by the Town Council 1904.' The plaque reflects the custom of the time that a married woman was formally addressed by her husband's full name, *Mrs James Raddlestone*. The fact that the wife is almost hidden behind her husband's name was brought home to me one day by a visitor who missed the all-important s at the end of *Mrs*, and asked me why on earth it was called *Granny's* Grave when it was a memorial to a man called James Raddlestone.

Feminist writers in particular believe that modern societies are fundamentally patriarchal, meaning that men are the movers and shakers. This has been the case for many centuries. Indeed, an ancient Jewish prayer—presumably only for men—gives thanks to 'our God, ruler of the universe who has not created me a woman'. If history is written by the victors, then in the battle of the sexes, history is written by men, and the role of women is downplayed. If women are not important, then their names are not worth recording.

For feminists, this comes out clearly in the Bible. The Book of Genesis in the Old Testament was written about 2500 years ago. You may remember the story of Lot's wife, who was turned into a pillar of salt when she looked back to see God's destruction of the cities of Sodom and Gomorrah. Although she is a key figure in the story, she is not named, but referred to only as Lot's wife. Better known perhaps are Noah and his three sons, Shem, Ham and Japheth, who sailed on Noah's Ark when God flooded the earth. However, although all four men were accompanied by their wives, the Book of Genesis doesn't name any of them. Come forward several hundred years to the time of the New Testament. The Gospel of St Matthew names the brothers of Jesus as James, Joses, Simon and Judas, but the sisters of Jesus are not named.

One thousand years after the New Testament was written, people in Britain began using surnames. The custom developed that after marriage a woman replaced her unmarried *maiden* surname (her father's) with her married surname (her husband's). The feminist explanation is that the change of name is symbolic of a husband's total domination of his wife. A delegate at a US Woman's Rights Convention in 1858 didn't pull her punches about this: 'the slavery and degradation of woman proceeds from the institution of marriage; by the marriage contract she loses the control of her name, her person, her property, her labor, her affections, her children and her freedom'. In the 1850s, ownership of slaves was still legal in the US, and so the word *slavery* had added meaning. Both slaves and wives lost their original names.

All this might sound a bit over the top—but less so when you look at the circumstances of married women at the time. For much of the nineteenth century in Britain, a woman lost her legal identity when she became a wife. She couldn't own property; her existing property passed to her husband, and anything she earned was legally her husband's. She had to be available sexually on demand and her husband could imprison her, like the 'mad wife' locked away by Mr. Rochester in *Jane Eyre*. Feminist writer Dale Spender points out that it was impossible for a wife to leave her husband as divorce was 'virtually unobtainable and any woman who left a marriage was deemed a "disobedient wife" and could be returned to her rightful owner—her husband'.

The subordinate status of women is reflected by the fact that the official British marriage certificate, which was introduced in 1837 and is still in use, requires details of the father but not the mother of the bride and groom—symbolizing the fact that in the nineteenth century marriage was a business arrangement between fathers. And as women didn't have the vote in the nineteenth century, they were not in a position to help elect a government to change these laws. The feminist argument that the change of name is symbolic of a husband's total domination of his wife now seems a pretty strong one.

William Camden was a scholar who was writing at the same time as Shakespeare, several centuries before the term *feminist* was even coined. He gives us one of the earliest insights into family names in a book published in 1605. The custom of a wife taking a husband's surname was well entrenched in England by this time, though Camden notes that in some parts of Europe women retained their own name. Note that I use the word *custom* above. The practice of a wife taking her husband's surname has always been a custom—and therefore voluntary, rather than something required by law. As we've seen time and again, the development of naming customs has often been erratic, and although the evidence is a bit patchy, it looks as if this naming custom has varied between different social groups and between different regions of Britain. Here are a few examples.

As a card-playing sociologist might say, class can trump gender. In this context, the usual custom of a wife taking her husband's name was often turned on its head when the wife had a higher social status than her husband. Rich parents who had only daughters were keen to see the family name survive. One way to do this was to have their son-in-law change his surname to theirs. One of the earliest examples goes back to the twelfth century when Robert Fitzmaldred married Isabel Neville. The Nevilles were a powerful and wealthy Norman family, and Isabel's grandfather had stipulated in his will that the surname Neville be continued after her marriage. Robert Fitzmaldred was more than happy to agree as it meant adopting an influential Norman surname while, at the same time, gaining control of Isabel's large landholdings. Isabel's grandfather would also have been happy as the Nevilles went on to be one of the most influential families in northern England.

More recently, the highest profile story of class trumping gender features Queen Elizabeth II and her husband, the former Prince Philip of Greece and Denmark. Elizabeth's surname is Windsor, which is also the name of the royal house, or dynasty. Philip's adopted surname is Mountbatten. When King George VI died and Elizabeth became Queen, Philip expected that the name of the royal family would change from Windsor to Mountbatten. There was a royal precedent as a century earlier when Queen Victoria married Prince Albert, his house name became that of the British royal family. However, Philip had some *heavy-duty* opposition that included his wife, Queen Elizabeth II, his mother-in-law, the former Queen Elizabeth, widow of George VI, his grandmother-in-law, the former Queen Maud, widow of George V—not to mention the prime minister, Sir Winston Churchill.

So, it's not surprising then that Philip didn't get to change the royal family's name to Mountbatten. According to biographer Gyles Brandreth, Philip was not happy, declaring somewhat unscientifically: 'I am nothing but a bloody amoeba. I am the only man in the country not allowed to give his name to his own children'. However, the power of this naming custom eventually showed through when, a decade after becoming queen, Elizabeth issued a statement approving limited use of the hyphenated surname Mountbatten-Windsor. It first appeared officially in 1973 when Elizabeth and Philip's only daughter married using the name Anne Mountbatten-Windsor.

As with so many other naming customs, brides taking their husband's surname started among the social elite in London, and slowly spread socially, from the wealthy to the poor; and geographically, from London in south-east England to Scotland in the far north, and Wales in the far west. In England by about 1400, it was the custom in the landed classes that on marriage a woman took her husband's surname. By 1500 the custom had been generally adopted, and by 1600, the time that William Camden was writing, the custom was well entrenched, though not universal. Indeed, in mid-nineteenth century Dorset it was common for a wife to retain her maiden name; and in late nineteenth century Wales, the custom was still observed by many working-class families. Even in the twentieth century there were still pockets of Britain where married women continued to be called by their maiden names. For example, this was the local custom in the 1950s in parts of Cumberland in north-west England.

The custom of a wife adopting her husband's surname took longest to be widely established in Scotland. At the end of the nineteenth century, generally throughout Scotland but especially among the working class in the north, a woman was always known by her maiden name. Even in the 1930s, Scottish gravestones, obituary notices and legal documents described a married woman first by her maiden name and then by her husband's name, such as "Mary Campbell, widow of John Stewart" or "Barbara Macdonald, wife of John Scott". One explanation focuses on the history of the legal framework in Scotland. Unlike other regions of Britain, Scottish law draws strongly on Roman legal traditions. This meant that in Scotland a wife retained ownership of the property she owned before marriage. 'Property' is often taken to include your personal name, and under Roman law a wife kept her maiden name. Although there was no specific mention in Scottish statutes about a wife keeping her maiden name, canny Scots lawyers realised any legal document that defined a wife only by her husband's surname might be open to challenge, and so both maiden and married names were included.

However, these examples are very much the exceptions to the custom that after marriage a woman adopted her husband's family name. This applied even when a woman was very much in the public eye. For example, in the mid-nineteenth century Elizabeth Barrett was one of the most admired poets in Britain, being shortlisted for the prestigious position of Poet Laureate following the death of William Wordsworth.

Nevertheless, after she married Robert Browning, a much less prominent poet, she changed her name to Elizabeth Barrett Browning, and it's by this name that she's remembered today. At about the same time, Jenny Lind was one of the world's most popular singers. Like today's rock stars, she did a national tour of the US, for which legendary promoter P.T. Barnum paid her the equivalent of $10 million. (Unlike most of today's rock stars, she donated the money to charity.) But in 1852, at the height of her fame, she married her German pianist Otto Goldschmidt—and promptly changed her professional name to 'Madame Otto Goldschmidt, late Jenny Lind'.

This last example illustrates the naming custom mentioned at the start of the chapter, the adoption by a married woman of the full name of her husband. The style depended on the title *Mrs* referring only to married women, something that didn't become firmly established among middle class British women until the start of the nineteenth century. For example, in a letter she wrote in 1801, Jane Austen refers to Mary, her sister-in-law who was married to her brother James, as 'Mrs James Austen'. The practice became widespread a few decades later among affluent women in the US. A feminist interpretation appears in the aptly named book *Mrs Man* by Una Stannard: 'Husbands used to assert mastery over wives by teaching women they were inferior beings. Now husbands assert mastery over wives by teaching women that they are not women until their life has been merged into that of a husband.' Stannard sees this as 'brainwashing'.

You might have noticed the rather odd phrasing in Jenny Lind's new stage name, 'Madame Otto Goldschmidt, *late* Jenny Lind'—suggesting that the original Jenny Lind had somehow died and been replaced by Madame Otto Goldschmidt. I'm sure that the author of *Mrs Man* would see the stage name as evidence of her brainwashing hypothesis, although the 'brainwashing' was not entirely successful.

In particular, the public began to refuse to accept the abrupt name changes of female entertainers and writers after they married. Many female actors, singers and writers responded to this public pressure by maintaining their own name in public, but using their husband's name in private. Jenny Lind was one of the first female entertainers to do this after she realised that her fans wanted to hear 'Jenny Lind' rather than 'Madame Otto Goldschmidt'. By the time the movies came along in the early twentieth century, this dual naming had become the standard practice for female actors. Mary Pickford was probably the most famous woman in the world in 1920. But when she married Douglas Fairbanks, although publicly she continued to be Mary Pickford, privately she was Mary Fairbanks or Mrs Douglas Fairbanks. And it wasn't just female entertainers who began using two names. A large number of doctors, lawyers and other professional women kept their own name at work, and adopted their husband's surname at home.

One woman who *definitely* was not brainwashed was Lucy Stone. She was a nineteenth century campaigner for women's rights in the US, who became well known for her refusal to change her surname after marriage. However, her views on women's rights were well ahead of her time, and her calls for women to keep their names after marriage went largely unheeded. But she did inspire the formation of the Lucy Stone League in 1920, which was dedicated to equal rights for women and men to retain or change their names. The League had some success initially, as the number of prominent married American women who used their own names doubled between 1915 and 1935. However, its success was short-lived. By the mid-thirties, the Lucy Stone League existed in name only as older members were subjected to increasing legal pressure to use their husbands' names, and in the scathing words of Una Stannard, 'the younger generation of college women were eager to become Mrs Whoevercamealong'.

Although World War II resulted in many more women in the paid workforce, when the war ended in 1945 there was a return to traditional values and customs, including women taking their husband's name on marriage. For the next quarter of a century the issue of a woman's married name was hardly on the public agenda—at the start of the seventies even Lucy Stone League members generally used their own name at work, and their husband's name at home.

However, the issue became part of the more general feminist agenda from the 1970s. Along with use of the newly created *Ms* title, keeping your own name after marriage became a badge of feminism. But by the end of the twentieth century only about one in four US women thought of themselves as feminists, meaning that the traditional custom of a woman changing her name when she married continued to have widespread support.

The marriage of George Clooney and Amal Alamuddin was one of *the* celebrity events of recent years. Mr Clooney, of course, is a high profile US actor. Ms Alamuddin is a UK lawyer who, according to the website of the chambers where she works, has represented high profile clients such as Julian Assange, and has been a member of a number of UN commissions. But the name *Amal Alamuddin* is no longer on the website; she is now listed as *Amal Clooney*. Much to the disappointment of many feminists, she has adopted her husband's family name at work and, presumably, at home too.

Is Amal Clooney (née Alamuddin) out of step with most twenty-first century brides? Well, no. In fact, just the opposite. In the UK, one recent survey revealed that over three quarters of brides-to-be planned to adopt their husbands' family name after marriage. Another survey, this one of Facebook's 33 million British users, analysed the names of married women whose husbands were also registered. There were three major results. First, it found that the custom of women using their husbands' surname is still very much alive and well in Britain in the twenty-first century. Second, it found that younger women are least likely to adopt their husbands' family name, though most still do so. And thirdly, it found that, regardless of age, very few women are keen to use a hyphen-ated name.

The traditional naming custom seems even stronger in the US. One recent official survey found that nearly 95% of married women had the same surname as their husband, compared to less than 5% who had a different surname, and only 1% who had either a hyphenated or double surname. There was the same age-related pattern as in the

UK results, with a whopping 97% of women aged sixty years and over having the same surname to their husbands, compared to 91% of women in their teens and twenties. Even women in the youngest category may have married over a decade ago, but US brides continue to follow the custom, with four out of five taking their husband's surname recently.

These figures are a bit of a puzzle. After all, these days most people support the right of an individual to develop his or her own identity—and your name is very much part of that. You might expect that the longer you have had your name, the more it becomes bound up with your identity, something which applies most obviously when a woman has 'made a name' for herself at work (such as the former Amal Alamuddin). This is important because over the last few decades the age of marriage for women (and men) has increased. In Britain in the early 1970s, brides had an average age of 26; forty years later the average age had gone up to 34. A name change is likely to be more troublesome in your mid-thirties than your mid-twenties.

However, it's possible that the above figures give a misleading impression of trends over time. Today, only about half of adults in the US are married compared to nearly three quarters half a century ago. Much of this change is the result of many more couples choosing to live together without marrying—something that only a few decades ago would have been generally condemned as 'living in sin'. It could be that women who at one time might have married but kept their maiden names are now rejecting marriage altogether—and so are not included in the statistics about married women. This, in turn, will increase the proportion of married women who adopt their husbands' surname. In other words, as the marriage rate goes down, the women who do marry are less of a cross-section of society. Instead, they are a more conservative group, who are more likely to support the traditional custom of a bride changing her name when she marries.

Another possibility is that the percentages are masking a tendency for women to adopt their husband's name at home, but keep their maiden name at work, following the lead given by Jenny Lind, Mary Pickford and many other women in the public eye in the nineteenth and twentieth centuries. A woman in a professional job who marries after a career spanning a decade or more is most likely to use this dual name strategy, not wanting to give up the name by which she is well known by colleagues and clients. A high profile example of someone with a dual name is Zara Phillips, who is a grand-daughter of Queen Elizabeth II. She is an accomplished horse rider who won a silver medal under the name Zara Phillips in the 2012 Olympics. She married former England rugby player Mike Tindall in 2011, and socially is known as Zara Tindall or Mrs Michael Tindall. In fact, 'Mrs Michael Tindall' is officially listed in the line of succession to the British throne—though she is sixteenth in line, and so, regretfully, *Queen Zara* (or would it be *Queen Michael*?) is an unlikely prospect.

J.K. Rowling is today's most successful British female author, having sold close to half a billion books. Rowling is her maiden name, which she went back to following her divorce in 1994. The first Harry Potter book was published in 1997, and six more hugely successful novels appeared in the next ten years. It was during this time that she married again, to Neil Murray. I'm sure that there was absolutely no discussion between author and publisher after her marriage about whether J.K. Rowling would become "J.K. Murray"—the *J.K. Rowling* brand was far too valuable. But in her private life she is Joanne Murray. Incidentally, J.K. Rowling has a long way to go to catch up to Agatha Christie, who has sold two *billion* books. Her writing career took off while she was married to Archibald Christie. She later divorced him, but by then the Agatha Christie name was just too deeply embedded in the public's mind to be changed. Consequently, although she was known privately as Agatha Christie for less than fourteen years, she was known professionally by that name for well over fifty years.

A slightly different story concerns British singing sensation Lily Allen. Following her marriage to Sam Cooper in 2011, she announced that she was changing her name to Lily Cooper. According to media reports, this was because she was a very traditional person who couldn't wait to be a good wife and mother. However, in 2013 she reverted to her maiden name, telling fans by changing her Twitter handle from *@lilyrosecooper* to *@lilyallen*. Perhaps, like Jenny Lind/Goldschmidt over 150 years earlier, she found that the public didn't really take to thinking of her as anything other than Lily Allen. One thing is sure—her recording company would have applauded her most recent name change before the release of a new album. In a telling newspaper interview in 2014, she explained: 'I'm two people. I'm Lily Allen the singer and music person. And Lily Cooper the wife and mother.'

However, I can't help feeling that I haven't really explained why such a large percentage of brides still adopt their husbands' surnames. Surveys show that the most common reason given by women for following this age-old tradition is because . . . it's an age-old tradition. And yet, tradition has not prevented the marriage ceremony itself from changing significantly in other ways. Twenty-five years ago the majority of weddings in Britain took place in church; now, only about one third of weddings are religious ceremonies. Even in the US, where religious belief is more widespread, only one third of brides now marry in church. An even bigger change to the institution of marriage is that it's now open to same-sex couples both in Britain and the US. Despite these upheavals to the custom of marriage, the tradition that the bride changes her surname remains firmly in place.

Feminists suggest that patriarchy—the social dominance of men over women—is still an important factor in explaining why the name-changing tradition has continued into the twenty-first century. Clearly, the family today is different from that in the nineteenth century when a husband's domination of his wife was open and legal. And the idea that a wife should merge her life into that of her husband, and so become 'Mrs John Smith', was generally abandoned as women began to play an increasingly important role in the workplace during the twentieth century. Almost the only time you now see a Mrs John Smith is when a bride marries a groom with a much higher public profile. For example, on the day of her wedding to Hugh Hefner, the publisher of *Playboy*, glamour model Crystal Harris announced on Twitter that 'Today is the day I become Mrs Hugh Hefner'. A rather different example is Lady Colin Campbell, one of Princess Diana's biographers. Her title and name stems from her marriage to Lord Colin Campbell. Although they were married forty years ago, and the marriage only lasted for just over a year, she continues to use her married name—and more importantly, perhaps, her married title, which adds a certain something when writing biographies of the royal family.

Despite their much greater public role, women are still expected to carry out their traditional private role as primary care giver in the family. It's likely that many brides-to-be are subjected to some subtle (and not so subtle) pressure to change their names. There's a general expectation that a wife will make sacrifices for the good of the family—such as giving up that part of her identity that is reflected by her maiden name. This obligation to make sacrifices even applies when a married couple divorce. The majority of divorced mothers in one study chose to keep their married surname, frequently citing children as the reason for doing so because they believed that it would make their children's lives easier. (The next chapter looks in detail at the very important issue of children and family names.)

Certainly, most men expect that a wife will take her husband's family name. One survey found that about two thirds of men would be upset if their wives kept their maiden names. One man echoed the sentiments outlined above telling journalist Robin Hilmantel: 'One family, one name. If she didn't take my name, I'd seriously question her faith in us lasting as a couple.' However, name-change for these men was a one-way street; almost all would refuse if their wife asked them to take her surname.

The few husbands who do change their name don't find it easy. Kris Dyer chose to become Kris Myddleton when he married Jo Myddleton, but in an interview with Sarah Harris, the Myddletons lamented 'just how old-fashioned the rest of the world is'. They were especially surprised that their friends were 'the fiercest reactionaries... They kept asking "Why?" People seemed vaguely disapproving as if we were breaking a sacred rule.' The 'sacred rule', of course, is that it's the bride who changes her name, not the groom, and people are likely to approve when the bride follows the rules. It's not just the disapproval of friends that name-changing husbands have to confront. If the Myddletons lived in the US rather than in Britain, they would find that husband Kris would have to negotiate a number of legal obstacles to adopt his wife's surname that would not have applied if Jo had wanted to adopt her husband's surname.

Of course, adopting the bride's maiden name is not the only option for a groom. Hyphenating the couple's surnames has been the most obvious possibility, though as pointed out earlier, this is not now a popular choice among women—and, I suspect, even less popular among men. For example, when *Big Bang Theory* star Kaley Cuoco married Ryan Sweeting she became Kaley Cuoco-Sweeting, but her husband didn't become Ryan Cuoco-Sweeting.

Other naming options seem even less popular. *Blended* or *meshed* names result from the blending into one word all or part of the surnames of husband and wife—such as when Miss Harley and Mr Gatts became Mrs and Mr Hatts; Mr Mole and Miss Clifton became Mr and Mrs Molton; and (perhaps less successfully) Mr Pugh and Miss Griffin became Mr and Mrs Puffin.

Even rarer are couples who decide to abandon both of their original surnames, and to adopt a completely new surname. Jonathan Camery-Hoggatt married Rebecca Jones, and they became Jonathan and Rebecca Jackson, a surname they liked because it's easy to pronounce and went well with their first names. Although some people supported their decision, others were downright hostile. Jonathan Jackson explains that 'Much resistance came from people we least expected—a handful of friends who advocate gender equality. They simply assumed Rebecca would take my name, so our decision threw them off-balance.' The reaction to Jonathan changing his surname was especially fierce, with one woman insulting him by saying that he must have a small penis.

You would think that homosexual couples wouldn't be influenced by the custom of a change of name, particularly as many gays and lesbians blame patriarchy for the long-term stigmatisation of homosexuality. However, homosexual couples do sometimes mark their marriage with a name change, and lesbian women take their partners' names more often than gay men, perhaps in part because it's customary for women to change their names on marriage.

A high profile lesbian couple are actor Portia De Rossi and talk-show host Ellen DeGeneres. During their marriage ceremony, De Rossi wore a traditional white wedding dress, and the couple exchanged rings. Portia De Rossi also made a legal application to change her name to Portia DeGeneres. These traditional trappings of marriage were as important for this homosexual couple as they are for many heterosexual couples. More generally, some same-sex couples feel that having a shared name gives their marriage more social status. According to Vicki Valosik, a family law attorney who specialises in same-sex issues, 'People do it for a need of acceptance in a larger world where there is one idea of what family looks like, and to fit into that box.' However, there are also other, sometimes darker, reasons why same-sex partners choose to have the same surname. Some US states have laws that specifically prohibit same-sex marriage, and so some homosexual couples who live in these states but who were married elsewhere may not want to be open about their relationship. Having the same surname allows them to avoid any potential animosity by giving the impression that they are sisters or brothers.

As with heterosexual couples, having the same surname is sometimes regarded as important when a homosexual couple decide to have children. In fact, another reason why lesbians are more likely than gay men to change their name when marrying is because they are more likely to have children.

SIXTEEN

Mr Tom Dixon, Mrs Tom Dixon & Tom Dixon Jr

Marriage, children and family names

You may recall from the last chapter that Lucy Stone was a nineteenth century feminist, famous for refusing to give up her own name when she married Henry Blackwell. When their daughter, Alice, was born in 1857, Lucy and Henry found that deciding on her given name was the easy part. The choice of surname was much more difficult. Henry Blackwell felt that, as his wife had brought the baby into the world, she had the right to give it her surname. As you can gather, he was not your typical nineteenth century husband, nor would he be now. Lucy Stone thought long and hard about her daughter's surname. In fact, baby Alice was nine months old before Lucy Stone decided on her full name—Alice Stone Blackwell: Blackwell was the child's surname, and Stone was her middle name. So, even Lucy Stone eventually went along with the custom of a married couple giving the husband's surname to their children. The story suggests that the custom of giving children their father's surname is even more strongly entrenched than the custom of a wife adopting her husband's surname.

*

When the Normans invaded England in 1066 most people used a *by-name* that described either what they did, where they lived, what they looked like, or who their father was. Most by-names came from a father's given name. Tom's son Dick might be known as Dick Tomson, and

Dick's son Harry might be known as Harry Dickson. Over the course of the next three centuries, non-inherited by-names were replaced by inherited surnames, but they continued the earlier emphasis on fathers' given names. Even today, the majority of the most popular surnames clearly reflect their origins as fathers' given names—either explicitly, as in Johnson; or in a shortened form, as in Johns; or in a more obscure form, as in Jones.

These are just the tip of an iceberg of surnames taken originally from fathers' by-names. Surnames developed in a very patriarchal society in Britain. As the husband was the head of the family, it followed that the family name should be his. A husband was legally regarded as the guardian of the family's children, with the duty to support them until they were adults, which was just as well as any property a wife had became her husband's when they married. In other words, legally the children were the father's. As such, he had a right of custody that the mother could not question. A husband could even appoint a *testamentary guardian* in his will. If the father died, the testamentary guardian took over his role, meaning that he could take the children of the widow from their mother's care. These custody laws lasted several hundred years, not being formally abandoned until the late nineteenth century. It's not surprising then that the custom became established that it was the father's surname that the children inherited. To do otherwise would have been unthinkable.

Having said that, naming children after their mother did happen occasionally. As well as Thomas, Dixon and Harrison, we have surnames such as Anson, son of Ann, and Babcock, son of Babs or Barbara. It's impossible to give definitive explanations of why surnames like these occurred. It may be, for example, that Ann had been a widow for many years, so her children took on their mother's name rather than their long-dead father's. Another explanation for the use of mothers' names is about how class sometimes trumps gender. An early example features Eustace FitzJohn, a man from a relatively humble background who, partly through judicious marriages, became a powerful figure in twelfth century England. After his marriage to an heiress, Beatrice de

185

Vesci, their son was named William de Vesci, taking his mother's family name and status.

One group of children who generally *were* given their mother's surname were *bastards* or *illegitimate* children. If the father was willing to support the child, then the child could take the father's family name. This tended to happen most famously with the 150 or so *royal bastards*, the acknowledged illegitimate offspring of kings. They often had the surname Fitzroy ('son of a royal') or included the king's name, such as Charles FitzCharles and his sister Catherine FitzCharles who were two of the fifteen royal bastards of Charles II. However, these royal bastards were the exception rather than the rule. In the more likely case where there was no acknowledgement of paternity by the father, then the child was given the Latin stigma *filius nullius,* 'child of no man'. As the husband was the guardian of his children with a duty to support them, he had the right to give them his family name. If the mother didn't have a husband, then the child didn't have a guardian—or a legitimate family name. Instead, the child was given the mother's surname.

In the sixteenth century, the first Poor Laws were passed, which led to an unmarried mother being able to get some financial support from the parish or borough for the care of her child. However, this quickly resulted in the local authorities complaining that they were overburdened with the care of large numbers of illegitimate children. This led to local officials doing their utmost to identify the fathers so that they could be pursued for maintenance money.

One way of highlighting a man's paternity was to record his name on the child's baptism register, such as this one from April 1595: 'Joane, whome we maye call Yorkkooppe, because she was the bastarde dawghter, as yet is commonlye reported, of one John Yorke and Anne Cooper.' The local church authorities clearly knew that the parents, John Yorke and Anne Cooper, were not married. They were probably illiterate, and so not aware that the clergyman had officially recorded the name of the child as *Joane Yorkkooppe,* a name that manages to blend both the given names and family names of both parents. A more common recording technique was to use the *alias* device. The entry Isabel Sandes *alias* Rigge gives the surnames of both parents of Isabel, though it's unclear which surname is the father's and which the mother's.

To increase their chances of getting some maintenance money, local authorities would sometimes pressure the mother to identify a *rich* man as the child's father, regardless of actual paternity. But the most general approach of the so-called Guardians of the Poor was to minimise the number of unmarried mothers and children in their 'care' by making sure that conditions were so harsh that only the most desperate would apply. They sentenced unmarried mothers to hard labour and whippings, and sent children to factory owners who used them as slave labour. Harsh conditions lasted at least until the turn of the twentieth century. In 1895 a six-year-old Charlie Chaplin (the future movie star) entered the Lambeth workhouse with his mother—and was promptly separated from her because she was seen to be a bad influence.

These harsh workhouse conditions were well known, and rather than enduring them, many unmarried mothers instead abandoned their babies. This eventually led to institutions being set up to look after these *foundlings*. Because these babies were left anonymously, staff at the foundling institutions had to decide on names for them. Captain Coram's Foundling Hospital, which was established in 1739, first chose 'courtly names' for the children, and when these names were exhausted chose names from 'persons of quality and distinction', 'eminent deceased persons', church officials, poets, philosophers, soldiers, and characters in popular novels. When the numbers of foundlings increased dramatically, hospital governors began naming them 'after the creeping things and beasts of the earth, or created a nomenclature from various handicrafts or trades'. In the nineteenth century, governors started naming children after themselves or their friends—but the scheme ended abruptly after some of the foundlings later claimed that they were the governors' children. From then on, the hospital prepared a list of 'ordinary names'. Other hospitals had a much simpler naming scheme. For example, the foundlings left at St Clement Danes all had the surname Clements; and those left at the St Lawrence hospital all had the surname Lawrence.

Other surnames came from where or when the babies were first found, including Coalhouse, Porch and Monday.

However, despite these exceptions, most illegitimate children have long been named after their mothers. It was because of this that a book on English surnames published in the 1870s caused quite a stir when the author included many examples of surnames that he argued were based on female given names. It was in the light of this long association between mothers' names and illegitimacy that in 1880 the US National Woman Suffrage Association debated the following resolution: 'That since man everywhere has committed to woman the custody and ownership of the child born out of wedlock, and has required it to bear its mother's name, he should recognize woman's right as a mother to the custody of the child born in marriage, and permit it to bear her name.' The resolution was passed, but I'm sure that none of the women at the meeting expected it to make much difference to the long-established custom of children having their father's surname. Indeed, feminists regard the custom about children's surnames as more deep-seated than the custom about wives' surnames.

It's also important to bear in mind the legal framework surrounding the naming of children. In the 1970s several US states required that the father's surname be included on a birth certificate of a child whose parents are married. But over the next decade or so, state officials generally came to recognise the common law right of married parents to give *any* surname they wanted to their children. Governments had a role only when divorced or separated parents disagreed—usually when the father objected to his surname being replaced by the mother, who had custody of the children.

Traditionally, US courts had regarded the father's surname as the child's 'natural', 'primary', 'time-honoured' or 'legal' name, and so had rarely consented to a name change. However, in a landmark decision in 1980, the Californian Supreme Court held that 'the rule giving the father, as against the mother, a primary right to have his child bear his surname should be abolished'. As a result, legal naming restrictions on surname choice began to be lifted towards the end of the twentieth century.

٭

The custom of naming the child of a married couple after its father has been the practice for a thousand years, and in the early years of the new millennium there is little sign that it is about to change. Indeed, giving a child its father's surname is so commonplace that when a couple who have the same family name (e.g. Mr and Mrs Smith) talk about what to call their new-born baby, the discussion is almost certainly limited to *given* names—the unspoken assumption being that the baby will have the parents' surname. However, for a couple where both husband and wife have retained their original surnames, the arrival of a child means that they have to make a decision about the baby's surname—as Lucy Stone and Henry Black-well found out in the 1850s. Over 150 years later, Lisa Kelly, a US university professor, found herself in the same situation. Both she and her husband retained their own names when they married, and so when their daughter was born they found themselves having to make identity choices for a new generation. This was not easy: 'the weighty stare of the ancestors became fixed upon us. "What will you do now?" the collective force of family, friends, and society seemed to ask as we gathered about the hospital incubator.'

Lisa Kelly's well-chosen phrase 'the collective force of family, friends and society' emphasises that when parents choose a surname, the decision is not made in a vacuum. Importantly, the arrival of a child marks the definitive move from couple to nuclear family—and the social conditioning that goes with this. The idea that a wife is the primary caregiver in a marriage takes on added significance when a child is born. One way for a wife to show she cares is by putting her family's needs above her own—and her husband's surname above her own when naming their children. Not surprisingly, in families where the wives have changed their surname to their husband's, almost all give their children the same surname. But even when a wife kept her own surname, more than nine out of ten children were named after their father, with no difference between boys and girls.

However, not far off half of the children with their fathers' surnames also have their mother's maiden name as a middle name. For example, 'Harry Potter' author J.K. Rowling has two children with husband Neil Murray: David Rowling Murray and Mackenzie Rowling Murray. Of course, it's very likely that many fathers will *strongly* object to having anything other than their own surnames conferred on their children—even if they have reluctantly accepted the fact that their wives have gone against tradition and kept their own names. Not every husband will be as enlightened as Lucy Stone's husband, Henry Blackwell. In the face of opposition from their husbands, it's probably not surprising that giving children their mothers' surname is still a rarity.

The practice of using the father's surname is still so universal, I'm sure many people assume it's a legal requirement for married couples. But, in fact, in the UK and US there are now few legal restrictions on parents when registering the family name of a child. The law in Britain is straightforward as an official government website explains: 'English law places no restrictions as to what surname may be registered for a child in the UK'. The situation is a bit more complicated in the US where each state is different, but in most states, parents have few restrictions when registering a surname for their child. A freeing of the remaining restrictions is likely as the only constitutionally watertight reason to restrict names is to prevent false implications of paternity—for example, to prevent a mother naming her child *Tom Dixon Harrison, Jr.* when Tom Dixon Harrison is not the father.

Incidentally, perhaps the most surprising restriction occurs in a handful of US states where parents are not allowed to register a name that includes letters with accent marks, such as *ñ, é* and *ç*. The most notable example is California, where the large Spanish-speaking population can't register traditional Spanish surnames such as Nuñez and Pérez (or

190

given names such as Lucía or José). According to one legal opinion, the ban is likely to be unconstitutional.

Given that there are few legal restrictions, in theory the decision about a child's family name is as open as the decision about a given name. What sort of naming options do twenty-first century parents have available to them should traditional surnaming become less popular? There are several possibilities. I'll use the example of a married couple called Harriet Jones and Tom Smith who have twins called Oliver and Amelia.

Most obviously, there's the traditional system of using only the husband's surname, so that the children are called Oliver Smith and Amelia Smith. This is referred to as *patrilineal* naming. Using only the mother's name, so that the children become Oliver Jones and Amelia Jones, is called *matrilineal* naming. Of course, if each parent retains his or her own surname, then regardless of which naming option they choose for their children, at least one parent will have a surname that is out of step with the other family members, as in the case of Tom Smith, Harriet Jones, Oliver Jones and Amelia Jones. This can lead to awkward situations, such as Tom Smith having to explain to a border official that he is indeed the father of Oliver Jones and Amelia Jones, the two children he is taking abroad on holiday.

Another option for Harriet Jones and Tom Smith is to hyphenate their surnames, so that the children are called Oliver and Amelia Jones-Smith (or Smith-Jones). However, hyphenating can often result in a dauntingly long name for a child starting school. And even when this is not an immediate problem, in the longer term it may lead to complications, such as when young Oliver Jones-Smith marries Emma Williams-Brown and they decide to start a family of their own...

A fourth option is to compound both parents' surnames, so that the children's family names become Smith Jones (or Jones Smith). This has the same problem as hyphenating them—plus the added difficulty that no one is really sure whether the surname consists of one word or two. Does young Oliver Smith Jones go under *S (Smith Jones)* or *J (Jones)* on a class register? In other words, is *Smith* a middle name, or the first part of the surname? Of course, both hyphenated and compounded surnames rely on the parents agreeing on which name should come first.

The fifth option is to match the parents' surnames to the gender of the children, meaning that the father's name is used with sons (e.g. Oliver Smith), and the mother's name is used with daughters (e.g. Amelia Jones). It has been called *bilineal* naming because there are two lines to each person's family tree, the male line and the female line. The father's surname is passed down to his sons, grandsons, and so on; and the mother's surname is passed down to her daughters, grand-daughters, and so on. The idea of matching a parent's surname to the gender of the children sounds very modern, but in fact there's some evidence that historically this was the custom in some regions of Britain, such as on the Welsh island of Anglesey.

Yet another naming option is to use *blended* or *meshed* surnames. These result from the blending into one word all or part of the surnames of husband and wife. This is yet another idea that, although sounding very modern, in fact goes back a long way—remember Joane Yorkkooppe, the illegitimate daughter of John Yorke and Anne Cooper, who was born in *1595*. I suspect that blended or meshed surnames these days are initially decided by marrying couples, who later give their new name to their children.

But on many occasions blending will be less than satisfactory. Joane Yorkkooppe would certainly have had to spell out her name, if anyone had been concerned about spelling during her lifetime. If Harriet Jones and Tom Smith decided to use this naming option, their children might be called *Josmith* (Jones + Smith) or possibly *Smines* (Smith + Jones). Both surnames do exist, but I'm sure most of the twenty or so people called Josmith in the US *White Pages* probably have to spell out their surname for people they have just met. And the one man in the US *White Pages* called Smines will certainly have problems.

The final option in this long list for children's surnames is to choose a surname unrelated to that of the father or mother. It can include, well, *any* name—TV celebrity, movie star, author, historical figure, birthplace, and so on. For example, Harriet Jones and Tom Smith might call their son Oliver King (after Tom's favourite author, Stephen King), and their daughter Amelia Kardashian (after Harriet's favourite TV celebrity, Kim Kardashian). Or perhaps the parents realised that Harriet became pregnant while on holiday on the Isle of Skye, and so they might give both children the surname Skye to commemorate their Scottish start in life.

Although this type of naming is perfectly possible in many jurisdictions, real-life examples are few and far between. One study by Susan Kupper of 'Lucy Stoners'—women who kept their birth name after marriage—found that only one of 170 US couples with children had opted for a completely new name for their children. The parents, whose surnames were Sheedy and Morea, gave their children the surname *Ailanthus*, the scientific name for the tree of heaven, because of the character of the tree, and because it sounded like a 'reasonable surname' rather than a 'cutesy' one. They had a lot of trouble at first getting accurate birth certificates, but a longer-term problem was the 'negative reactions' of the family who 'simply refuse to acknowledge the children's name.'

Same-sex couples might be expected to be most open to different naming possibilities, but in a study of lesbian couples only one in twenty adopted a new surname completely unrelated to their existing surnames, which they then gave to their children. Celebrities are another group with a more adventurous approach to naming their children, but I can think of only one example (and an old one, at that) of parents giving a child a *surname* unrelated to their own. The actor Troy Garity is the son of Oscar-winning actress Jane Fonda and prominent political activist Tom Hayden. Both parents wanted to make sure their son was not burdened by either of their well-known surnames, and so they gave him his paternal grandmother's name, Garity. Instead of unusual surnames, celebrities often decide on unusual *given* names for their children, and then follow tradition by choosing the family name of one of the parents, most often the father. To give just a few recent examples, Bodhi Ransom Green is the son of Brian Green and Megan Fox; Ace Knute Johnson is the son of Eric Johnson and Jessica Simpson; and Bear Blaze Winslet is the son of Kate Winslet and Ned Rocknroll (the former Ned Smith).

So, the thousand-year-old custom of a married couple giving the father's surname to their children seems set to continue well into the new millennium. And yet many other long-established traditions related to marriage and the family have quickly changed as social values have changed. Getting married in church is now a minority interest and same-sex marriage is becoming socially and legally acceptable. One other social trend that may well have an important bearing on the father's surname tradition is the rapid growth in the number of marriages ending in divorce, a trend which started during the last quarter of the twentieth century and looks set to continue in the twenty-first century. Some figures are worth mentioning here. British government statisticians estimate that more than four in ten marriages now end in divorce. Wives initiate two in every three divorces. Nearly one in three people getting a divorce have been married before, meaning they have had two marriages and two divorces. Nearly half of divorcing couples have at least one child living with them at the time.

The increasing level of divorce will inevitably result in more *blended families*, as divorced people with children re-marry. Most often, it is the mother who will be the main carer of children from a previous marriage. If she re-marries, the tradition of a wife adopting the surname of her husband becomes even more problematic as the wife is likely to want to retain the same name as her children. A bachelor friend of mine recently married someone who had two children from a previous marriage. As mother and children all had the same surname, my friend and his new wife decided that it made a lot of sense for him to change his surname to theirs so that everyone in the family has the same name. Importantly, of course, my friend had no children of his own when he married; if he had, he might have been reluctant to change his surname to one that was different from theirs, symbolically cutting himself off more from his biological children. I suspect that even among men without children who marry women with children, my friend might well be in a minority when agreeing to change his surname to that of his new wife and her children. Nevertheless, it's an increasingly common scenario that can only serve to disrupt a custom about surnames that came about when it was almost impossible to obtain a divorce.

The recent figures about divorce and remarriage show British actor Kate Winslet to be almost mainstream in terms of her marital history. She has been married three times, first to film director Jim Threapleton, with whom she had a daughter, Mia Honey Threapleton; then to another director, Sam Mendes, with whom she had a son, Joe Alfie Winslet Mendes; and most recently to businessman Ned Rocknroll, with whom she has had a son, the previously mentioned Bear Blaze Winslet. She therefore has three children, each with a different surname, two of whom have the surname of men she has left behind. In contrast, her third child has her own family name, making the mother-son link clear and, as a bonus for her, also helping to ensure that her family name is passed on to future generations.

As people begin to realise just how many marriages end in divorce, they might begin to view marriage as a medium-term rather than a long-term arrangement. If more celebrities like Kate Winslet begin to flout the 'rules' not only about given names but also family names, it might be a signal for an increasing number of ordinary folk to do likewise. Bilineal naming might become something more than a little-known phrase in a book. However, there are a lot of *might*'s here. If this scenario is to play out, there will have to be a decline in the custom of wives adopting their husbands' surnames. There are some small signs that twenty-first century women are starting to retain their own surnames after marriage. For example, one recent study showed that a *majority* of US women who married in a civil ceremony (rather than a religious one) retained their own names. However, I suspect that '*Hello, My Name Is . . .*' will be into its umpteenth edition before giving a child its father's surname loses its place as the preferred choice for the majority of parents.

PART FOUR...

The story of name titles

SEVENTEEN

Mr Thomas, Mrs Dixon and Ms Harris

Social titles

People often add other information to their given name and family name. Paul McCartney, former Beatle and the world's most successful songwriter, is more formally known as Sir Paul McCartney, MBE. Similarly, fans of James Bond may know that his 'obituary' refers to him as Commander James Bond, CMG, RNVR. *Sir* Paul McCartney, *MBE* are honorary titles, granted by the British government for his services to the music industry. The *Sir* before his name shows that Queen Elizabeth II awarded him a knighthood; and the *MBE* after his name shows that he is a Member of the Most Excellent Order of the British Empire. *Commander* Bond, *CMG, RNVR* are professional titles that tell you James Bond's rank in the Royal Naval Volunteer Reserve where he performed his duties with such outstanding bravery and distinction that he was made a Companion of the Order of St Michael and St George. I'm sure that there are many more men in Britain named Paul McCartney and James Bond, but most of them will be known simply as *Mr* Paul McCartney and *Mr* James Bond. This part of '*Hello, My Name Is* ...' is about the titles that we add to our personal names. This chapter focuses on the common-or-garden social titles like Mr and Mrs. The next chapter looks in detail at professional and honorary titles like Commander and Sir.

These days, of course, all men can give themselves the social title Mr, but several centuries ago it had much more limited use. In the

Middle Ages, the title 'Master' was used as a way to identify men of high status—those with property or learning. However, as there was no cost to using the title, over time more and more men gradually adopted it, and by the 1500s it was used by nearly all men of any social standing.

Around the same time, two other developments occurred. First, the title began to be used with the family name, as family names themselves became more important. Secondly, the abbreviation Mr became increasingly common. William Shakespeare includes the title several times in his plays, including 'Mr Fang', a character in *King Henry IV, Part II*. The first collection of Shakespeare's plays appeared in 1623 under the title *Mr. William Shakespeare's Comedies, Histories, & Tragedies*. Over time, the 'Mr' abbreviation came to be pronounced as 'Mister' rather than 'Master', and by the beginning of the eighteenth century 'Master' and 'Mr' were seen as two different words. At first, as happened with Master, the title Mr was used only by upper-class men, but it wasn't long before the title spread socially and, by the nineteenth century, Mr was a formal and polite term for any man.

As use of Mr became more widespread, the title Master became more restricted. In the final two decades of the nineteenth century, the only adults in Britain still using it were old men in rural backwaters. When that generation died out, the title Master was used only with boys. And it wasn't used with all boys: in poor families children were called by name; in rich families the servants addressed boys as Lord or Mr; it was only in middle class families that the title Master continued to be used. However, even this restricted use was short-lived, and by the 1930s the title Master for boys was seen as old fashioned, and used only by servants. As the number of servants declined rapidly following World War II, there was a similar rapid decline in the use of Master as a title for boys. By the early 1970s, Master was restricted to small boys up to about eight years of age, and even they generally disliked it. It may have hung on more tenaciously in the US. One modern American etiquette book, *Emily Post's Etiquette,* suggests that young boys have the title Master until the age of six or seven; for the next decade or so they have no title;

then in their late teens they become Mr. However, I suspect that outside etiquette books the reality is that the title Master has now gone the way of men's cloaks and bowler hats.

The title *Mrs* has a similar history to *Mr*. In the sixteenth and seventeenth centuries, *Mistress* was the title given to women with status and authority, such as when King Henry VIII addressed Anne Boleyn as 'Mistress' to show his respect for her rank. Over time, 'Mistress' began to be superseded by the abbreviation 'Mrs'. As happened with Mr, the abbreviation gradually took on a different pronunciation from the original word, and Mrs and Mistress became two different words, with Mistress gradually being completely superseded by Mrs as a social title. Like their menfolk, women lower down the social scale began to copy the upper class and started giving themselves the title Mrs, until eventually it became used by women at all levels of society.

For a long time the title did not specify anything about age. Seventeenth century English poet John Milton had a daughter whose tombstone read 'Mrs Kathern Milton', although she was less than six months old when she died. The title also said nothing about the marital status of its holder. Applying the title Mrs only to married women came about very slowly. In fact, well into the nineteenth century many women continued to be called Mrs even though they were single. The title Mrs was used for unmarried female servants in upper class households at least into the late nineteenth century. For example, one unmarried English lady declared in 1889 that her own housekeeper 'has been *Mrs* for years, though she was never married, and though she looks with just scorn upon the inferior animal and all his works'. (The last comment, I think, was a reference to *men*.)

A fictional example of the custom appears in one of Agatha Christie's few non-crime novels, *Giant's Bread*, written under the pen name Mary Westmacott. It is set initially in a wealthy household at the end of the nineteenth century. Vernon is a young sickly boy who has a nurse called Mrs Pascal: 'Vernon never cogitated on the possibility of a Mr Pascal. Not that there was any such person. The Mrs was a tacit recognition of

Nurse's position of authority.' The writers of the TV series *Downton Abbey* suggest that the custom continued into the twentieth century at the highest level of British society. Fans will recall that the person in charge of all the female servants at the Earl of Grantham's country house is Mrs Hughes, although there is no suggestion that there has ever been a Mr Hughes. Her title reflects her status as head housekeeper, not her marital state.

The title *Miss,* another abbreviation of mistress, also has a long historical development. Early in seventeenth century England it was used as an insult to describe a woman of loose morals, regardless of whether she was married or unmarried. For example, a seventeenth century book has the title *Dutch Whore, or the Miss of Amsterdam.* Surprisingly, however, in the 1660s it began to be used by young girls, though they stopped using it in their teens, and changed to the title Mrs. It wasn't until about 1750 that Miss was well established as a title for unmarried women, regardless of age. It's likely that upper and, later, middle class families used the title to highlight the 'marriageability' of their daughters to potential suitors. In fact, naming customs went a stage further, with the oldest, and therefore most marriageable, daughter, distinguished from her younger sisters by name. In Jane Austen's *Pride and Prejudice* (1813) the five unmarried Bennet sisters, Jane, Elizabeth, Mary, Catherine and Lydia, all have the title of 'Miss', but the oldest, Jane, is 'Miss Bennet' while the younger sisters are known, for example, as 'Miss Elizabeth' and 'Miss Lydia'.

As happened with Mr and Mrs, the use of the title Miss by families of high status encouraged its use by those of lower status. By the middle of the eighteenth century, Miss was the standard title among unmarried women, particularly younger unmarried women.

Apart from Mr, Mrs and Miss, the only other traditional social titles used before a name are what social scientists call *kinship* titles, because they show the family relationship of the title holder. Nineteenth century novels are full of characters with kinship titles: Cousin Phillis, Sister Deane, Uncle Phillips, Aunt Polly, Grandmother Smallweed, and so on.

Today, we use kinship titles much less. Some, such as Cousin, Brother and Sister, largely disappeared during the twentieth century. Others, such as Aunt and Uncle, have managed to hang on. For example, in Britain in the 1960s it was quite unusual for nephews and nieces to address their aunts and uncles only by their first name. Half a century on, there seems to be a feeling that these kinship titles are rather old fashioned. In the online forum Etiquette Hell there's a long discussion set off by a 32-year-old woman who uses the traditional titles with her aunts and uncles. However, her twelve-year-old nephew thought that he was too old to call her Auntie, leading her to wonder if she is being old-fashioned. The consensus among fellow members was that she wasn't, but the fact that she needed to ask the question suggests that in the not-too-distant future Aunt Polly might go the same way as Cousin Phillis.

Some people also apply the label 'old-fashioned' to the various traditional kinship titles of grandparents, such as Grandad and Grandma. The thinking is that many of today's baby boomer grandparents look younger, feel younger, and act younger than their predecessors—though perhaps *every* new generation of grandparents thinks this. Apparently, many boomers want their grandchildren to see them more as special friends, and want a title that sounds more fun and modern. Another argument is that as divorce and remarriage become more common, and as people are living longer, a child is more likely to have more than two sets of grandparents, not to mention great-grandparents. Having different titles for grandparents could make things less confusing. To help them, there's a *Big Book of Grandparents' Names,* which include hundreds of alternative titles for grandparents. Similarly, an online 'Ultimate guide to grandparent names' lists dozens of 'trendy' names such as G-Mom and G-Daddy; and 'playful' names such as Dizzy and Grumpy, though it's easier to see them used as free-standing names, such as Grumpy, rather than as titles before a given or family name like Grumpy Bob or Grumpy Green.

It's not just family members who can have kinship titles. You may well have an 'Auntie Jane' or an 'Uncle Jack' who is not a sister or brother of one of your parents. Instead, they will be long-term family friends you have grown up with. Social scientists have a term for this: *fictive kinship*. The practice seems quite common but, like many social customs, it varies a good deal between social groups, being most common in poorer communities. It's widespread use among African-Americans can be traced back to the slave era when parents could be sold to different plantation owners, leaving their children behind to be looked after by their 'aunts' and 'uncles'.

All the social titles mentioned so far come before the person's name as prefixes. However, *generational titles* appear after a person's name, as suffixes. In Britain, suffixes like II, III, and IV are seen as the preserve of royalty, and refer to the number of monarchs with the same name. Thus, the current Queen is the second monarch named Elizabeth, although some Scots object to the title 'Elizabeth II' as Elizabeth I was *not* Queen of Scotland. The most popular royal names are Henry and Edward, each of which has been used by eight kings, including the much-married King Henry VIII, and the unmarried King Edward VIII, who abdicated to marry.

In the republican USA these Roman numerals are more widely used. If a grandfather, father and son all have the same given names, then they might well add I, II and III after their names. Similarly, if parents give their son, very rarely their daughter, exactly the same name as his father, they may use the title *Junior* (usually shortened to *Jr*) for the son and *Senior* (*Sr*) for the father. These naming customs have been particularly important among high status families. For example, one quarter of the twenty US presidents in office since 1900 have this kind of suffix, including Barack Hussein Obama II. Other influential men with generational titles include business leader and philanthropist, and one of the world's richest men, Bill Gates, also known as William Henry Gates III; Thomas Cruise Mapother IV, better known as movie star Tom Cruise; and Marshall Bruce Mathers III, better known as the rapper Eminem.

Strict use of these generational titles can get very tricky. The Sr/Jr titles can only be used when both father and son are living. If the father (let's call him Tom Dixon, Sr) dies then his son is no longer Tom Dixon, Jr. But he may replace Jr. with the Roman numeral II; and the former (now deceased) Tom Dixon, Sr becomes Tom Dixon I. Of course, if Tom Dixon II decides to give *his* son the same name, then Tom Dixon II could become Tom Dixon, Sr and the new addition to the family would be Tom Dixon, Jr. *Or,* Tom Dixon II might decide to keep the 'II' title, and so his son would then be Tom Dixon III. *Or,* he might decide to keep both his Sr and II titles, and become Tom Dixon, Sr, II, and name his son Tom Dixon, Jr, III ...(!)

Bill Gates' father's birth certificate recorded him as 'William Henry Gates III', his father and grandfather both having the same name. However, he officially changed his name to 'William Henry Gates, Jr.' to avoid being made fun of when he joined the army. But when he continued the family tradition of giving his son, Microsoft Bill, his own name he called him 'William Henry Gates III', even though it would appear that the new addition to the family should have had the title IV and/or Jr. (but Jr only if his grandfather was deceased). It's clear why many families don't follow these often-confusing naming rules. The most recent edition of the long-running US etiquette book, *Emily Post's Etiquette*, advises readers to use common sense and avoid confusion by keeping a generational title when a grandfather or father dies.

One clear naming rule that families do generally follow is to avoid using a suffix when the son's name is not *exactly* the same as his father's. For example, George Walker Bush, the 43rd US President is not a Junior because he has almost, but not quite, the same name as his father, George Herbert Walker Bush, the 41st US President. One celebrity who decided to short-circuit the custom about generational titles is former world heavyweight boxing champion George Edward Foreman, now better known for his George Foreman grill. He has five sons, each of whom is named George Edward: George Edward, Jr, George Edward III, George Edward IV, George Edward V, and George Edward VI. Not surprisingly, the family use nicknames to distinguish them, with the oldest, of course, being called Junior.

Naming your son after you and adding the title 'Junior' can be immensely satisfying if you are the father, but can be a burden on the son who may feel like a minor version of his father. One study found that the percentage of Juniors among mental patients was three times higher than in the general population.

Use of the title Junior dates back at least to the sixteenth century. In 1776, three of the 53 men who signed the American Declaration of Independence were Juniors. The use of Roman numerals as post-nominals started in the US around 1800. Like many social customs, generational titles were started by rich families who wanted to highlight the continuity of ownership of a family business. Families lower down the social pecking order then began to copy the practice in the twentieth century. For example, Curtis James Jackson III, better known as rapper 50 Cent, was born in 1975 in a poverty-stricken neighbourhood in New York City. His mother added the Roman numerals 'III' in honour of her father and uncle. This widespread take-up of generational titles in turn meant that they became less popular among the elite, so that today they are rarely seen. Half a century ago, nearly one in ten of the men in the US Congress had the title *Sr, Jr* or *II* after their names; now, only a handful of Congressmen use a generational title. This decline among the elite has been mirrored by a similar decline in the population generally.

Finally, in this review of traditional social titles, there are the suffixes *Esquire* (abbreviated to *Esq*) and *Gentleman (Gent)*. According to the *Oxford English Dictionary*, originally an esquire was 'A young man of gentle birth, who as an aspirant to knighthood, attended upon a knight, carried his shield, and rendered him other services' (the dictionary doesn't specify which ones). Over time, the historical link between esquires and knights was lost. Instead, esquires became the top layer of the gentry. Below them in terms of social standing were 'gentlemen', who added the title *Gent* after their names. According to a sixteenth century document, a gentleman was someone 'who can live idly, and without manuall labour', but the distinction between esquires and gentlemen was never clearly defined, and by the nineteenth century the title *Gent* had pretty much been replaced by *Esq* as more and more men began to use the higher-status term.

As a result, Esquire became simply a social title of general respectability.

Nevertheless, it served to distinguish respectable men from the rest, and so addressing someone as Mr rather than Esquire could cause great offence among those who thought themselves to be particularly respectable. Richard Atkins was a magistrate in the new British colony of New South Wales in the late eighteenth century. When he received a letter addressed to *Mr* Richard Atkins rather than Richard Atkins, *Esq*, he felt so insulted that he refused the request of the letter-writer, and sniffily concluded his reply saying that he would return unopened any further letters addressed to 'Mr Richard Atkins'. The same sentiment still comes through well over a century later in Lady Troubridge's *Book of Etiquette,* published in the 1930s. She suggested that it was very discourteous to address letters to one's friends with the title Mr rather than Esq In her view, Mr was appropriate only on letters to tradesmen. However, I suspect that Lady Troubridge was reflecting her own rarefied social circle rather than British society in general. (I'm confident that she didn't have any friends who were tradesmen.)

Certainly, by the late twentieth century in Britain, the title *Esq* had largely disappeared, just as the title *Gent* did 100 years earlier. Nowadays, only the most traditional organisations still use Esquire. Even Buckingham Palace has restricted its use. For example, in the 1960s the Palace announced that 'Ringo Starr, Esq (Richard Starkey, Esq), Member of *The Beatles*, had been awarded an MBE. Half a century later, MBE recipients are listed by name only, the Esquire title being reserved for the most prestigious appointments, such as judgeships.

In the US, use of the title Esquire took a very different path. Historically, the term was extended to include not just someone who attended a knight, but others in official capacities, such as sheriffs, justices of the peace, and lawyers. Over time, only lawyers continued to use the title, and now the title Esquire after a person's name in the US shows that he or she is a lawyer.

*

Hello, My Name Is ...

The English language has not treated men and women equally in terms of social titles. Historically, all men had the title Mr, regardless of whether they were single or married. In contrast, the titles available to women distinguished between those who were single (Miss) and those who were married (Mrs). Over the last few decades, many people have suggested that this unequal treatment should end. There are a number of ways to do this, none of them easy as language 'rules' are not the same as, for example, road rules. Politicians can pass a law that requires motorists to change from driving on the right-hand side of the road at 5.00am to driving on the left-hand side of the road at 6.00am (as happened in Samoa on September 7th, 2009) but people can choose to ignore language 'rules' if they don't agree with them. That's why significant changes in language come about gradually as more people know them and become comfortable with them. So, what changes might allow us to treat men and women more equally?

The simplest option is to stop using social titles such as Mr, Miss and Mrs. Instead, we would use just our names. This has been happening slowly over the last century or so, beginning in the US. It moved across the North Atlantic to Britain by the 1930s, perhaps as a result of the Prince of Wales (soon to be King Edward VIII) who made first names acceptable in high society. It's now common to answer the phone and hear someone you've never met address you by your given name: "Hello John. I'm Jodie from A1 Insurance...". Not everyone is happy about total strangers using their given name. An elderly relative of mine interrupts the caller in mid-flow to insist, 'The name's Mr Smith, not John'. Even Americans are strongly divided about it. *Washington Post* columnist William Raspberry stirred up a hornets' nest when he wrote about how annoyed he was at strangers calling him by his first name. Following the blizzard of responses to his article, he concluded that there were only two kinds of people in the US—those who call strangers by their first name, and those who strongly resent it.

Another way to treat women and men more equally in terms of social titles is to *simplify* the titles used by women from two (Miss *and* Mrs) to just one (Miss *or* Mrs). This would be used by all women, single and married, in exactly the same way that all men, single and married, use the title Mr. You could argue that at a time when marriage itself has declined in importance, a system of titles that downplays marital status is appropriate. This was the option taken in Germany, where the same types of social titles were traditionally used: *Herr* for all men, *Frau* for married women, and *Fraulein* for unmarried women. Germans picked what they saw as the higher status female term, Frau, and applied it to all women. Forms began listing Herr and Frau as the only options; the title Fraulein disappeared. Within a few years, Fraulein had almost gone from spoken usage. It may be that the same thing will happen in France following the government's decision in 2012 to ban the use of Mademoiselle on official forms, leaving only Madame as the social title for all women.

English-speaking countries took a different path to treat men and women equally in terms of social titles. We added the title *Ms* to Miss and Mrs to allow women to use a title that, like Mr for men, applies to both single and married women. Ms was occasionally used as an abbreviation of 'mistress' as far back as the seventeenth century, but it was re-discovered in the 1940s when feminists proposed that men's and women's titles be made more equal by substituting Ms for both Miss and Mrs. This was a revolutionary proposal, coming at a time when two in five Americans still disapproved of women wearing trousers in public.

In 1970, the annual conference of the US National Organization for Women adopted a resolution advocating the use of Ms. In 1972, *Ms* magazine was launched in the US, the editors explaining that women who use the title Ms wanted to be seen as more than simply their father's daughter or their husband's wife. Feminists saw the single title Ms as uniting women rather than dividing them into unmarried and married. The term also helped to get people talking in general about equal opportunities for women.

Agitation about the use of the title Ms was one small part of the hot political issue of women's rights in the 1970s, especially in the US. For example, some women refused to register as voters because electoral laws didn't allow the use of the title Ms. The electoral laws were eventually changed, beginning in New Jersey in 1972; and around the same time government organisations in general began recognising Ms as an acceptable title.

In the media, although the most high-profile development was the publication of *Ms* magazine, much more important was the steady change in the policies of individual newspapers. One of the biggest obstacles to making Ms a standard title for women was the refusal of the *New York Times* to use the term. In fact, it wasn't until June 1986 that this newspaper changed its policy, arguing that the title Ms had now become part of the language. In part, Ms became part of the language because it fitted better into an increasingly common situation where women retained their original family name after marriage. When Geraldine Ferraro married John Zaccaro but retained her original name, it wasn't appropriate to call her either *Miss* Geraldine Ferraro, because she was married, or *Mrs* Geraldine Ferraro, because she was married to Mr Zaccaro. *Ms* Geraldine Ferraro was a much better title. And because in 1984 Geraldine Ferraro was a candidate for the vice-presidency of the United States, her social title was a public issue as well as a private matter.

The move to introduce the title Ms as a replacement for Miss and Mrs led to some very heated, and some very strange, debates in the 1970s and '80s. One of the strangest arguments put forward by the conservative side is worth quoting at length from a book with the impressive title *Sexist Language: A Modern Philosophical Analysis*. In it, Michael Levin makes the following comment: 'a man has to know, when encountering a new female, if she is eligible for his overtures... The Miss/Mrs device signals the male immediately as to the potentials for his future relations with this new female... Miss/Mrs has come about through its evolutionary value.' This is from a US philosophy academic at a New York university, and I'm pretty sure that he said it in all seriousness. I must admit that it hadn't occurred to me that these social titles had 'evolutionary value'.

In the short term, use of Ms by supporters of the women's movement led to the title quickly coming into general use. For example, as early as 1973, a Gallup poll in the US showed that 30% of people approved of

Ms as an alternative to Miss or Mrs. But this initial surge of popularity came at a longer-term price, as the idea quickly developed that if you called yourself Ms you must be a feminist. The image of feminists as men-hating women's libbers didn't last long. What did last was the perception that women who use the title Ms are more achievement-oriented, more assertive, and colder than women who use either Miss or Mrs. By the end of the twentieth century only about one in four women labelled themselves as feminists—and, not surprisingly, about the same proportion used the title Ms.

The use of the title Ms has become more complicated over the last few years. For example, an increasing number of women now use different titles in different situations. They may use Ms at work, because of the stereotype of Ms as more business oriented; but use Mrs at home, to tap into the title's traditional association with the family. You can view this either as a clever use of the variety of titles available, or simply as a way to avoid making a hard decision about a preferred title. I'd put myself in the first camp as I vary my title depending on where I am. At work, I'm *Dr*, to reflect my academic qualification. Away from work, I'm *Mr*, to avoid being mistaken for a member of the medical profession. ('Dr Burdess, come quickly! Someone's having a heart attack on the aircraft.') However, I can see that this is not how feminists saw the future use of Ms way back in the 1970s.

Feminists from the 1970s would be even more shocked to find that, rather than disguising a woman's marital status, the title Ms is now often seen to give *more* information about the holder's marital status. It's mainly older divorced and separated women who use the title Ms. In contrast, a large majority of married women prefer the traditional title Mrs, and very few use Ms. As a result, many younger women believe that the title Ms is for unmarried women who are too old to use the title Miss.

It looks as if the Germans were right. We should have gone down the same path and selected Mrs as a social title for all women. History is on its side: at one time *all* women had the title Mrs. Or we could have borrowed the French title Madame to be used for all women. It's already a title for several high status positions, from the Queen down. One of my favourite TV shows at the moment is *Madam Secretary,* the main character being Secretary of State, one of the highest positions in a US president's administration. (She is fourth in line for the top job should the president die.) However, hindsight is a wonderful thing. Instead, it looks as if we're stuck with Miss/Mrs/Ms for the foreseeable future.

Another way to treat women and men equally is for everyone to have the *same* social title, such as *Citizen* or *Comrade.* Unfortunately, in history these terms are often closely linked to totalitarian governments. In the eighteenth century, during the French Revolution all titles that even hinted at the nobility were abolished, including Monsieur, literally, 'My Lord', and Madame, 'My Lady'. Instead, the revolutionaries used the term *Citizen.* They re-named the deposed King Louis XVI as 'Citizen Louis Capet', before they chopped off his head. Though, to be strictly accurate, the men who led the French Revolution saw women as second-class citizens, and were keen to distinguish themselves from their female revolutionaries. They therefore used the title *Citoyen* for a man, and *Citoyenne* for a woman.

Similarly, the social title *Comrade* is closely associated with the twentieth century Soviet Union. So, in George Orwell's novel *Animal Farm*, a satire on the Soviet Union, the animals all refer to each other as 'Comrade'. Given their history, Citizen and Comrade stand no chance of adoption as social titles in English-speaking countries in the near future. Nor, I think, does the universal title *Person.* About the only thing it has going for it is that it doesn't have any historical baggage, but that's not saying a lot. The only gender-free social title I've seen that might stand a chance of adoption is the single letter *M* (pronounced *em*), though so far it only gets a mention only in specialist books about non-sexist writing.

Some people see the big advantage of a title such as Comrade to be that it treats everyone the same, regardless of whether they are men or women, single or married. They argue that your sexual and marital status is no-one's business but yours and your sexual partner's. Others argue that we use social titles precisely to give out information about ourselves, and

212

they should do this as accurately and fairly as possible. It's now gener-ally accepted that not everyone classifies themselves as either male or female. To reflect the fact that there are shades of grey, the UK Deed Poll Service, a British company specialising in helping people change their names, recently introduced a new title, *Mx* (pronounced 'Mix'). The company saw it 'as an option for people who do not identify themselves as either male or female and, therefore, feel a gender specific title such as Mr or Miss is inappropriate and unsuitable for them'. However, the company cautioned that they were 'unable to guarantee' that all govern-ment departments, companies and organisations will recognise the new title. *Misc* (pronounced 'Misk') is another possible gender-neutral title.

Let me end the chapter on a whimsical note. If social titles provide infor-mation about a woman's marital status, then to be fair men should also have two social titles, depending on whether they are single or married. Just as we have the titles Mrs for married women and Miss for single women, we could for example have the titles *Mr* for married men and *Master* for single men. Or it could possibly be *Mar* for married men and *Sin* for single men. There have been several other suggestions over the years, none meant to be taken really seriously, or if they were, then their authors will have been sadly disappointed. You might be able to think of better titles. All have absolutely *no* chance of success.

EIGHTEEN

Major Tom, Dr Dick and Lady Harriet

Professional and honorary titles

This chapter looks first at the huge range of professional titles, such as *Admiral, Bishop* and *Dr*, which are used by members of military, religious and medical organisations; and then at some of the many honorary titles like *Sir* and *Lord*, which are awarded by governments.

Many people use professional titles at work. They serve to show that the title-holder belongs to a professional body, holds certain professional qualifications, or has reached a certain level in the professional hierarchy. *Professor* Stephen Hawking is probably the world's most famous living scientist, the 'Professor' title reflecting the fact that he is a senior academic. Less well known perhaps is Steven V. Silver *ASC*, whose name is at the end of each episode of the TV comedy series *Big Bang Theory*. He appears in the credits as Director of Photography, and the ASC after his name shows that he is a member of the American Society of Cinematographers. Directors of photography in cinema and television can join this elite body only when invited, and so cinematographers are keen to show off their membership with the professional title. Now that I've pointed out a couple of examples, you'll probably start to see professional titles everywhere.

The title we are most familiar with is *Dr*, which we usually expect to see before the name of the person we go to for medical advice. The link in the English language between the title Dr and medicine goes back in history to at least the 1300s. In his *Canterbury Tales,* Geoffrey Chaucer refers to a 'doctour of phisik' (doctor of medicine)—though his curative powers in part depended on the study of astrological signs. But medical professionals were not the only ones to claim the title Dr. In Latin, *doctor* means 'teacher' rather than healer, and universities have awarded doctorates since the thirteenth century. Today, a doctorate is usually awarded to candidates who have done original research over the course of several years, and it's an essential qualification for any ambitious young university academic.

In the US and Canada, the distinction between the two types of doctor, medical and academic, has been done away with by awarding students who complete a four-year graduate program in medicine with a doctorate, a Doctor of Medicine (MD). (Rather pompously, the letters are often reversed in the suffix MD, an abbreviation of the Latin phrase *Medicinæ Doctor.*) In the UK and other Commonwealth countries, universities often award medical graduates with bachelor degrees, usually Bachelor of Medicine and Bachelor of Surgery. Of course, these medical graduates still use the traditional title of Dr when they start practising medicine.

Such is the status, and income, of medical doctors, that many other health care professions have also taken on the title Dr. Again, in most parts of North America this has happened by awarding a doctorate to students who complete a four-year graduate program in, for example, dentistry, optometry, pharmacy, physiotherapy, osteopathy or chiropractic. In Britain and other Commonwealth countries, other health care professionals have instead often opted to adopt Dr as a courtesy title. For example, in the mid-1990s, the professional body for dentists in the UK simply changed its ruling on professional misconduct to allow dentists to give themselves the courtesy title Dr if they wished, providing that they didn't mislead anyone into thinking that they were anything other than dentists. Though I suppose it would have been less misleading simply not to use the title Dr.

However, not all medical practitioners give themselves the title Dr. Last week, I consulted a surgeon who used the title Mr. I mentioned this to a cousin of mine who told me that the physician he'd just consulted (we're a very unhealthy family) used the title Dr. This curious practice of different medical specialities using different titles is rooted in the history of the medical profession in Britain. For several centuries, it was firmly divided into two distinct groups, *physicians* and *surgeons*. Physicians were university trained, treated their rich patients with drugs and advice, and regarded themselves as the elite medical group. In contrast, surgeons trained as apprentices, and their business was much more brutal and bloody as they performed surgery without anaesthetics. Originally, surgery was done by clergymen, but when a thirteenth century papal decree prohibited them from shedding blood, they began to supervise barbers to do the surgical work because of their skill with razors! These *barber surgeons* lasted several centuries, and are symbolised by the red and white poles traditionally displayed outside British barbershops—red for blood and white for bandages.

Barber surgeons who specialised in surgery formally separated from barbers in the middle of the eighteenth century, when what was to become the Royal College of Surgeons was formed. Because their qualification was awarded by the College rather than a university, surgeons couldn't use the title Dr. Instead, they adopted the title *Mr*, which at the time was used only by upper-class men. This was also the time when the traditional second-class status of surgeons was gradually changing, and they began to see themselves as at least the equal of, if not better than, physicians. They even created a new unofficial College category of 'pure surgeon' to distinguish themselves from the general practitioners who had College membership. Only pure surgeons could use the front door of the College, the others had to go round the back. Being addressed as Mr became a hallmark of a pure surgeon. The title became a badge of honour rather than a put-down.

Historically then, British physicians have used the title Dr, and surgeons have used the title Mr. This is why today in the UK when doctors become members of the Royal College of Surgeons, the convention is that they change their title from Dr to Mr, Mrs, Miss or Ms, to emphasise their medical status as surgeons. A similar tradition applies in Ireland, parts of Australia, and New Zealand. The practice may be anachronistic, but most surgeons are happy to keep it. One survey showed that two thirds of male surgeons wanted to keep their Mr title, though female surgeons were more evenly divided about being known as Miss, Mrs or Ms.

Pretty much all professionals have educational qualifications or are members of professional groups, and thus are able to add titles after their name. The aim, of course, is to enhance their professional image. For example, I've just been to see my family doctor—let's call him Bill Feelgood. Professionally, he's known, much more imposingly, as Dr William Feelgood, MB (Melb), BS (Melb), DRANZCOG, FRACGP, FACRRM. The first three titles show that Bill has a Bachelor of Medicine (MB) from the University of Melbourne (Melb), a Bachelor of Surgery (BS) also from the University of Melbourne, and a Diploma from the Royal Australian and New Zealand College of Obstetricians and Gynaecologists (DRANZCOG). The final two sets of letters show that he is a fellow of the Royal Australian College of General Practitioners (FRACGP) and the Australian College of Rural and Remote Medicine (FACRRM). Of course, it's highly unlikely that any of Bill's patients have a clue about what these professional titles mean. But that's not important. What *is* important is the professional image that the titles project—not only is Bill Feelgood a doctor (clearly shown by the Dr title before his name), but he must be a pretty good one considering all the letters after his name.

Nursing is another health profession where history continues to have a major impact on professional titles. The word *nurse* originally meant a woman who breastfed someone else's baby. Later the term was widened to mean a woman employed to look after young children; and later still to a woman who cared for others, young and old. This was fine during the nineteenth century when the nursing profession began to expand rapidly, as almost all hospital nurses were women. As a result, senior nursing roles also had feminine titles. *Matron* was the title of the chief nurse in a hospital. In the thirteenth century, the word matron meant a married woman, and later the term widened to mean a woman having the characteristics usually associated with the mother of a large family, or a matriarch. She was responsible for all the nurses and domestic staff, overseeing all patient care, and the efficient running of the hospital. Lower down the nursing hierarchy were *sisters* who were in charge of individual wards. The term comes from the fact that much of the early nursing work was done by nuns who used the title Sister.

Although replaced in part by more modern titles such as 'director of nursing' and 'charge nurse', the traditional titles Matron and Sister have continued into the twenty-first century. For example, although the British National Health Service scrapped the position of matron in the 1960s, matrons were brought back in 2001 to be in charge of wards, with responsibility for managing ward budgets. In Australia, Sister has come to mean the same as a registered nurse, denoted by the suffix RN, despite the fact that male registered nurses are much more common in the twenty-first century than they were in the nineteenth. Registered nurses routinely use the title Sister when introducing themselves or a colleague; even male nurses sometimes answer the telephone saying 'Sister speaking'. I suspect that the historical titles Matron and Sister will be around for a good deal longer.

Large formal organisations such as the armed forces, police and churches have a hierarchical structure, with members at each level having a different title. With over half a million members (double that if you count reservists), the US Army is an excellent example of such a formal organisation. It uses a dozen titles to identify two dozen ranks. From most to least senior, the title *General* is used by generals, lieutenant generals, major generals and brigadier generals; and the title *Sergeant* is used by master sergeants, sergeants first class, staff sergeants and sergeants. This clearly defined system becomes less clear when members from several national armies are in a single multinational force. To help clarify matters, organisations like the North Atlantic Treaty Organisation have rank codes that make it clear, for example, that a Private First Class in the US Army is equivalent to a Lance Corporal or Lance Bombardier in the British Army, and so all have the title Private.

Employers sometimes recognise their best employees by giving them awards. Most of the time, these awards don't result in letters after the employee's name. But when the employer is the government, and the service being awarded is something really special, then the award might result in letters after your name. Best known are the gallantry awards for military personnel, the most famous being the Victoria Cross. It is awarded 'for most conspicuous bravery, or some daring or pre-eminent act of valour or self-sacrifice, or extreme devotion to duty in the presence of the enemy'. Recipients of the award can add the letters VC after their name. Less than a score of people have received a Victoria Cross since the Second World War. Several other less well-known military awards for gallantry allow recipients to add letters after their names. One level down from the Victoria Cross are the Distinguished Service Order (DSO) and Conspicuous Gallantry Cross (CGC). And at the third level are the Distinguished Service Cross (DSC) for acts of bravery during combat operations at sea, the Military Cross (MC) for bravery on land, and the Distinguished Flying Cross (DFC) for acts of bravery in the air.

Awards for gallantry aren't restricted to military personnel. They include the George Cross (GC), the George Medal (GM), and the Queen's Gallantry Medal (QGM). Although much less well known, the George Cross is equal with the Victoria Cross as the highest award for gallantry. The difference is that the George Cross is for gallantry *not* in the presence of the enemy. As a result, the award is also open to civilians, though most recipients are still military personnel. Other bravery awards aimed at specific occupational groups include the Queen's Police Medal (QPM) and the Queen's Fire Service Medal (QFSM), which are awarded for gallantry or distinguished service.

Widening the scope of the award to include distinguished service also brings in a range of other awards reserved for specific occupation groups, including senior officers in the military, members of the diplomatic service, and people providing personal service to the sovereign. For example, at the time of writing the head of the British Army is General Sir Peter Wall, GCB. He became a Knight Grand Cross of the Order of the Bath (GCB) when he was listed in the Military Division of the Order of the Bath in the Queen's Birthday Honours List.

This mention of the Birthday Honours List takes us neatly into *honorary titles*. I would imagine that every government in the world honours its citizens by presenting them with awards—a cynic might say they're a cheap way of acknowledging people's achievements. To fit the discussion into a few pages, I'll focus on just a few of the many British honorary titles.

The British government has one of the most complex systems of honorary titles, which goes back to before the Norman Conquest of 1066. Harold, the last Anglo-Saxon king of England, held the title Earl Harold of Wessex before his coronation. As every English schoolboy knows, King Harold was killed at the Battle of Hastings fighting William of Normandy. The victorious King William demanded that his supporters send him money and knights for his army. In return, he gave them land and titles. Of course, over time the honours system became largely ceremonial, although much of the historical hierarchy remains. It is still headed, or *crowned*, by the royal family, followed by peers and baronets, then knights and dames, and finally those whose honour allows them to add letters after their name, but not a title before it.

At the top of the British pecking order are members of the Royal Family, who are close relatives of the British monarch, Her Majesty Queen Elizabeth II. Members of the Royal Family include about two dozen people who have the title *Royal Highness*. They include the Queen's husband, His Royal Highness [HRH] The Duke of Edinburgh; her children such as HRH The Prince of Wales; her daughters-in-law such as HRH The Duchess of Cornwall; some of her grandchildren, their spouses and children such as HRH The Duke of Cambridge, HRH The Duchess of Cambridge, HRH Prince George of Cambridge; and the Queen's cousins and their wives, including HRH The Duke of Gloucester. According to the official 1917 declaration, 'the children of any Sovereign of the United Kingdom and the children of the sons of any such Sovereign and the eldest living son of the eldest son of the Prince of Wales shall have and at all times hold and enjoy the style, title or attribute of Royal Highness.' As you can see, honorary titles are not straightforward!

As it stands, the wife of a British king has the title Queen. For example, when Prince William becomes King William V, his wife will be Queen Catherine. However, the husband of a reigning queen does not have the title King. In fact, he has no automatic right to any title. Queen Victoria's husband, Albert, was given the title Prince Consort, a title that Queen Elizabeth II's husband, Philip, refused. Eventually, ten years after his marriage, the Queen gave him the title 'Prince of the United Kingdom'. In 2013, the British government changed the ancient laws of royal primogeniture, which grant males a greater right to the throne than their female siblings, so that now a monarch's eldest child, regardless of sex, will be next in line to succeed. There is some support also to update the titles of the spouses of a monarch, treating them equally regardless of sex. So, the wife of a reigning king would have the title Princess Consort, and the husband of a reigning queen would be Prince Consort. If this occurs, then King William V's wife would have the title Princess Consort rather than Queen.

Next down from the Royal Family are *peers,* who according to *Burke's Peerage & Baronetage* are divided by 'order of descending relative seniority' into dukes, marquises, earls, viscounts and barons. The female equivalents are duchess, marchioness, countess, viscountess, and baroness. The correct form of address for a marquis, earl, viscount and baron is *Lord*; and for a marchioness, countess, viscountess and baroness it is *Lady*. Dukes and duchesses keep their original titles, and they are addressed as 'Your Grace, the Duke [or Duchess] of ...'. This distinguishes dukes and duchesses, the grandest peers, from the rest. William the Conqueror, King William I, was also the Duke of Normandy, and for several centuries monarchs appointed dukes only from members of the royal family. This practice also applies now. You may (or may not) have noticed that following his wedding, Prince William became the Duke of Cambridge, an English title, the Earl of Strathearn, a Scottish title and Baron Carrickfergus, a Northern Irish title. The last person from outside the royal family to become a duke was Hugh Grosvenor, who in 1874 became Duke of Westminster.

Traditionally, peerages are hereditary, being handed down to the oldest surviving son. So, the current Duke of Westminster, Gerald Grosvenor, is the first Duke's great-grandson. He is the wealthiest Englishman, with a fortune of several billion pounds, which in part comes from land he owns in Westminster in the heart of London. Monarchs can also elevate peers to higher levels of seniority in the peerage. For example, past generations of the current Duke of Westminster were once marquises, and before that earls, viscounts and barons. So, Gerald Grosvenor is not only 6th Duke of Westminster, he is also 8th Marquess of Westminster, 9th Earl Grosvenor, 9th Viscount Belgrave and 9th Baron Grosvenor.

Outside the royal family, virtually all new peerages are *life peerages,* which apply only during the life of the peer. Over the last half-century, successive governments have created well over a thousand life peers. What became one of the most controversial life peerages went to English novelist and former politician Jeffrey Archer, who became 'Baron Archer of Weston-super-Mare'. Later, a court found him guilty of perjury and perverting the course of justice, and he spent two years in jail. However, a life peerage cannot be withdrawn without the permission of the peer, and he is still Lord Archer.

Confusingly, although barons are members of the peerage, *baronets* are not, and so don't use the title Lord—though a baronet's wife is referred to as *Lady.* A baronet has the title *Sir* before his name, followed by the suffix *Bt,* to show that he is a baronet and not just a mere knight. A baronetcy is a hereditary title that goes back to the seventeenth century, when King James VI and I saw it as a good way to raise funds. Sir Richard Grosvenor, the great-great-great-great-great-great-great-great-great grandfather of the current Duke of Westminster was one of the first baronets. In the nineteenth century, baronetcies were conferred on engineers and similar professionals who had performed distinguished service, but who nevertheless were seen as not from the upper echelons of society, and so not quite worthy of a peerage.

However, with the introduction of life peerages, there has been only one new baronetcy in the last half century. Denis Thatcher, husband of former British Prime Minister Margaret Thatcher, was made a baronet in 1990, and became Sir Denis Thatcher, Bt. When he died, his son became Sir Mark Thatcher, 2nd Bt. To be precise, he became

The Honourable Sir Mark Thatcher, 2nd Bt, 'The Honourable' being a courtesy title that came to him when his mother was made a baroness. Now that his mother has died, I'm not sure whether or not Mark is still *Honourable*—life can be complicated when your father was a baronet and your mother was a baroness. After the Honourable Sir Mark Thatcher, 2nd Bt had been found guilty of involvement in an attempted coup in Africa, there were calls that he be stripped of his baronetcy; but like Baron Archer of Weston-super-Mare, he still has his honorary title.

If the Royal Family is Division 1 of British society, the peerage is Division 2, and the baronetage is Division 3, then Division 4 is the *knightage* (the word comes straight out of *Burke's Peerage*). Knights, of course, play an important role in British history and mythology, the most famous being King Arthur and his Knights of the Round Table. However, unlike peerages and baronetcies, knighthoods have never been hereditary. A knight is addressed as *Sir*, as in Sir Paul McCartney. His wife has the title *Lady* McCartney. However, Sir Paul is still a *knight bachelor*, the title having nothing to do with his marital status, but with the fact that he is in the lowest division of knights.

By comparison, knights who hold their titles in any of several orders of chivalry add letters after their name showing which order they belong to. Members of the Most Honourable Order of the Bath might add KCB (Knight Commander of the Bath) or, even better, GCB (Knight Grand Cross of the Order of the Bath). For example, the head of the British Army, General Sir Peter Wall, was recently promoted from a KCB to a GCB. By the way, *Bath* refers to the bathing that once formed part of the ceremonial preparation of a candidate for knighthood.

There is no female version of a knight bachelor—no 'knight spinster'. The equivalent of a knight is a *dame*, and dames are created as one of the higher classes of an order of chivalry. These days, a female recipient becomes a Dame Commander of the Order of the British Empire. In 2003 Queen Elizabeth II made British actor Helen Mirren a Dame Commander of the British Empire. She thus became Dame Helen Mirren, DBE. A few years later, Helen Mirren won an Oscar for best leading actress in the movie *The Queen*—playing Queen Elizabeth II. Over the years, many female celebrities have been awarded the title of dame, including actors Dame Maggie Smith and Dame Elizabeth Taylor, authors Dame Agatha Christie and Dame Barbara Cartland, and opera singers Dame Nellie Melba and Ann Murray DBE. Note the absence of *Dame* before Ann Murray's name. She is from Ireland, which is not a member of the Commonwealth and so, rather confusingly, her DBE is an 'honorary' award. This means that although she can add the letters DBE after her name, she can't add the title *Dame* before her name. Nellie Melba (1861-1931) was an Australian operatic soprano who in 1918 was one of the first women to become a DBE—not for her singing, but for her charity work during the First World War. A decade later, she was elevated to the highest class of the Order of the British Empire, a Dame Grand Cross, and thus became Dame Nellie Melba GBE.

The wife of a knight can take the title *Lady*, but the husband of a dame has no honorary title. Similarly, the female partner of a lesbian dame does not have a title, nor does the male partner of a gay knight. Sir Elton John's male marriage partner is *Mr* David Furnish. Of course, the number of people affected is very small but, particularly with the end to royal primogeniture and the introduction of same-sex marriages, it seems reasonable to change the UK honours system to treat the partners of all knights and dames equally.

Most people who appear on an Honours list do not get titles such as Baron, Sir or Dame to put in front of their names. For many years now, the vast majority of honours recipients have received awards in the lower classes of the Most Excellent Order of the British Empire, and become either a Member of the British Empire (MBE), an Officer of the British Empire (OBE), or a Commander of the Most Excellent Order of the British Empire (CBE). So, for example, just as in 1965 Paul McCartney and the rest of the Beatles received MBEs, in 2006 all of the Ashes-winning England cricket team received MBEs—apart from the captain,

Michael Vaughan, who already had an MBE, so he was promoted and awarded an OBE.

Thankfully, it's not just celebrities who are honoured with MBEs and OBEs. For example, the chances are that you haven't heard of Ella Edgar, MBE, who was awarded an MBE for her services to Scottish country dancing; or Tony Warburton, MBE, whose award was in recognition of his services to owl conservation. The idea was extended recently with the revival of the British Empire Medal, known as 'the working class gong' (an old British army term for a medal). It's designed to encourage people to volunteer to help with various good causes at the local level. Among the first recipients was a waitress, Mrs Patricia Carter. The Birthday Honours List explains that she received her award 'For services to the Hospitality Industry'.

PART FIVE...

The story of professional names

NINETEEN

Joanne Rowling, J.K. Rowling and Robert Galbraith

Pen names

Not long after the last Ice Age, when I was on the brink of becoming a teenager, I became interested in pop music. BBC radio didn't play much pop music then, so I spent a good deal of time trying to listen to the only alternative, Radio Luxembourg. The Radio Luxembourg transmitter struggled to keep the signal strong enough to reach my hometown, but when the atmospheric conditions were right, I was able to hear the latest pop songs. I can still remember liking not only the music but also the names of the performers. While my friends and I all had very ordinary, boring names, the names on Radio Luxembourg *sounded* exciting—names like Billy Fury, Rory Storm and Marty Wilde. Call me naïve (well, I was), but at the time I didn't think for a moment that these might not be their real names. I found out later they were all professional names—that Billy Fury was actually Ron Wycherley, Rory Storm was Alan Caldwell, and Marty Wilde was Reg Smith.

Ron Wycherley/Billy Fury was performing 50 years ago, but the use of professional names goes back at least 1500 years, to when Mercurius chose the name John II on being elected pope because he thought it was wrong for a pope to be named after a Roman god. And the custom of adopting a papal name still applies, Jorge Mario Bergoglio becoming Pope Francis after his election in 2013. At the other end of the spectrum, criminals often adopt new identities, including new names, when on the run from the police. Ronald Biggs is Britain's best-known fugitive. He was on the run for 36 years following his part in the Great Train Robbery, and used several false names (and some cosmetic surgery) during his round-the-world escape to Brazil. Other well-known professional names are the pen names used by writers, and the stage names used by actors and other entertainers. The last two chapters of '*Hello, My Name Is . . .*' look at these, starting with pen names.

*

This last year, I read a few new novels, and re-read rather more old favourites. One of the new novels was an enthralling, though rather gory, crime novel called *The Silkworm* by Robert Galbraith. I've also re-read one of my favourite novels, the light-hearted and gore-free *Coming Up for Air* by George Orwell, which has the memorable opening line 'The idea really came to me the day I got my new false teeth.' Another old favourite of mine is the science fiction classic *Day of the Triffids* by John Wyndham. It's set in a world where virtually everyone is blind and where there are marauding, intelligent, man-eating plants. The plot is far-fetched, but Wyndham is such a good writer that the novel works. Finally in my list of recently read books is the Lewis Carroll classic, *Through The Looking-Glass*, the second Alice in Wonderland book. I can't help quoting Humpty Dumpty, who asks Alice what her name means: '"MUST a name mean something?" Alice asked doubtfully. "Of course it must," Humpty Dumpty said . . .'

Robert Galbraith, George Orwell, John Wyndham and Lewis Carroll all have one thing in common—yes, you've guessed it, they are all pen names. You might well ask why an author would want to substitute a pen name for his or her own name. Isn't seeing your name in print one of the big thrills of being a writer? Well, yes, but it hasn't stopped hundreds of writers from using pen names. One website lists over 10,000 pen names used by 4000 authors, alphabetically all the way from Matthew Arnold to Stefan Zweig.

Clearly, there are a multitude of reasons for using pen names. Early in his career, Isaac Asimov (1920-1992) was invited to write a juvenile science fiction novel that could be sold as a television series. The thought of a longrunning, lucrative TV contract was inviting to the impoverished young writer. 'What bothered me, though', explains Asimov, 'was that all the television I had seen was uniformly awful. What good would millions of dollars do me if I were ashamed of its source?' (This is not a sentiment you often hear!) He took his publisher's advice and used a pen name.

Asimov's publishers also urged him to change his Jewish given name and Slavic family name, suggesting that given the high level of racism and anti-Semitism among the book-buying public, 'a simple American name might lead to greater reader acceptance'. This time, Asimov refused. However, another writer from a Jewish background, Harold Rubin, *did* see the financial benefits of a name change. As Harold Robbins, he became a top-selling author, selling twice as many books as J.K. Rowling (so far). He wrote his first novel, *Never Love a Stranger*, published in 1948, while he worked at Universal Studios, which routinely changed actors' names to disguise their Jewish background.

Harold Robbins and George Orwell are both pen names, but that is probably all these two writers have in common. George Orwell today is best known for two novels, the nightmarish *Nineteen Eighty-Four*, and his self-styled 'fairy tale' about tyranny, *Animal Farm*. His birth name was Eric Blair, and he had a very upper-middle-class upbringing, being a pupil at the elite Eton College, and an officer in the Indian Imperial Police in Burma. Illness led him to return to England, and while recuperating he completely rejected his earlier life. He wanted to be a writer, and not just any kind of writer, but one whose work would not be well received by his former Eton chums and Imperial Police colleagues. His first book, the semi-autobiographical *Down and Out in Paris and London,* is about poverty in two of the world's richest cities.

One way of proclaiming this new life was to use a new name in his writing. At the end of 1932, when *Down and Out* was close to publication, he wrote to his agent listing several possible pen names including P.S. Burton, Kenneth Miles, H. Lewis Allways and, the one 'I rather favour', George Orwell. He doesn't say *why* he rather favours George Orwell, but clearly his agent went along with his preference. It's odd to think that in some parallel universe, H. Lewis Allways is one of the greatest of all British writers.

Lee Child is also a pen name. As with Orwell, the adoption of the pen name Lee Child marked a major life-change. Lee Child's real name is Jim Grant. He worked for a television company for many years, but following a very long, intense period of conflict with a new management group, he and many of his colleagues were sacked. In his 40s, and jobless for the first time in his life, Grant decided to channel his anger into a new venture, and started writing his first Jack Reacher novel. To mark this change, he adopted a new name, explaining that from his work in television, 'I saw how it was often a valuable psychological boost, you know, new job, new name, personal reinvention'. Unlike Orwell he didn't choose his writer's name randomly. Jim discovered that nearly two-thirds of the authors in the *New York Times* best-seller lists had last names that started with C, and that the pen name *Child* would put him neatly between Raymond Chandler and Agatha Christie. He not only wanted to be a writer; he wanted to be a *best-selling* writer.

The preponderance of best-selling authors with names starting with C, now boosted by the addition of Lee Child, has not gone unnoticed elsewhere in the publishing industry. Martyn Waites, a moderately successful British crime writer, was one day having coffee with his publisher who told him that the company lacked a female thriller writer. Without thinking, Martyn volunteered to fill the gap. Clearly, he would have to have a female first name, but the publisher also wanted a new surname, 'a surname beginning with C because shoppers' eyes are naturally drawn to ... where books by "C" authors live.' Martyn Waites and his publisher eventually came up with the name Tania Carver which, as well as having the right initial letter, also gives the prospective reader a good idea about what sort of storyline to expect ...

So far, I've looked at a handful of pen names, meaning that there are several thousand more left. Fortunately, many of them are the result of three goals that together are pursued by pretty much all writers. First, they want to see their current manuscript *published*. Secondly, they want to *write* more books. Thirdly, they want to *sell* more books, to boost their egos and their incomes. Substituting a pen name for their own name is likely to happen if it increases the chances of achieving one or more of these goals.

These days, we rarely give a second thought about whether an author is a man or a woman because we see writing as something that men and women can do equally well. But it wasn't always like this. It's only about 150 years ago that a leading British philosopher, John Stuart Mill, observed that women writers are 'a disturbing element' in a civilised society. This strong taboo against women writers was also evident when in 1837 Charlotte Brontë wrote to the poet Robert Southey asking him for advice on her poems. (Robert *Who?* I can hear most readers saying.) His reply was that 'Literature cannot be the business of a woman's life and it ought not to be'.

At this time, men believed that *any* intellectual pursuit was beyond a woman's capabilities. Higher education was even seen as harmful to women's health. A publisher would likely dismiss out-of-hand a woman's manuscript and if, by chance, it were published, book sales would be minimal as potential buyers would be put off by the female authorship. In addition, many members of the author's social circle would avoid her because she had done something that women were not meant to do. To get around this bigotry, some female authors in the early nineteenth century submitted their manuscripts anonymously, and later in the century submitted their manuscripts under a male pen name.

During her lifetime, all of Jane Austen's novels were published anonymously. Her first book *Sense and Sensibility* (1811) was 'By a Lady'; and her second novel *Pride and Prejudice* (1813) was 'By the author of *Sense and Sensibility*'. Her final two novels, *Persuasion* and *Northanger Abbey*, were published after her death in 1817. Although again showing no author on the title page, each book included a 'Biographical notice of the author' written by Jane Austen's proud brother, Henry, in which he announced that the author was Jane Austen.

Later, several women writers in the nineteenth century got around the taboo on female authors by using masculine pen names. The French novelist Aurore Dupin used the pen name George Sand; and English novelist Mary Anne Evans published as George Eliot. Even in the early twentieth century, Australian-born novelist Ethel Richardson still found it necessary to use a masculine pen name, Henry Handel Richardson. Most famous are the three Brontë sisters, though their original male pseudonyms are now largely forgotten. Charlotte, author of *Jane Eyre,* used the pen name Currer Bell; Emily, author of *Wuthering Heights,* used the pen name Ellis Bell; and Anne, author of *The Tenant of Wild-fell Hall,* used the pen name Acton Bell. The given names Currer, Ellis and Acton are all from Yorkshire, where the sisters lived. However, the authors' real names were made public by Charlotte in the 'Biographical notice' she added to the second edition of Emily's *Wuthering Heights,* which was published in 1850, not long after the deaths of both Emily and Anne. Charlotte Brontë explains that the sisters chose these 'ambiguous' names because they knew that 'authoresses are liable to be looked on with prejudice'.

A less extreme way for a female author to hide her gender is to use only the initials of her given name. For example, Edith Nesbit (1858-1924) was a prolific children's author in the late nineteenth and early twentieth centuries using the name 'E. Nesbit'. She's probably best known today for *The Railway Children*, which was first published in 1906. You might expect that the use of a male pen name by a female author is now long gone. Well, not quite. Consider, for example, J.K. Rowling, the British author of the hugely successful Harry Potter series. The use of the *J.K.* initials was the idea of Rowling's British publishers, Bloomsbury. She had submitted the manuscript of the first Harry Potter book using her full name, Joanne Rowling. However, the publishers told her that 'we think boys will like this book but we're not sure that they'd pick it up if they think a woman wrote it'. All that Rowling was concerned about was that the book was published—'I would let them call me Enid Snodgrass if they published the book'. Bloomsbury wanted to disguise the fact that she was a woman by using only the initials of her given names. As she had only one given name, she added the middle name Kathleen, after her favourite grandmother, and became J.K. Rowling. As it turned out, two months after Bloomsbury published the book, J.K. Rowling was on national television, and no one bothered that the author was a woman.

The issue is still with us. In 2015 Catherine Nichols sent her novel to literary agents, who are the usual link between new authors and major publishers. She found that when she used her own name, she received favourable responses from only two of fifty agents. But when she sent exactly the same novel to fifty different agents using a male pen name, she received seventeen favourable responses. There's even a term for bias against women's writing—*gynobibliophobia*.

What about men using female pen names? Here we have the flip side of the J.K. Rowling story: men writing romantic novels, a genre where most readers and authors are women. For example, under the pen name Madeleine Brent, British writer Peter O'Donnell (1920-2010) wrote romances that had strong female characters and a largely female readership. Peter O'Donnell kept his real identity a closely guarded secret— even his US publishers didn't know about it. When he replied to a letter addressed to 'Miss Madeleine Brent', his wife signed it to give it a female touch. Of course, when he won the Romantic Novelists Association's novel of the year award, Madeleine/Peter wasn't able to personally receive it. The romantic novel of the year award goes back to 1960, and *all* the winners are women—or perhaps there are more men like Peter O'Donnell hiding their identity behind female pen names. Clearly, in this genre, being female was a big advantage, and it is still.

Following in the footsteps of Peter O'Donnell/Madeleine Brent is Bill Spence who, in 1994, started writing romantic novels under the pen name Jessica Blair. It was his publishers who came up with the pen name. According to Bill Spence, 'they pointed out that more women than men read and buy books, and they felt that a woman's name as an author would be better for marketing purposes'. When they asked him to use a female pen name, his response was 'You don't say no to publishers.' Over twenty Jessica Blair books later, the novel *The Road Beneath Me* was shortlisted for the best 'Epic Romantic Novel' award. It didn't win, but if it had Bill Spence would have attended the award ceremony, as he hasn't made a secret of the fact that he's a man. (But would he have had a better chance of *winning* if, like Peter O'Donnell, he had kept secret the fact that he was a man?)

Here's one final interesting twist on this idea of needing a female name if you're going to be a successful romantic novelist. Terry Gerritsen's first book was a romance novel. However, her publisher felt that as Terry was usually a man's name, readers might be put off buying the book. So, following Bill Spence's advice, 'Don't say no to publishers', Terry Gerritsen 'feminized' her name to Tess Gerritsen. She went on to write nine romances under that name. Later, she moved into writing thrillers, a genre where the gender of the author is of no importance. Having built up a fan base with her earlier novels, she kept the pen name.

Writing anonymously or using a pen name is also useful when the publication of a book could get the writer into trouble with government authorities or other groups. Politics, religion and sex tend to be the most controversial topics and, in the past, authors often wrote about these either anonymously or under a pen name to avoid detection. A classic example is the eighteenth-century French writer François-Marie Arouet, who is much better known as Voltaire. He adopted this pen name after his release from the Bastille for criticising the monarchy and the Catholic Church, which was not a wise move at the time. He spent much of his life keeping one step ahead of the authorities.

A contemporary of Voltaire was Scotsman David Hume (1711-1776), often regarded as the greatest philosopher in the English language. However, his atheistic views so offended powerful people in the Scottish establishment that they often blocked his appointment to university positions. Anxious not to make life more difficult for himself, for twenty-five years he held off publishing his greatest work, the sexily titled *Dialogues Concerning Natural Religion*, which suggested that the order we see in nature is a result of chance rather than divine intervention. He was on his deathbed before he decided to go ahead and publish. As it turned out, Hume's supporters were still so concerned about its reception that the book didn't come out until three years after his death, and the first edition didn't include the name of either the author or publisher.

In the twentieth century, the Russian political and economic writer Vladimir Ilich Ulyanov adopted a range of pseudonyms to escape the attention of the tsar's police. The one he would later make famous was Lenin. This was standard practice at the time for Russian revolutionaries. His fellow revolutionary, Stalin, used twenty different names in his writing.

Probably the only thing that Lenin and Stalin have in common with British novelist Andy McNab is that he too uses a pen name to protect himself from his political enemies. It's his military work in Northern Ireland that makes him a potential target, and led him to adopt a pseudonym. He was serving in the British Army when he killed a member of the IRA, and later joined the Special Air Service where he served with a clandestine group identifying IRA active service units. However, like all successful writers these days, he has to promote his work in the media. This has led him to appear on TV with his face in shadow; and his official website 'photo' shows him in silhouette. Of course, it may well be that with the passage of time his life is no longer threatened. Or, perhaps not. If nothing else, his anonymity is still a valuable trademark.

One writer who did *not* hide his identity, but almost certainly wishes he had, is Salman Rushdie, the British author of *The Satanic Verses*. The novel appeared in 1988, and many Muslims denounced it as blasphemous. A few months after the book came out, Rushdie went into hiding when a senior Muslim cleric issued a *fatwa*, which called on Muslims to kill those involved in the publication of *The Satanic Verses*. A Muslim organisation then offered a reward of $US1 million to any Muslim who killed Salman Rushdie. The fatwa has not been carried out, but is still in force. In 2012, Rushdie wrote a memoir of the decade he spent in hiding. It's called *Joseph Anton* after the alias he used during this time. The alias comes from the names of two of Rushdie's favourite writers, Joseph Conrad and Anton Chekhov. Rushdie comments: 'I made it the title of the book because it always felt very strange to be asked to give up my name, I was always uncomfortable about it, and I thought it might help dramatise, for the reader, the deep strangeness and discomfort of those years'.

Sex has long been another controversial subject. In the past, an author whose real name appeared on the cover of an erotic book usually ended up in court. For example, John Cleland, the author of the most famous eighteenth century erotic novel, *Fanny Hill,* used his own name. He was promptly charged with obscenity, had his book banned, and made no money from the sale of illegal copies. Not surprisingly, later writers who wanted to keep their freedom, and income, chose to publish anonymously. They include the writer of the curiously named *The Autobiography of a Flea,* published in 1887, which is narrated, believe it or not, by a flea that moves between the bodies of the main characters in the story. Even more unbelievable is that it's still available online.

Fast-forward to France in the mid-1950s when the author and publisher of the erotic novel *Story of O* were charged with obscenity. However, only the publisher appeared in court because the author used an untraceable pen name. It wasn't until forty years later that Anne Desclos admitted she was the author. Her boyfriend had told her that he thought no woman was capable of writing an erotic novel, and she wanted to prove him wrong. Eventually, the courts dismissed the obscenity charges, but a publicity ban was put in place for some years. The novel came in for considerable criticism, some feminists seeing it as the ultimate objectification of women. The woman who is the main character doesn't even have the dignity of a proper name; instead, she's known only by the letter O—which could stand for *Object* (or worse).

The *Story of O* was the inspiration for a similar French novel, *Emmanuelle*, which was published a couple of years later. It's about the sexual exploits of the wife of a French engineer in Bangkok. Because of fears of prosecution, initially the book had no author's name on the cover; it then appeared under the pen name Emmanuelle Arsan, hinting that it was autobiographical. A later story was that the author was the wife of a French diplomat in Bangkok. Later still, it turned out that her husband, Louis-Jacques Rollet-Andriane, was the author. He wrote his soft-core books under a pen name because he believed it would harm his career as a diplomat. When it looked as if he would be discovered, he claimed that his wife was the author. After all, she was the wife of a Frenchman living in Bangkok, and the book was about the wife of a Frenchman living in Bangkok.

English language versions of the *Story of O* and *Emmanuelle* appeared soon after the liberalisation of the obscenity laws. They were quickly followed by other sexually explicit mainstream books such as the best-selling *The Sensuous Woman* by 'J', *The Sensuous Man* by 'M', and the spoof *The Sensuous Dirty Old Man* by 'Dr A'. By this stage, of course, pen names were a marketing device rather than a way to avoid legal problems. For example, the front cover of *The Sensuous Dirty Old Man* featured a picture of the author (Isaac Asimov) with a bra over his eyes, to hide his identity. He even appeared on television with the bra, 'It was the silliest thing I ever did' is his rueful comment.

Although there's now no need for authors of sexually explicit novels to hide their names from the law, they may still want to use a pen name for other reasons. This was the case most recently with E.L. James, author of the hugely successful *Fifty Shades of Grey* trilogy, sometimes described as 'mummy porn' because of its popularity with older women readers. E.L. James is the pen name of British author Erika Mitchell. She used a pen name because she was 'trying to stay under the radar' so that she could 'maintain normality for her husband and two teenage sons', which was relatively easy to do when her work was a little-known online book. She points out that her sons had not read the books, 'I'd be mortified, and they'd be mortified ... It'd be far too embarrassing.' But staying under the radar became impossible when the online publication morphed into a literary sensation, generating a six-figure book deal and a multi-million dollar Hollywood film contract.

Many other authors adopted pen names for much less dramatic, but no less important reasons, like earning enough to live on while they struggled to get established as a writer. Early in their writing career, many authors write in their spare time, supported by the income from their 'real' job. Keeping this job is important, and these novice writers don't want their employers reacting negatively to any publicity that might result from their writing. This is most likely, of course, if the writers are drawing on their experiences at work, or if the genre they are working in is at odds with their other work. As we've seen, this was what happened with French diplomat Louis-Jacques Rollet-Andriane, who wrote erotic novels as a sideline. Here are a few more examples.

Charles Lutwidge Dodgson (1832-1898) was a nineteenth century British mathematician who spent all his working life tutoring at Oxford University. Not surprisingly, his widespread fame is not based on his mathematical books, such as *Symbolic Logic Part I*. He's not much better known for his contributions to the theory of elections, such as *Principles of Parliamentary Representation*. Instead, his fame comes from novels and poetry written primarily for children. Dodgson had been writing poetry and fiction since his early days at Oxford, but kept it separate from his professional writing by using a pen name. He had written to the editor of a magazine where he had submitted some poetry with various suggestions for a pen name: Edgar Cuthwellis and Edgar U.C. Westhill were anagrams of Charles Lutwidge; and Louis Carroll and Lewis Carroll were both based on Charles Lutwidge. The editor chose Lewis Carroll, and Dodgson used this for all his subsequent poetry and fiction. This includes, of course, *Alice's Adventures in Wonderland* and *Through the Looking-Glass*, which he originally started writing to amuse a colleague's ten-year-old daughter, Alice Liddell.

A twentieth century example is David John Moore Cornwell. He's a British writer of espionage novels, though like all top spies he uses a false name, John le Carré. His writing career spans over half a century, his first novel coming out in 1961. At the time, Cornwell was working for MI6, a branch of British military intelligence, doing the sort of things spymasters do—organising break-ins, conducting interrogations, running agents, tapping telephones and so on. He told his employer that he was writing a spy novel and, not surprisingly, his superiors insisted that he didn't use his real name. In fact, it's incredible that they permitted him to write at all. In answer to queries about how he decided on the name, he tells the story that he saw the name *le Carré* above a tailor's shop in London, but more recently has admitted that he actually can't remember where the name came from. It didn't take long for le Carré to earn enough money from his writing to allow him to leave MI6. His third novel, *The Spy Who Came in from The Cold*, was a huge hit in 1963, which was during the Cold War when there was enormous public interest in spies and spying. By this time, of course, the le Carré pen name was fixed in the public's mind; going back to his real name simply wasn't an option.

Not long after le Carré's spy came in from the cold, a veterinary surgeon called Alf Wight was busy writing about a vet who went out into the cold in a series of highly successful books, loosely based on his many years as a vet in north Yorkshire. The books were then serialised for BBC television in the hugely popular *All Creatures Great and Small*. However, Alf Wight didn't write under his own name; instead he used the pen name James Herriot. He did this because when he first started writing he saw himself as 'a working vet whose hobby happens to be writing'. The professional body that Alf belonged to, the Royal College of Veterinary Surgeons, 'frowned on any form of advertising or publicity that drew undue attention to its members'. A pen name also helped him to avoid writs from the real people he based his characters on.

Alf Wight picked James Herriot as a pen name almost as randomly as Cornwell picked the name le Carré. The first part was easy, as Wight's own first name was James, though everyone called him by his middle name. The last name was trickier. At first, he thought about adopting the name James Walsh, but found that there was a vet with that name on the British veterinary register. Later, he was watching a soccer match on television, and one of the goalkeepers was a Scottish player called Jim Herriot. He had such a good game that the young writer, who had been brought up in Scotland, decided it must be a good omen, and adopted James Herriot as his pen name. It wasn't long before James Herriot the writer became a lot more famous that Jim Herriot the footballer. The two Herriots eventually met, with James giving Jim a signed copy of one of his books, and Jim giving James one of his Scotland football jerseys.

Literature can be classified into several types or *genres*: comedy, romance, science fiction, and so on. Sometimes, writers who are already established in one genre use different names when they begin writing in a different genre. This can be helpful to readers because then they aren't misled by an author's established name into buying a book in a genre that they dislike. It's also helpful to booksellers, because they don't have to worry about shelving books by the same author in different parts of the store. It's helpful to established authors because, if all goes well, it can result in them selling more books, and if all does *not* go well, the pen name protects an author's established 'brand' name.

The idea is not new. A classic example is Scottish writer Sir Walter Scott (1771-1832) who for twenty years wrote only poetry. His best-known lines come from his 1808 poem *Marmion*: 'Oh! what a tangled web we weave/ When first we practise to deceive!' But the income of even a successful poet is not large and so, in part because he needed the money, Walter Scott began writing novels. At the time there was a tremendous stigma attached to writing fiction. Indeed, a 'horror of fiction' continued into the twentieth century, with young boys being advised to avoid reading these 'worthless books'. Walter Scott was very anxious about how the public would react. So much so, in fact, that he published his first novel, *Waverley*, anonymously in 1815, just as Jane Austen had done a few years earlier. *Waverley* was a success, but Scott continued to use his own name only when writing poetry. For almost the rest of his writing career, the front cover of each of his novels proclaimed that it was 'By the Author of *Waverley*'. He was nicknamed 'The Great Unknown', and guessing the identity of the author became the first great marketing stunt. The 'horror of fiction' disappeared during the early years of the twentieth century, but the use of pen names by authors writing in different genres didn't. Here are a few interesting examples I've been able to track down.

Some pen names are easy to spot, most obviously when the pen name appears on a book cover alongside the author's established name. This happened with Ruth Rendell (1930-2015), one of Britain's biggest-selling crime writers, who started writing in the 1960s and is best known for her series of crime novels featuring Chief Inspector Wexford. In the mid-1980s she began using the name Barbara Vine, with some of her early covers stating that the books were by 'Ruth Rendell writing as Barbara Vine'. At the end of the first two Barbara Vine novels there's a letter to her readers signed 'Ruth Rendell'. She starts by explaining that she has two given names, Ruth and Barbara, and that some people know her as Ruth and others know her as Barbara. So far, she says, all her books have been written by Ruth, but she also wanted the 'more feminine' Barbara to be heard: 'It would be a softer voice speaking at a slower pace, more sensitive perhaps, and more intuitive'.

Other authors use pen names that are very much like their own names. For example, Scottish author Iain Banks (1954-2013) used his own name for his mainstream novels, and Iain M. Banks when writing science fiction. John Wyndham (1903-1969) was the most popular science fiction writer of his time in Britain. His birth name was John Wyndham Parkes Lucas Beynon Harris, and he used several combinations of these as pen names. Before the Second World War, he wrote as John B. Harris, John Beynon Harris, John Beynon, Wyndham Parkes and Johnson Harris. With six names to choose from, he had lots of options.

Many of his stories were 'space operas' that appeared in American pulp science fiction magazines. However, after the war his writing changed, featuring ordinary people in extraordinary situations on Earth, such as in *The Day of the Triffids*. Wyndham wanted a new name to reflect his new style, and all his post-war novels are published under the name John Wyndham. He took the pen name idea one step further with his novel *The Outward Urge*, which is a hard science fiction story about space exploration. Wyndham appears to use a co-writer, Lucas Parkes, to help with technical and scientific details, but in fact Lucas Parkes is another pen name derived from the author's six real names. The additional name is there to caution readers not to expect a 'typical' John Wyndham story.

In most cases the pen name is used as a cover for the established name. For example, Anne Rice is best known for her 'Vampire Chronicles' series, especially her first novel, *Interview with the Vampire*, which was made into a movie. Actually, Anne Rice was given the name Howard O'Brien at birth, Howard being her father's name (though he called himself Mike—families can be so complicated). Not surprisingly, the young Miss Howard O'Brien didn't like her given name, and started calling herself Anne when she started school. Rice is her married name. However, the name Anne Rice does not appear on the original covers of her erotic novels, which she wrote under the pen names A.N. Roquelaure and Anne Rampling. The *Sleeping Beauty* trilogy, originally put out under the pen name A.N. Roquelaure, was re-issued in 2012 in the wake of the success of *50 Shades of Grey* with the author shown as 'Anne Rice writing as A.N. Roquelaure'.

US author Orson Scott Card has received many awards for science fiction writing. Wanting to establish an identity beyond science fiction, in 2004 Card wrote a family drama called *Zanna's Gift: A Life in Christmases* under the name Scott Richards. The good news for Card was that it was well received. The bad news for Card was that it didn't take long for word to get out about who Scott Richards really was. As the game was up, the front cover of the 2008 re-issue of *Zanna's Gift* says the author is 'Orson Scott Card writing as Scott Richards'. After this failed attempt at using a pen name, Card promised that 'If I try the pseudonym gambit again, you can be sure that it will be untraceable'. Of course, it may be that he's *already* using an untraceable pen name . . .

The idea of using different pen names for different genres applies particularly when an author writes for both adults and children. An excellent example is Daniel Handler. Handler's books are definitely adults-only, with one review listed on the back cover of his novel *Watch Your Mouth* describing it as 'One of those ... incest-comedy gothic Jewish porn opera novels'. Handler explains that he 'tried to make the sexual parts really sexual and the scary parts really scary in order to have some conflict with the humor'. However, to many young readers, Daniel Handler is much better known as Lemony Snicket, the author of the hugely successful series of thirteen children's novels known as 'A Series of Unfortunate Events'.

J.K. Rowling has also written for both children and adults. The 'Harry Potter' fantasy books are aimed primarily at younger readers and were published under her own name. The 'Cormoran Strike' crime novels, published under the pen name Robert Galbraith, are certainly aimed at adults. As I mentioned at the start of the chapter, the gore in her *Silkworm* book left at least one adult reader (me) feeling a bit queasy (and the follow-up, *Career of Evil*, even queasier). The pen name helps make sure that younger readers don't pick up a Cormoran Strike novel thinking that he's another graduate of Hogwarts School of Witchcraft and Wizardry. But there's more behind the Robert Galbraith pen name than that.

With sales of Harry Potter books in the hundreds of millions, J.K. Rowling is one of the very small band of authors for whom writing under a pen name is not driven by the urge to sell more books. Her first post-Potter novel, *The Casual Vacancy*, was published under her own name, and there was tremendous anticipation before its release; critics 'were all waiting desperately to attack it' is how one literary agent put it. Without the celebrity authorship, the first Robert Galbraith book, *The Cuckoo's Calling*, was judged entirely on its merits. In fact, one publisher turned the book down, just as a string of publishers turned down the first Harry Potter book in the 1990s. *The Cuckoo's Calling* came out to good reviews and moderate sales, selling 1,500 copies. Rowling and her publishers tried very hard (perhaps too hard) to disguise the real author. Robert Galbraith was even given a fictional biography on the book cover: 'Born in 1968, Robert Galbraith is married with two sons ...'

However, it took only three months for the true identity of the author to be revealed. Following an anonymous tip, the London *Sunday Times* called in the help of computer linguistic experts who confirmed that there were marked similarities between *The Cuckoo's Calling* and Rowling's previous books. The fact that 'both' authors had the same publisher, same agent and same editor confirmed their suspicions. When asked, Rowling admitted that she had used the Robert Galbraith pseudonym, and it had been 'such a liberating experience! It has been wonderful to publish without hype or expectation and pure pleasure to get feedback from publishers and readers under a different name.' Of course, once the real author's name was revealed, the book became a best-seller, as did the follow-up, *The Silkworm,* where in an 'Acknowledgements' page at the back of the book, Rowling comments that 'Writing as Robert Galbraith has been pure joy'.

One of the few authors who can claim bigger sales than J.K. Rowling is Agatha Christie. Only Shakespeare is likely to have sold more than Christie. In 1930, when her career as a crime novelist was well and truly established, she published the first of six semi-autobiographical family dramas under the pen name Mary Westmacott. Mary was one of Christie's middle names, and Westmacott was the name of some distant relatives. Unlike J.K. Rowling's short-lived anonymity, Christie was able to hide her identity until 1946. According to one of her biographers, Gillian Gill, when it finally became public knowledge, 'Christie was wounded and outraged.' This had nothing to do with book royalties; in fact, the Westmacott novels sold poorly. Rather, it was the fact that writing as Mary Westmacott was for Christie 'a release, a self-indulgence, a pleasure'. By comparison, she saw writing the mystery novels as 'an immense chore, a bore, a painful and uncongenial effort', which she did purely for the income it brought. The personal satisfaction she got from writing in a different genre comes through clearly in her autobiography where she describes one of the Westmacott novels, *Absent in the Spring*, as the 'one book that has satisfied me completely ... the book that I had always wanted to write ... [It] was written as I meant to write it, and that is the proudest joy and author can have.'

US horror writer Stephen King is one of the few current authors who can almost match J.K. Rowling's sales figures, and he too has used a pen name.

It happened early in his long career, when publishers generally thought that the book-buying public would buy only one book a year from the same author. But Stephen King's imagination worked much faster than one book per year. He's produced over eighty novels, short-story collections and non-fiction in a career spanning fifty years. Having published his third book in January 1977, he was able to convince his publisher to put out a 'straight fiction' book under the pen name Richard Bachman later that year. To throw readers off the scent, one of the Bachman books is dedicated to his 'wife', who is credited with taking the photograph of her 'husband' that appears on the dust jacket. (It's not Stephen King.) However, as King points out 'you can change your name but you can't really disguise your style', and after five books the true authorship was made public.

Initially, the Richard Bachman pen name was primarily to help the bank balance of a hungry young author. But later the pen name became more than this. For one thing, there was less pressure on King when writing as Richard Bachman. King's explanation that 'I think I did it to turn the heat down a little bit' is echoed several decades later by J.K. Rowling's comment above about writing 'without hype or expectation'. He also used the pen name as a sort of real-life experiment to find out how much his career was based on talent and how much on luck. If success was all to do with talent, then the Bachman books should have done as well as the King books. Stephen King suggests that they didn't because of the difference in the marketing of the King and Bachman books.

Later, the Bachman pen name allowed King to play intellectual games with his readers. For example, at the start of his novel *The Dark Half*, published not long after his pen name became known, King tells us in an 'Author's Note' that he is 'indebted to the late Richard Bachman for his help and inspiration'. The plot of *The Dark Half* revolves around an author who for many years used the pen name George Stark to write super-violent pulp thrillers. He decides to stop using the pseudonym, but his 'Dark Half', George Stark, does not go along with the idea of being killed off ...

Mention of Stephen King's *The Dark Half* reminds me of one interesting real-life struggle between an author and his pseudonymous self. US author John Sandford started his writing career as a journalist under his real name John Camp. In fact, he won a Pulitzer Prize for some of his news stories. At first I thought that the Sandford/Camp dual naming was another example of a writer using different names to distinguish his work in different genres, but it was a bit more complicated than that. In the late 1980s, Camp sent two books under his own name to the same publishers. They decided to publish both, but asked him to use a pen name for one of the books to avoid the marketing problem of having two different books written by the same author coming out at the same time. So, one book, *The Fool's Run,* came out under John Camp's own name; and the other, *Rule of Prey,* came out under the pen name John Sandford. Each turned out to be the first in a series of books, but the one under the Sandford pen name was much more successful. So much so, in fact, that the publishers later re-issued *The Fool's Run* and the follow up in the series under the Sandford name. In other words, the pen name took over from the author's real name.

TWENTY

From Marilyn Monroe to Charlize Theron

Stage names

Noel Coward's advice was 'Don't put your daughter on the stage, Mrs Worthington', and for most of the history of the stage, actors and acting have had a very poor reputation. Long ago in ancient Rome, authorities instantly *executed* soldiers who became actors. Roll the camera forward two millennia, and although executions were long gone, in nineteenth century America the 'age-old prejudices continued to cling to actors'. The men were still seen as drunkards, and the women still had 'loose morals'. Because of the social stigma attached to acting, actors often used stage names to protect their family names. However, this stigma began to decline in the late nineteenth century, and now applies only to actors in pornographic movies. Ron Jeremy, one of the top US porn stars (so I'm reliably informed) was told by his father: 'If you want to get into this naked, crazy business, so be it, but if you use the family name again, I'll kill you'.

In the early years of silent movies, motion picture companies never divulged their actors' names. In part, this was because they realised that a famous actor would demand to be a well-paid actor (and they were right, of course). In addition, many theatre actors were reluctant to have their names associated *too* closely with movies, which they saw as a big come-down in the profession. After all, in silent movies *all* parts were non-speaking parts. As a result, fans had to refer to movie actors by the name of the studio that produced their movies. For example, fans knew the actress Florence Lawrence simply as the 'Biograph Girl' following her appearances in Biograph Studio films.

The system began breaking down when a rival studio realised the commercial importance of movie stars. Once it had persuaded Florence Lawrence to sign with them, it began publicising her by name. It was from this point that the star system was born, and by 1913 even Biograph realised that the old system was doomed. Mary Pickford, one of the actresses they had under contract, quickly became one of the biggest names in the early star system, matched only by Charlie Chaplin. Their rising stars were reflected in their rising salaries. By 1915 both were earning an astronomical $10,000 per week, or about $12 million a year in today's money.

However, the studios still had tight control over many actors who appeared in their films. They did this by erasing an actor's previous identity, including their original name and personal history, and replacing it with a new identity that the studio could legally control. Probably the first fabricated movie star was Theda Bara. Her real name was Theodosia Goodman, the daughter of a Jewish tailor from Cincinnati. But in the publicity material, she was 'born in the shadow of the Sphinx', the daughter of a European artist and an Arabian princess, who was weaned on serpents' blood, and who had occult powers. The studio said that her stage name was an anagram of 'Arab Death' though, in fact, it seems to have come from a childhood nickname, Theda, and part of her grandfather's name, Baranger. The fabricated biography supported her on-screen roles. In her first starring role she played a wicked seductress billed as 'The Vampire'. The movie is largely forgotten, but Theda Bara gave the word *vamp* to the English language.

Although the manipulation of movie actors became much more subtle as the movie industry, and movie fans, became more sophisticated, an actor's career often, but by no means always, involved a change of name. The original reason to adopt a stage name, the stigma attached to acting, was no longer important, but studios, agents and the actors themselves were all keen to have stage names in keeping with their on-screen roles.

Probably the two best-known examples are Marilyn Monroe and John Wayne, who both used stage names. Marilyn's birth name, Norma Jeane Mortenson is fairly well known, as is John Wayne's birth name, Marion Morrison, but how common are stage names among all movie stars during the last 100 years?

It's impossible to look at all the thousands of actors who have worked in the movie business over this time. So, to make the task more manageable, I'll focus on that elite group of stars who have won the most prestigious award in the film industry, the Academy Awards for 'Leading Actor' and 'Leading Actress' that are presented each year by the Academy of Motion Picture Arts and Sciences. The awards are usually known as *Oscars*, though no one quite knows why. In total, 79 men and 74 women have won leading actor and leading actress Oscars. The difference in the number of men and women receiving the award is because of the number of multiple award winners. Nine men have each received two or more leading actor Oscars, the most successful being Daniel Day-Lewis who has won three. Thirteen women each have won two or more leading actress Oscars, the most successful being Katharine Hepburn who has won four, her final one being awarded nearly fifty years after her first.

Judging from the names of these 153 Oscar winners, it's clear that Marilyn Monroe and John Wayne are very much in a minority in terms of their use of stage names. In fact, only nine of the 153 stars have stage names that are completely different from their real names. The five men are Jamie Foxx, Ben Kingsley, John Wayne, Charlton Heston and Ray Milland, and the four women are Susan Hayward, Shirley Booth, Joan Crawford and Jennifer Jones. A much more common practice is for stars to keep at least some connection with their real name. Nicholas Coppola uses the stage name Nicholas Cage, and Natalie Hershlag uses the stage name Natalie Portman. And the changes can be more subtle than that. Barbara Streisand became Barbra Streisand, and Reg Harrison became Rex Harrison. A single letter can make all the difference!

Marilyn Monroe and John Wayne are not quite so unusual when you compare them to other stars working in the same era. This is because there has been a marked change over time in the use of stage names. In the first forty years or so, movie stars were much more likely to adopt stage names than movie stars in the last forty years. From 1928 to 1969, almost half the Oscar winners changed their original name to some degree, including seven whose stage names are completely different from their original names. In contrast, from the 1970s onwards, just one in ten Oscar winners used any sort of stage name, including two which are so minor as to hardly count: Richard Dreyfus became Richard *Dreyfuss*, and Jayne Fonda became *Jane* Fonda. (Her full birth name is Lady Jayne Seymour Fonda, a name she always disliked: "Lady'! That was actually what they *called* me! ... I didn't want to be anything resembling a lady. To make matters worse, there was that 'y' in the Jayne.') Only two Oscar winners from the 1970s onwards, Ben Kingsley and Jamie Foxx, have completely new stage names. Clearly, these days it's much less important to have a stage name in order to help a movie career. This then raises the question as to *why* stage names have become less important.

One explanation focuses on the range of roles actors play. As we've seen, in the early days of cinema, actors and studios thought it was important that an actor's name matched the type of role he or she played on the screen. Marilyn Monroe's sexy image and John Wayne's tough-guy image are two excellent examples. More recently, there is much less typecasting. In many respects Charlize Theron is a latter-day Marilyn Monroe, including appearing in *Playboy*, and ranking high in polls to find the world's sexiest women. But unlike Marilyn, Charlize Theron has won a leading actress Oscar for her very unglamorous portrayal of a female serial killer in the movie *Monster*. I have great difficulty imagining Marilyn Monroe in this role, and I suspect I'm not the only one.

Similarly, John Wayne's very typecast roles in westerns and war movies contrast with Daniel Day-Lewis's much more varied roles. He won his first leading actor Oscar in *My Left Foot* playing an artist with cerebral palsy who can paint with his only controllable limb, his left foot; he won his second playing a ruthless businessman in *There Will Be Blood*; and he won his most recent Oscar playing the American president in

Lincoln. Similarly, the only other actor to win two leading actor Oscars in the twenty-first century, Sean Penn, won his first in *Mystic River,* playing an anguished father seeking revenge for his daughter's murder; and he won his second in *Milk,* playing the first openly gay man in the US to be elected to political office. Veteran actor Rod Steiger certainly appreciated that actors now have to be much more flexible: 'When old actors come up to me and say, "I don't know if I should do this role. It might be bad for my image." I say, "That's tough that you only have one image."'

When typecasting declines, the need for a stage name to fit the type-cast also declines. This decline in typecasting in part is a result of a major shake-up of the movie studio system that began in the middle of the twentieth century. It was then that the US Supreme Court ordered the major studios to end their tight control over the production, distribution and exhibition of movies. At the same time, television began to have a major impact on cinema box-office returns. As a result, studios began hiring stars on a picture-by-picture basis rather than locking them into long-term contracts. This, in turn, meant that studios became less involved with maintaining the long-term image of actors. Instead, stars began to take more control over their own PR.

During his conversation with Norma Jeane Dougherty, the casting director from 20th Century Fox made the point that her stage name needed to 'have some class'. Norma Jeane Dougherty, Gladys Smith, Phylis Isley, Thelma Ford and Edythe Marrenner were all names that the studios saw as lacking class, or glamour. Their stage names, Marilyn Monroe, Mary Pickford, Jennifer Jones, Shirley Booth and Susan Hayward, all had more star appeal, being names that were fashionable at the time. Similarly, among men the birth names Marion Morrison, Reginald Harrison and Reginald Truscott-Jones had less star appeal than their stage names, John Wayne, Rex Harrison and Ray Milland. The idea of *class,* in a Hollywood sense, also became less important over time. In fact, the most recent Oscar winner to adopt a more 'classy' stage name is Ellen Burstyn who won the leading actress award way back in 1974, and she had changed her name from Edna Rae Gillooly much earlier still, in 1960.

One explanation for this change in the use of stage names is to do with changes in the movies themselves. In the 1920s, most movies were silent melodramas; in contrast, many movies today depict their characters with total realism. With total realism, the need to have stars whose names have *class* is not as important. The 'godlike' stars in silent movies have been replaced by the 'real people' we see on the screen today. The glamorous stars of the past needed glamorous, or classy, names. The more realistic stars of today need real names—and their own names are usually fine.

Another major reason why stage names have become less important is to do with the increasing acceptance of 'ethnic' names—which in Hollywood means names that are not of Anglo-American origin. Although they overlap, there are two basic reasons behind a studio's decision to replace an ethnic name: to make a name easier for fans to use; and to disguise an ethnic background.

Generally, studios wanted actors to have names that were easy for fans to pronounce and remember. In the 1920s, MGM rejected the French-sounding birth name of American starlet Lucille LeSueur. MGM argued that many fans would have difficulty pronouncing her last name, and when they did the chances were that it would sound like *sewer*, which in turn might then remind them of Lucille's 'notorious sexual past'. Following a competition among fans to find a new name, Lucille LeSueur became Joan Crawford, a name she hated. In the 1940s, Marilyn Monroe had to get rid of her Irish last name, Dougherty, because 20th Century Fox thought it was too difficult to pronounce. Other leading actress Oscar winners who had similar name changes include Claudette Chauchoin, who became Claudette Colbert; Anna Maria Louise Italiano, who became Anne Bancroft; and Sofia Villani Scicolone, who became Sophia Loren.

Among the leading male Oscar winners, Hungarian-born Pál Lukács, not surprisingly, became Paul Lukas when, like many European actors in the 1920s, he came to Hollywood to make his fortune in films. The arrival of the talkies stalled his career because of his heavy European accent, but gradually his English improved, and he ended up winning an Oscar playing an anti-Nazi role. In contrast, Paramount studio allowed German star Emil Jannings to continue using his European stage name. It was easy to pronounce, and didn't sound too German, an important point as only a few years earlier Hollywood had churned out 'Hate the Hun' films during the First World War. Jannings is the only man to receive a leading actor Oscar for performances in silent movies. However, he couldn't make the leap to talkies. He returned to Germany where he appeared in several Nazi propaganda films, and Hitler made him an 'Artist of the State'. Needless to say, his career ended with the fall of Nazi Germany. (There's a reference to this in Quentin Tarantino's movie *Inglourious Basterds*.)

Studios also used stage names to disguise an actor's ethnic background. In particular, anti-Jewish sentiment, or anti-Semitism, has a long history, going back to Biblical times. European migrants brought anti-Semitism to the US, and it became especially strong during the Great Depression of the late 1920s and 1930s. Many of the leading figures in the movie business were Jewish, and their reaction was to stop making films about Jews and Jewish life. The studios also downplayed the involvement of Jewish actors in their movies by replacing any Jewish names with Anglo stage names.

Among Oscar winners, the clearest example is Paul Muni. In the 1920s, he established a major reputation in US theatre under his own name, Muni Weisenfreund. Looking to start a film career, he met with Fox studio's executive producer Sol Wurtzel and Winfield Sheehan. According to his biographer, Jerome Lawrence, the conversation they had showed the studio's determination to press ahead with stage names, even for established actors. Muni Weisenfreund was not happy about a name change, but Wurtzel simply told him that 'It's been decided'. They suggested he use his given name as a surname, a ruse that the actor immediately saw through: 'People'll pronounce it 'Mooney', and everybody'll think I'm an Irishman.' When he saw that he'd lost the argument about his new surname, the actor attempted to get them to agree to the given name Philip, in honour of his father. But Sheehan felt that 'Philip Muni doesn't sound right', and suggested the name Paul instead: '"Paul Muni. It's a beautiful name," Wurtzel insisted, "and to me, it sounds like a star's name."' So, Paul Muni it was.

Of course, Muni was right. Executive producer Sol Wurtzel *would* have preferred that audiences saw Mooney/Muni as Irish rather than Jewish, despite the fact that many studio moguls, including Sol Wurtzel and his boss at Fox studios, William Fox (whose birth name was Vilmos Fried), were themselves Jewish. This highlights just how widespread anti-Jewish feeling was at this time, and the studios ignored it at their commercial peril. Revenue from the sale of movies overseas were particularly susceptible as in 1934 Hollywood films with Jewish actors and actresses were banned in Hitler's Germany, and this was extended across most of Europe as Nazi troops marched across the continent during the Second World War.

The use of stage names to disguise Jewish ethnicity continued in the US after the Second World War. As a result, Judith Tuvim, the granddaughter of Jewish migrants from tsarist Russia, became Judy Holliday, winner of the leading actress Oscar in 1950. According to Milly Barranger, she was 'made-over' by Fox studios for Hollywood stardom: 'She was given softer makeup, a more flattering hair style, and a new name. Since Tuvim sounded too Jewish for Hollywood success in the forties, she was redubbed *Holliday*, a translation of her Hebraic family name.' To complete the transformation, her Jewish given name, Judith (meaning 'woman from Judea'), was shortened to the more neutral-sounding Judy. Like many other performers, Judy Holliday was caught up in the anti-communist activities of US Senator Joseph McCarthy in the 1940s and 1950s. She was questioned because she was Jewish and descended from Russian immigrants, characteristics that according to McCarthy marked out entertainers as having 'a susceptibility to Communism'.

Looking wider than Oscar winners, many other Jewish actors adopted non-Jewish stage names during this early period of cinema history. They include Danny Kaye (whose birth name was David Daniel Kaminsky), Tony Curtis (Bernard Schwartz), Jerry Lewis (Jerome Levitch), Kirk Douglas (Issur Danielovitch) and Edward G. Robinson (Emanuel Goldenberg). Of course, like Paul Muni, some actors were very unhappy about hiding their Jewish origins. One Jewish actor's autobiography starts with the comment that it is 'the life and times not of Edward G. Robinson but of Emanuel Goldenberg'. The name change 'was unpleasant, somehow a denial of my beginning, somehow unfaithful to my mother and father and five brothers'. The actor regarded the *G* in his stage name as 'my private treaty with the past', because it was the initial of his original family name.

More recently, however, it has been individual actors rather than film studios who have been the main agents behind replacing ethnic names with more Anglo stage names. British actor Ben Kingsley was born in Yorkshire, where his father was a doctor of Indian descent. Kingsley's original name was Krishna Bhanji, which he used in the mid-1960s when he auditioned for the Royal Academy of Dramatic Art in London. He describes the audition as follows: 'I was sitting there waiting to go on with my audition piece and someone said, "Christina Blange?" I said, "I think that's me."' He was so flustered that he failed the audition. His pragmatic father then suggested that he should call himself 'something a bit more English'. Kingsley went on to receive a leading actor Oscar for his portrayal of the leader of the Indian independence movement in the movie *Gandhi*. In one of those quirks of history, Kingsley's family originally came from the same Indian village as Gandhi.

The concerns of a pragmatic father also led to a name change for British actress Helen Mirren. Her Russian-born grandfather was an emissary for the Russian tsar in Britain during the First World War, and wasn't able to return home when the tsar was overthrown during the Russian revolution. In the 1950s, his British-born son, Vasily Mironov, changed the family name and anglicised the given names of his children because he didn't want foreign names 'to make obstacles for his children'. Hence, when she was a child, Ilyena Mironov

257

became Helen Mirren, who went on to be awarded a leading actress Oscar.

Similar sentiments are still occasionally heard. The 2015 best actress Oscar winner Brie Larson adopted a stage name instead of using her family name Desaulniers, which she inherited from her French-Canadian father. Living in California, as a child she grew tired of people mispronouncing her surname, and decided to change it to something easier. The name Larson comes from her mother's Scandinavian branch of the family, and was also the name of the actress's favourite doll when she was a child. She used this stage name from the start of her acting career, when she was a young teenager.

Generally, actors in recent decades have been under much less pressure to use stage names that disguise their ethnic origins. Oscar winners Leonardo DiCaprio, Robert de Niro and Al Pacino all retained their Italian family names; and Dustin Hoffman and Richard Dreyfuss kept their original Jewish names. In fact, we hardly notice when the lead roles in movies are played by actors with 'ethnic' names like Renee Zellwegger or Arnold Schwarzenegger. Today, even actors with decidedly difficult ethnic names are inclined to keep their original name rather than adopt a stage name. Chiwetel Ejiofor and Gugu Mbatha-Raw are British actors whose parents migrated from Africa. Like Ben Kingsley, they may have had difficulty with their names but, unlike Kingsley, they have gone on to successful acting careers without adopting stage names.

Name changes do still occur now and again, but they have little to do with hiding an ethnic identity. Natalie Portman was the winner of the 2010 Best Actress Oscar for her role in *Black Swan*. Portman is a stage name, her birth name being Natalie Hershlag. When she was only thirteen, she got a starring role in a major film, and in order to protect their privacy, the family decided that Natalie should adopt a stage name. The change had nothing to do with hiding her Jewish background. Indeed, another prominent actress, Whoopi Goldberg, *adopted* a Jewish stage name believing it would get her further in Hollywood than her birth name of Johnson—though combining it with a first name based on a whoopee cushion was unusual, even for Hollywood.

A final, very unusual story about stage names concerns Jamie Foxx, who in 2004 won the leading actor Oscar for his performance as musician Ray Charles in the movie *Ray*. Jamie Foxx is the stage name of Eric Marlon Bishop. His stage name has its origins well before the start of Foxx's film career. He started performing as a stand-up comedian, and his last name, 'Foxx', is a tribute to Redd Foxx, an African-American comedian. In terms of the first part of his stage name, Eric Bishop noticed that theatre managers always placed women before men when drawing up the evening's roster of stand-up comics. Wanting to appear on stage as early as possible, he chose 'Jamie' because it could be a woman's name. As the previous chapter shows, using a professional name to hide an *author's* gender is not uncommon, but I wouldn't be surprised if Jamie Foxx is the only *actor* to do this.

Actors can use virtually any stage name, though there are a few exceptions. Most importantly, from the time their names were first publicised by the studios, actors at the start of their career have had to make sure that their stage names are not already being used by other actors. There are various performing arts unions such as the Screen Actors Guild-American Federation of Television and Radio Artists (SAG-AFTRA) and the Actors' Equity Association in the US, and Equity in the UK. These unions keep lists of members, and refuse to register the professional name of a new member if it's the same as, or very similar to, that of an existing member. There's a huge number of actors and would-be actors: SAG-AFTRA has 160,000 members, the Actors' Equity Association has 49,000, and Equity in the UK has over 30,000 entries in its directory of professional names.

This problem of duplicating names has been around since the 1920s. I mentioned earlier that MGM rejected the French-sounding birth name of starlet Lucille LeSueur. Studio mogul Louis B. Mayer came up with the idea of letting fans pick a new name for his starlet. The fan magazine *Movie Weekly* ran a competition under the title 'Name Her and Win $1,000'. The original winner of the $1000 prize was a reader who submitted the name 'Joan Arden', and Lucille LeSueur duly became Joan Arden. However, MGM then found that the name Joan Arden was already registered to an extra working for MGM, and she threatened to sue. The studio then had to go to the second-place entry, Joan Crawford, a name the actress hated, complaining that Crawford sounded like *crawfish*. The reader who submitted this name won $500, which seems a bit mean-spirited on the part of MGM—though it was still a decent prize for this time.

You can't use a name that's already been taken even if it's your own birth name. For example, British actor Stewart Granger's real name was James Stewart, but he couldn't use this because there was an Oscar-winning American actor with this name. The same thing happened more recently with American actor Michael Keaton, whose birth name is Michael Douglas, but he couldn't use it because there was an established, Oscar-winning, actor with the same name. After reading about the actress Diane Keaton, the younger Michael Douglas decided on the stage name Michael Keaton simply because it sounded good. Interestingly, the actress who inspired him, Diane Keaton, was originally called Diane Hall, but she had to change her last name because there was another actress named Diane Hall already registered with Actors' Equity. Most recently, the 2014 best actress winner, Julianne Moore, had to change her birth name, Julie Anne Smith, when she registered with the Screen Actors Guild as every variation of her name was already taken. She eventually combined her two given names and assumed her father's middle name as a surname. You can check whether your name is already taken by a British actor by searching for it on the Spotlight website (spotlight.com).

One of the few occasions when an aspiring actor *can* use the same name as an existing actor is when they are two generations of the same family. Over the years, there have been several examples of a son using the same stage name as his father. (I can't find any mother-daughter examples.) The earliest father-and-son combination was Douglas Fairbanks and Douglas Fairbanks, Jr., both of whom at one stage were working in silent films. Fairbanks senior was one of the big three names in the earliest days of movie making, along with Charlie Chaplin and Mary Pickford, whom Fairbanks married.

Other father-son namesakes are less high profile. They include Lon Chaney, another star in silent films, and Lon Chaney, Jr., who is most remembered for his monster movies. Currently, there are Ed Begley, Sr. and Ed Begley, Jr.; Robert Downey, Sr. and Robert Downey, Jr.; and Cuba Gooding, Sr. and Cuba Gooding, Jr. In these examples, use of the family name is clearly an advantage for the sons. In fact, Lon Chaney, Jr. initially used his original name, Creighton Chaney, before a producer persuaded him to change to Lon Chaney, Jr. as a marketing ploy. Chaney Jr. was uncomfortable with the change, but he went ahead because he was sure that the famous name could help his career. It did.

❋

I started 'Hello, My Name Is...' by looking in the most general way at personal names. I want to end by focusing on the names of just two people, Marilyn Monroe and John Wayne. In many ways, they can lay claim to being the biggest stars in the history of cinema. The names we know them by are stage names, names that both actors were at first not keen to adopt.

Marilyn Monroe died half a century ago after starring in only a dozen or so films, but her celebrity status is as evident now as it was in her heyday. A poll showed Marilyn Monroe to be one dead celebrity that Britons would most like to meet (beaten only by Jesus, Princess Diana, Shakespeare and Albert Einstein!). Recently I've read about the release of some photographs that Marilyn posed for in 1946, discovered that US singer Mariah Carey had named her daughter Monroe after her, and seen up-and-coming movie star Kate Upton described as a 'Monroe-esque beauty'. Marilyn Monroe is one of only a handful of celebrities who most people immediately recognise from just their first name, hence the movie *My Week with Marilyn*. And she is possibly the only one whose original name, Norma Jeane, is also widely known, in part because of the lyrics of Elton John's tribute song, *Candle in the Wind*.

If Marilyn Monroe is the epitome of the screen sex goddess, then John Wayne epitomises rugged masculinity. It's many years since John Wayne died; his last movie was released in 1976; and his only leading actor Oscar was way back in 1969, but John Wayne is still one of the top ten favourite movie stars in the US. His movie career stretched over half a century, starting with uncredited bit parts in silent movies in the 1920s. Altogether, he appeared in almost two hundred films, mainly westerns and war movies, and if we can measure popularity by box office receipts, John Wayne is probably the most popular actor in cinema history.

Marilyn Monroe was born in 1926. The name on her birth certificate is Norma Jeane Mortenson. It's likely that her mother, Gladys, chose the name Norma Jeane because it reminded her of a child she had cared for when she worked as a nanny. The family name, Mortenson, was legally correct as Gladys was still married to Edward Mortenson when Norma Jeane was born. However, he wasn't Norma Jeane's father as Edward and Gladys had separated well before she became pregnant. The identity of Norma Jeane's biological father has never been settled. Gladys used the name Baker herself, and also baptised her youngest child as Norma Jeane Baker. In the mid-1920s, when divorce carried a significant social stigma, it was more acceptable for Norma Jeane to have the same family name as her mother. Gladys was mentally unstable, and Norma Jeane spent much of her childhood in foster homes and orphanages. Faced with the prospect of otherwise being homeless, she married Jim Dougherty a couple of weeks after her sixteenth birthday, and became Norma Jeane Dougherty. In 1944, a photographer was making an army training film where the 18-year-old Norma Jeane helped assemble military equipment for World War Two. He asked her to pose for photographs and she started modelling using the name Jean Norman.

According to Randy Taraborrelli, one of her many biographers, two years later she met Ben Lyon who worked for 20th Century Fox studios as director of casting. She was offered a contract, but there was a problem—her name. (Readers named Dougherty may want to skip the next bit.) Ben Lyon told her that Dougherty was too difficult to pronounce, was 'too much like a child's', and had to be changed. Instead, he said, 'We need something that will offset your vulnerability but will have some class to it.' At first Ben Lyon suggested the name Carole Lind, possibly after Carole Lombard, a big movie star in the 1930s. However, although they tried it for a while, they decided that it wasn't quite right.

It's a bit surprising that 20th Century Fox didn't consider using her modelling name, Jean Norman, as a stage name. That's the name Norma Jeane herself would have chosen, in part because she would have shared a name with her cinema idol Jean Harlow, the 'Blonde Bombshell' of the 1930s. The most likely reason why Ben Lyon ignored Jean Norman as a possible stage name is that it had already been taken. There was a long-established singer named Loulie Jean Norman who would have already registered her name with one of the performing arts unions, making it unavailable for anyone else to use. It's also possible that the studio wanted to distance their new signing from Jean Norman, the pin-up and cover girl, and so a new name was needed. A third possible explanation is that by not using her preferred stage name, Ben Lyon was highlighting that 20th Century Fox were in charge.

Ben Lyon was thumbing through casting books with Norma Jeane looking for alternatives, when he suddenly came across the name Marilyn. He had known Marilyn Miller, one of the most popular Broadway musical stars of the 1920s and early 1930s. Norma Jeane reminded him of her, and he thought that *Marilyn* would be a perfect name for her. Norma Jeane was 'okay with it but not thrilled', complaining that 'I don't even know how to spell Marilyn!' In one of those curious twists of fate, Marilyn Monroe later also became Marilyn Miller when she married playwright Arthur Miller. Marilyn Monroe and Marilyn Miller both died in their 30s after often-unhappy lives.

Norma Jeane had no problems about dropping the family name Dougherty, which she had used for less than four years after marrying

Jim Dougherty. And by this time the marriage was all but over. But a surname wasn't decided until, according to her autobiography, she had a discussion with a long-time family friend, Grace Goddard, who told her that the name Marilyn 'fits with' with her mother's maiden name, which was Monroe. Norma Jeane hadn't heard the surname before, but after she heard that the family was related to the US President Monroe, she declared that Marilyn Monroe was 'a wonderful name'.

It's not surprising that Norma Jeane didn't know that her mother's maiden name was Monroe. Norma Jeane and her mother, Gladys, had lived together for only brief periods, when her mother used the family name Baker, the name of her first husband, Jasper. This was despite the fact that, when Gladys and Jasper divorced after a short, unhappy marriage, he took away their two children, Norma Jeane's half-sister and half-brother.

For most of her life, Norma Jeane's grandmother, Della, also used her first married name, Monroe. Again, this is surprising as the often-violent marriage ended with her alcoholic husband's madness and death. Norma Jeane is likely to have remembered nothing of her grandmother, Della Monroe, who died when Norma Jeane was only fourteen months old. However, she may have heard the story about how her sick and delusional grandmother tried to smother her one-year-old granddaughter while she was sleeping. With this family background, it's astonishing that Norma Jeane should have wanted to use Monroe as part of her stage name even if, in her mind, it did link her with a US president. Later on, for very different reasons, her name was linked to another US president, John F. Kennedy.

Grace Goddard's comment that Marilyn 'fits with' Monroe shows that she had an ear for stage names. Movie actresses often used the same initials for both parts of their stage names because it was memorable and sounded glamorous. For example, Beverly Bayne was a major star in the silent movies of the 1910s and 1920s. In the 1930s and 1940s, a dozen leading ladies had alliterative names, including Claudette Colbert, Deanna Durbin, Greta Garbo, Jennifer Jones, Rosalind Russell and Sylvia Sidney. Alliterative stage names were also used by some of Marilyn Monroe's contemporaries, such as Doris Day in the US, Brigitte

Bardot in France, Diana Dors in Britain, Claudia Cardinale in Italy, and Melina Mercouri in Greece.

Of course, Marilyn Monroe is best known for her sexy screen presence. In fact, she has been voted 'sexiest screen star of all time'. Way back in Chapter 1, I mentioned Roy Feinson's idea that words 'evoke a particular emotional resonance' because of how they sound and how our faces look when we're saying them. He points out that we make the *m* sound at the start of *Marilyn* by pursing our lips, as in kissing. Even the shape of the letter *m*, says Feinson, is reminiscent of a woman's breasts. And when you place an *m* close to the letter *r*, 'the definitive symbol for all things sexually robust', the result is a name that radiates a 'warmly sensual glow'.

If all this is true (and it's a big IF), then it's clear that Marilyn Monroe's stage name was an inspired choice. Using the same reasoning, the decision to change Marion Morrison's name to John Wayne was just as inspired.

John Wayne was born in 1907, a huge 13-pound baby who his mother believed almost killed her. The name on his birth certificate is Marion Robert Morrison. His two given names are after his two grandfathers, Marion Mitchell Morrison, and Robert Emmett Brown. His mother, Molly, called him Bobby, after her father. However, in 1912 Molly gave birth to a second son, and decided to name the baby Robert Emmett after her own father. She told her older son that from now on his name would no longer be Marion Robert. Instead, it would be Marion Mitchell, after his paternal grandfather. His baby brother would now be called Bobby. The five-year-old was confused.

In 1914, the seven-year-old Marion Morrison moved with his family from Iowa to California. They were at the very end of the pioneering era of the westward expansion of European settlement, and as a result the family ended up farming very poor land on the edge of the Mojave Desert. It was hard country for the most skilled of farmers, and Marion's father wasn't one of these. In fact, he had no experience of farming. After a couple of years, the jackrabbits, rattlesnakes, heat and dust drove them out, and the family moved to Glendale, an outer suburb of Los Angeles.

Marion is one of a handful of names that American parents give to both girls and boys. Marion was the 50th most popular girls' name and the 65th most popular boys' name in 1914. As one of his many biographers, Michael Munn, points out, having what can be a girl's name, Marion Morrison had a difficult time at school: 'I got into a lot of fights at school because my classmates laughed at my mid-western accent and especially at my goddamn name'. However, in Glendale Marion got a dog called Duke. He couldn't take the dog to school, so he left it at the fire station, which he passed on the way to school. Eventually, the fire-fighters began calling Marion 'Big Duke' and the dog 'Little Duke'. Over time, 'Big Duke' became simply 'Duke' to everyone except his mother. 'I was real glad to be rid of that goddamn name' was John Wayne's comment.

Duke Morrison then attended the University of Southern California (USC) on a football scholarship, and it was through football that he met the movie actor Tom Mix. Tom Mix starred in cowboy films made by Fox studios in nearby Hollywood, and he arranged for Duke to get a summer job at Fox carrying props. The summer job became permanent when, because of an injury, he lost the football scholarship and had to leave USC. Although his main living was still a props man, he also worked as an extra, and eventually his name, Duke Morrison, appeared in the credits of a 1929 movie called *Words and Music*.

Duke Morrison's big break came with the introduction of sound to cowboy movies. A film director at Fox, Raoul Walsh, realised that the silent movie stars were too unrealistic and too old for the part of a wagon train scout he was trying to fill. The young, good-looking, six-feet-four-inch Duke Morrison caught Walsh's eye on the movie lot. Walsh and Fox executives Sol Wurtzel and Winfield Sheehan met with Walsh later, and eventually decided to give Duke a contract. (You may recall that Sol Wurtzel and Winfield Sheehan were the same two executives who decided on Paul Muni's stage name.) However, according to biographer

Maurice Zolotow, Wurtzel and Sheehan didn't like the name Duke Morrison. Walsh had just read a book about a general of the American Revolution called Mad Anthony Wayne, and suggested the stage name *Anthony Wayne*. But Sheehan thought it sounded 'too Italian'. Walsh then proposed *Tony Wayne*. But Wurtzel thought it sounded like a girl's name. Finally, Sheehan came up with *John Wayne*. 'It's American', said Wurtzel. 'You betcha', said Walsh. And so John Wayne it was.

Duke Morrison/John Wayne was not present at the meeting, and when he met Fox executive Winfield Sheehan in his office the next day he made it clear that he didn't want to change his family name. But he was in no position to dig his heels in. He was a stage-hand and movie extra who was being offered a film contract. Despite resenting what he saw as the arrogant attitude of the studio bosses he eventually signed, and became 'John Wayne' on a salary of $75 a week, but he disliked his new name and low salary. His family and oldest friends still called him Marion Morrison. His more recent friends called him Duke Morrison. According to biographers Roberts and Olson, 'It took him years to grow accustomed to the name *John Wayne* and he never answered to *John*'.

John Wayne's film career did not have the best of starts. At a personal level, people kept mixing up John Wayne with two other actors at Fox, John Payne and Wayne Morris. Once, John Payne (who looked a bit like John Wayne) attended a film industry presentation in Mexico, and it was only after hearing the speeches that he realised they thought he was John Wayne. However, John Payne made a gracious acceptance speech, and was awarded the statue, which he later refused to give up, despite the fact that it was engraved 'John Wayne'. Much more importantly, John Wayne's first big film, *The Big Trail*, was a big flop, and Fox studios went bankrupt after the Wall Street crash. It wasn't long before Fox chose not to renew his contract, and John Wayne was unemployed. It was nearly a decade later, after being in countless Z-grade westerns, that he appeared in the movie *Stagecoach* and the rest, as they say, is history.

NOTES

Researching your personal name

With the number of given names in the hundreds of thousands, and the number of surnames in the millions, the personal names specifically mentioned in '*Hello, My Name Is ...*' represent no more than an ice crystal on the tip of an iceberg of names. Not surprisingly, the chances are that neither your given names nor your surname have been mentioned. As many of you will be interested in finding out more about your personal name, I've listed a few websites where you can do research to find out where and when your given and family names have been recorded. The recommended websites are based largely on official documents, and are free to use.

In 1997 the US Social Security Administration made available to the public part of its huge database of names of social security cardholders. As a social security card acts like an ID card in the US when dealing with government agencies, banks and other institutions, the database of cardholders includes virtually all US citizens, and goes back over one hundred years. The US Social Security Administration's website address for baby names is ssa.gov/OACT/babynames.

Searches you can do include the following:

for any given year, you can find the most popular 1000 boys' and girls' given names

for any given decade, you can find the most popular 200 boys' and girls' given names

for the last 100 years, you can find the most popular 100 boys' and girls' given names for any given name, you can find how its popularity has changed over time in terms of its rank in the top 1000 names.

There are also more detailed tables for each year going back to 1880, each table showing every name given to at least 5 boys or 5 girls. The most recent tables list over 30,000 names. As well as national data, you can also view names by state.

In Britain, the Office for National Statistics publishes information on baby names, though the website is rather less user-friendly than the US equivalent, and the available information less comprehensive. Their website address is ons.gov.uk. If you search for 'baby names', you'll find annual statistical bulletins going back to 1996, and separate Excel spreadsheets showing every name registered at least three times in the year for boys and girls. There is also a single file listing the top 100 names for boys and girls for ten-year periods between 1904 and 1994. These publications show data for England and Wales. Statistics for Scotland going back to 1998 are on the National Records of Scotland website at nrscotland.gov.uk. Search for 'babies' first names'. Statistics for Northern Ireland going back to 1997 are on the Northern Ireland Statistics and Research Agency's website at nisra.gov.uk. Search for 'baby names'. There is a *Full Baby Names List* file containing all registered names, including those given to just 1 or 2 babies.

These official websites don't usually publish information about surnames. This is not because the information isn't available—when people apply for a social security card or register a birth, they are required, of course, to give a full name. Rather, the issue is the usefulness of such data. Given the strongly held custom that a child is named after its father, a surname is not 'popular' in the way a given name is popular. Generally, we are not interested in how many babies named Smith or Jones are born each year. Instead, we want to know how many people there are *altogether* named Smith or Jones. This information is much harder to come by.

Traditionally, a government census involved asking questions of everyone, including their full name. The US Census Bureau did collate surname data from their 2000 census. You can find the results by accessing the Bureau's website at census.gov and then searching on 'surnames' to find the report *Frequently Occurring Surnames from the Census 2000*. The Bureau lists approximately 150,000 surnames that are held by at least 100 people. Unfortunately, the Bureau didn't repeat their research on surnames in the 2010 Census. The year 2000 results are now rather dated, but bear in mind that the relative frequency of different surnames changes very slowly, the new births always being added to the much larger pool of existing surnames.

It's also important to note that other methods of finding the number of people with particular surnames are rather flawed. For example, the traditional method is to count surnames in the white pages of a telephone directory. The US White Pages website (whitepages.com) will do this for you. According to their figures, not surprisingly, the most common US surname is Smith (2.8 million entries) and the second most common is Johnson (2.1 million). However, all telephone directory entries relate to households of varying size, not individuals; and as an increasing proportion of the population (especially younger people) use only mobile phones and tend not to be in the telephone directory, its usefulness as a source of surname data is going down.

Another traditional source of information about surnames are the electoral registers that list the names and addresses of people eligible to vote; you may see a voting official with one of these when you go to vote. Unfortunately for researchers in Britain, in 2001 there was a change in the law that allowed people to opt out of the publicly available electoral register. It's estimated that about 30 per cent of voters have taken this option, making the electoral register much less useful as a tool for surname research in Britain. Faced with an absence of really good data, researchers have to make the best of a less-than-ideal situation and combine as many different sources as they can find to come up with a reasonably comprehensive list of surnames.

I've found that the most valuable source of information online for British surnames is the 'Great Britain Family Names Profiling' website (gbnames.publicprofiler.org) which presents the results of a project carried out by a number of groups including University College London, mainly using data from the (pre-opting out) 1998 electoral registers. It provides statistical information plus maps of the distribution of surnames across Great Britain. It also shows surname data from the 1881 census returns so that you can see the geographical changes over a century or so. The Public Profiler site also has a link to worldnames.publicprofiler.org that includes 8 million different surnames from 26 countries, including the US, Canada, Australia, New Zealand and Ireland. For example, it shows that the country where you are most likely to meet someone called Smith is Australia, where they make up 1.2 per cent of the population. More locally, the Smiths are most commonly found in part of the South Island of New Zealand, where about 2 per cent of inhabitants are called Smith.

In late-breaking news (as they say), National Records of Scotland (NRS) have just published lists of the most common surnames in Scottish birth, marriage and death registers, going back to 1975. The 2015 list starts, as expected, with Smith, and lists over 2000 surnames that appeared at least 10 times on official registers. However, the NRS cautions that the surnames from these registers 'may not be representative of the surnames of the population of Scotland as a whole'. Bearing this in mind, you can find these surname lists by searching the NRS website (nrscotland.gov.uk) for 'most common surnames'.

The following pages list some of the hundreds of sources I've consulted when writing '*Hello, My Name Is…*' The authors vary alphabetically all the way from Abel to Zolotow; and historically sources go back to 1605 (or *much* further back if you count the references to the Old Testament in the Bible). The enormous breadth of material is reflected in the many autobiographies and biographies, which include (alphabetically!) those by or about the following people: 50 Cent, Isaac Asimov, Jane Austen, the Beatles, Victoria Beckham, Ronald Biggs, Lewis Carroll, Agatha Christie, John Cleese, Bill Clinton, Arthur Conan Doyle, Queen Elizabeth II, Bill Gates, Kris Jenner (formerly Kardashian), Rob Roy MacGregor, Marilyn Monroe, George Orwell, J.K. Rowling, William Shakespeare, Sitting Bull, Joseph Stalin, Charlize Theron, Harry Truman, Booker T. Washington, Malcolm X and Frank Zappa. However, the heading '*Select* Bibliography' means that there are other sources I've consulted but, to make the bibliography manageable, have not included. I am grateful for the help of all the authors whose work I consulted, which made writing '*Hello, My Name Is…*' so enjoyable.

Select bibliography

50 Cent & Kris Ex, *From Pieces to Weight: Once upon a Time in South-side Queens*, Simon & Schuster, New York, 2006.

'A man named Sue is dead', *New York Times*, 30 June 1980, p. D14.

"A.J.M.", 'Mrs. or Miss', *Notes and Queries*, 7th series, vol. vii, no. 163, pp. 104-5.

Ernest L. Abel & Michael L. Kruger, 'Taking thy husband's name: the role of religious affiliation', *Names*, vol. 59, issue 1, March 2011, pp. 12-24.

Academy of Motion Picture Arts and Sciences, *The Official Academy Awards Database*, 2016, online.

Peter Ackroyd, *The History of England: Volume I: Foundation*, Macmillan, London, 2011.

Richard D. Alford, *Naming and Identity: A Cross-Cultural Study of Personal Naming Prac*tices, HRAF Press, New Haven, CT, 1988.

Elsie Agnes Allen, *A World of Baby Names*, Hinkler Books, Heatherton, Vic, 2006.

Kathryn Almack, 'What's in a name? The significance of the choice of surnames given to children born with lesbian-parent families', *Sexualities*, vol. 8, 2005, 239-254.

Lizette Alvarez, 'Picked baby's name? Not so fast in Denmark', *New York Times*, 9 October 2004.

Gary Amos & Richard Gardiner, *Never Before in History: America's Inspired Birth*, Pandas, 1998.

Ancestry Europe, 'Goodbye Mr Chips'—*Nation's Extinct And Endangered Surnames Revealed*, 2013, online.

Hello, My Name Is . . .

Christopher P. Andersen, *The Name Game*, Simon and Schuster, New York, 1977.

Deborah J. Anthony, 'A spouse by any other name', *William & Mary Journal of Women and the Law*, vol. 17, 2010-2011, pp. 187-222.

Leonard R.N. Ashley, *What's in a Name?* Genealogical Publishing, Baltimore, 1989.

Isaac Asimov, *I, Asimov*, Doubleday, New York, 1994.

Isaac Asimov, *In Joy Still Felt: The Autobiography of Isaac Asimov 1954-1978*, Doubleday & Company, New York, 1980.

Isaac Asimov, *In Memory Yet Green: The Autobiography of Isaac Asimov 1920-1954*, Doubleday & Company, New York, 1979.

Wendy Atkins-Sayre, 'Naming women: the emergence of 'Ms' as a liberatory title', *Women and Language,* vol. 28, no. 1, pp. 8-16.

Tara Bahrampour, 'A boy named Yo, etc; name changes, both practical and fanciful, are on the rise', *New York Times*, 25 September 2003.

Michael Bakewell, *Lewis Carroll: A Biography*, Mandarin, London, 1997.

Howard F. Barker, 'Surnames in the United States', *American Mercury*, June, 1932, pp. 223-30.

Emma Barnett, 'Couples fuse surnames in new trend: "I now pronounce you Mr and Mrs Puffin"', *Telegraph*, 9 November 2012, online.

Milly S. Barranger, *Unfriendly Witnesses: Gender, Theatre and Film in the McCarthy Era*, Southern Illinois University, 2008.

Victoria Beckham, *Learning To Fly*, Penguin, London, 2001.

Beowulf in Hypertext, McMaster University. online.

Ronald Biggs, *Odd Man Out*, Pan, London, 1995.

Christopher Bigsby & Don B. Wilmet, 'Introduction', in Don B. Wilmeth and Christopher Bigsby (eds),

Cambridge History of American Theatre, Volume I, Beginnings to 1870, Cambridge University Press, 1998.

C.W. Bingham, 'Nick-names', *Notes and Queries*, 23 December 1865, pp. 517-518.

George F. Black, *The Surnames of Scotland: Their Origin, Meaning and History*, Birlinn, Edinburgh, 1999.

Blood, Bandages and Barber Poles, BBC, 2002, online.

Select Bibliography

Lesley Bolton, *The Complete Book of Baby Names*, Sourcebooks, Naperville, Illinois, 2009.

Books and Book Collecting, *A.K.A., Also Known* As, not dated, online.

Bounty, *Name Blame*, not dated, online.

Bounty, *Noise about Names*, 2011, research report kindly supplied by Bounty.

Bounty, *Parents "Regrets" over Kids' Names*, 2011, online.

Bounty, *Surnames as Firstnames*, 2012, online.

Neil Bowie & G.W.L. Jackson, *Surnames in Scotland over the Last 140 Years*, General Register Office for Scotland, 2003

William Dodgson Bowman, *The Story of Surnames*, George Routledge & Sons, London, 1932,

danah boyd, *What's in A Name?*, not dated, online.

Sarah Bradford, *The Reluctant King*, George Weidenfeld & Nicholson, St Martin's Press, New York, 1990.

Gyles Brandreth, *Philip and Elizabeth: Portrait of a Marriage*, Century, London, 2004.

Robert Briffault, *The Mothers: A Study of the Origins of Sentiments and Institutions, Vol. 1*, George Allen & Unwin, London, 1927.

British Baby Names: Times Births 2013, 2014, online.

Charlotte Brontë, 'Biographical notice of Ellis and Acton Bell', in Emily Brontë, *Wuthering Heights*, 1850.

Richard Brooks, 'JK the cuckoo in the crime novel nest', *Sunday Times*, 14 July 2013, p. 18.

Jonathan Brown & Oliver Duff, 'The black sheep of the family? The rise and fall of Hitler's scouse nephew', *The Independent*, 17 August 2006.

John Brownlow, *Memoranda, or the Chronicles of the Foundling Hospital*, CUP, 2013 (first published 1847).

Bill Bryson, *One Summer: America 1927*, Doubleday, London, 2013.

Bill Bryson, *Shakespeare*, HarperPress, London, 2007.

Bill Bryson, *Mother Tongue*, Hamish Hamilton, London, 1990.

Burke's Peerage & Baronetage, Burke's Peerage, London, 106th edn, 1999.

John Southerden Burn, *The History of Parish Registers in England*, John Russell Smith, London, 2nd edn, 1862.

Patrick Butler, 'Analysis: the matron', *Guardian*, 4 April 2001.

Enzo Caffarelli, 'Italian family names', in *Dictionary of American Family Names*, Patrick Hanks (ed.), OUP , Oxford, 2003, pp. lxix-lxxii.

Franklin Institute, *Call Me Alexander Graham Bell*, not dated, online.

William Camden, *Remains Concerning Britain*, edited by RD Dunn, University of Toronto Press, Toronto, 1984 (originally 1605).

Catherine Cameron, *The Name Givers: How They Influence Your Life*, Prentice Hall, Englewood Cliffs, NJ, 1983.

Margaret Cannell, 'Indian personal names from the Nebraska and Dakota regions', *American Speech*, vol. 10, no. 3, October 1935, pp. 184-187.

Orson Scott Card, *Zanna's Gift,* Hatrack River: The Official Web Site of Orson Scott Card, online.

Dale Carnegie, *How To Win Friends and Influence People*, Angus & Robertson, London, 1984.

Lewis Carroll, *Through the Looking-Glass*, Millennium Fulcrum Edition 1.7, Project Gutenberg, online.

Centrelink, *Naming Systems of Ethnic Groups: A Guide*, Commonwealth of Australia, Canberra, 2000.

Michelle L. Ceynar & Joanna Gregson, 'Narratives of keepers and changers: women's postdivorce surname decisions', *Journal of Divorce and Remarriage*, vol. 53, 2012, pp. 559-580.

'The challenges and limitations of assimilation: Indian boarding schools', *Brown Quarterly*, vol. 4, no. 3, Fall 2001, pp. 1-5.

R.W. Chapman, *Names, Designations & Appellations*, Clarendon Press, 1936.

Lee Child, *Is Lee Child Lee Child's Real Name?* FAQs, Official Site of Lee Child and Jack Reacher, online.

Nicholas J.S. Christenfeld, 'Don't yet name your child P.I.G.: reply to Morrison and Smith', *Psychosomatic Medicine*, vol. 69, no. 8, 2007, pp. 823-24.

N. Christenfield, D.P. Phillips & L.M. Glynn, 'What's in a name: mortality and the power of symbols', *Journal of Psychosomatic Research*, vol. 47, no. 3, 1999, pp. 241-254.

Select Bibliography

Agatha Christie, *Autobiography*, Fontana, 1978.

Clan Gregor Society, *Our History*, 2016, online.

Danae Clark, *Negotiating Hollywood,* University of Minnesota Press, 1995.

Nick Clark, "I turned down "Robert Galbraith"': Editor admits rejecting JK Rowling's secret novel', *Independent*, 14 July 2013.

John Cleese, *So, Anyway…*, Random House, London, 2014.

Bill Clinton, *My Life*, Vintage, New York, 2005.

Richard Coates, 'Onomastics', *The Cambridge History of the English Language, Volume 4,* edited by

Suzanne Romaine, CUP, 1998, pp. 330-372.

Computershare Voucher Services, *What's in A Name? New Parents Prefer To Keep It In The Family*, 2011, online.

Dalton Conley, 'Raising E and Yo Xing Heyno Augustus Eisner Alexander Weiser Knuckles', *Psychology Today*, vol. 42, no. 2, March/April 2010, pp. 80-87.

Will Coster, *Baptism and Spiritual Kinship in Early Modern England*, Ashgate, Aldershot, 2002.

Michael Crummett, *Tatanka-Iyotanka: A Biography of Sitting Bull*, Western National Parks Association, 2002.

Bryan Curtis, 'The curious case of Lee Child', *Grantland*, 20 December 2012, online.

Brian Dakss, *What's in A Baby's Name?* CBSNEWS, 13 August 2007, online.

Danish Justice Ministry, *Navnelister*, 2009, online.

Barbara Davies, 'Mummy porn…', *Daily Mail* 18 April 2012.

Hayley Davies, 'Sharing surnames: children, family and kinship', *Sociology*, vol. 45, no. 4, 2011, pp. 554-569.

George Deaux, *The Black Death 1347*, Hamish Hamilton, London, 1969.

Daniel DeFoe, *The Life and Adventures of Robinson Crusoe*, W. Taylor, London, 1719.

Yvonne Demoskoff, *Yvonne's Royalty Home Page*, 2005, online.

Kenneth L. Dion, 'What's in a title? The Ms stereotype and images of women's titles of address',

Psychology of Women Quarterly, 1987, vol. 11, pp. 21-36.

David Dorward, *Scottish Surnames*, HarperCollins, Glasgow, 1995.

Doughty Street Chambers, *Amal Clooney*, 2014, online.

D.C. Douglas, 'Companions of the Conqueror', *Journal of History*, vol. 28, no. 108, September, pp. 129-147.

Shana Druckerman & Sean Dooley, *Fifty Shades Of Grey Author: Hit Books Were 'My Midlife Crisis'*, ABC News, 17 April 2012, online.

Siobhan Duck, 'What's Poppin in your head, Angel?', *Herald Sun* [Melbourne], 17 October 2011, p. 19.

The Duggar Family, not dated, online.

Leslie Alan Dunkling, *What's in a Name?* Rigby, Adelaide, 1977.

Leslie Dunkling, *The Guinness Book of Names*, 7th edn, Guinness Publishing, London, 1995.

R. Dymond, 'Curious Christian names', *Notes and Queries*, 16 January 1875, p.52.

"E.D.", 'Married women's surnames', *Notes and Queries*, 13 August 1887, p. 127.

Elvis Australia, *Elvis Presley Family History*, 2015, online.

Erfolgswelle Naming Agency, *Creation of New First Names*, 2015, online.

Ernest A. Ebblewhite, 'Married women's surnames', *Notes and Queries*, 9 June 1888, p. 451.

Patricia Erens, *The Jew in American Cinema*, Indiana University Press, Bloomington, 1984.

Etiquette Hell, *Using Auntie And Uncle Titles*, 2011, online.

C. L'Estrange Ewen, *A History of Surnames of the British Isles*, Kegan Paul, Trench, Trubner & Co, London, 1931.

Roy Feinson, *The Secret Universe of Names: The Dynamic Interplay of Names and Destiny*, Penguin, Camberwell, VIC, 2004.

David N. Figlio, 'A boy named Sue: disruptive children and their peers', *Education, Finance and Policy*, vol. 2, no. 4, Fall 2007, pp. 376-394.

Raymond Firth, Jane Hubert & Anthony Forge, *Families and Their Relatives*, Routledge & Kegan Paul, 1969.

Ian Fleming, *You Only Live Twice*, Signet, 1964.

Select Bibliography

Alison Flood, 'Salman Rushdie reveals details of fatwa memoir,' *Guardian*, 12 April 2012.

Carlin Flora, 'Hello my name is Unique', *Psychology Today*, vol. 47, issue 2, March/April 2004, pp. 44-50.

Nancy Gentile Ford, *Americans All: Foreign-born Soldiers in World War I*, Texas A&M University Press, College Station, TX, 2001.

Robert A. Fowkes, 'Welsh naming practices, with a comparative look at Cornish', *Names*, vol. 29(4), December 1981, pp. 265-272.

James George Frazer, *The Golden Bough: A Study in Magic and Religion: Part II: Taboo and the Perils of the Soul*, 3rd edition, Macmillan, Basingstoke, 1911.

Roland G. Fryer & Steven J. Levitt, 'The causes and consequences of distinctively Black names', *Quarterly Journal of Economics*, vol. CXIX, issue 3, August 2004, pp. 767-805.

Douglas A. Galbi, *Long Term Trends In Personal Given Name Frequencies In the UK*, 2002, online.

Brian Gallagher, 'Mary Christmas, Belle Ringer & Miss L. Toe', *Ancestry Blog*, 27 December 2014, online.

Fraser & Fraser, *Ghoulish Halloween Names*, 2013, online.

Joshua Gamson, *Claims to Fame: Celebrity in Contemporary America*, University of California Press, Berkeley, 1994.

Robert F. Gardiner, 'Married women's surnames', *Notes and Queries*, 8 October 1887, p. 298.

General Register Office for Scotland, *Popular Forenames in Scotland, 1900-2000*, 2011, online.

George V, 'A proclamation', *London Gazette*, 17 July 1917, p. 7119.

Tess Gerritsen, *Writers and Secret Identities*, 2007, online.

Nancy Gibbs, 'Mrs, Ms or Miss: addressing modern women', *Time*, 26 October, 2009.

Gillian Gill, *Agatha Christie: The Woman and Her Mysteries*, Free Press, New York, 1990.

John Gillingham, 'Britain, Ireland, and the South', in *From the Vikings to the Normans*, ed. Wendy Davies, Oxford University Press, Oxford, 2003, pp. 203-232.

Gretchen E Gooding & Rose M Kreider, 'Women's marital naming choices in a nationally representative sample', *Journal of Family Issues*, vol. 3, no. 5, 2011, pp. 681-701.

Richard Griffith, Arthur Mayer & Eileen Bowser, *The Movies*, Columbus Books, London, 1981.

Fred Lawrence Guiles, *Norma Jeane: The Life and Death of Marilyn Monroe*, Grafton Books, London, 1986.

Robin Gwynn, 'England's "first refugees"', *History Today*, issue 5, 1985, pp. 22-28.

"H.L.L.D.", 'Surnames as Christian names', *Notes and Queries*, 20 May 1922, p. 397.

J.R. Hammond, *A George Orwell Companion*, Macmillan Press, London, 1982.

Daniel Handler, *Beatrice Interview*, 2000, online.

Patrick Hanks, 'The present day distribution of surnames in the British Isles', *Nomina*, vol. 68, 1992, pp. 79-98.

Patrick Hanks, 'General introduction', in Patrick Hanks (ed.), *Dictionary of American Family Names*, OUP, Oxford, 2003, pp. ix-xxii.

Patrick Hanks, Kate Hardcastle, & Flavia Hodges, *A Dictionary of First Names*. Oxford University Press, 2006.

Patrick Hanks & Flavia Hodges, *A Dictionary of Surnames*, OUP, Oxford, 1988.

Patrick Hanks, Flavia Hodges, A.D. Mills, & Adrian Room, *The Oxford Names Companion*, OUP, Oxford, 2002

Robert Hanks, 'Andy McNab: the hidden face of war', *The Independent*, 19 November 2004.

James Hannaham, 'The family that sings together ...', *Village Voice*, 15 August 2000.

Harris Poll, *He Was Both Captain Phillips and Walt Disney and Tom Hanks is also America's Favorite Movie Star* Harris Interactive, 2014, online.

Sarah Harris, 'No one understood why I took my wife's surname', *Independent on Sunday*, 17 August 2008, p. 39.

Simon Hattenstone, 'I made a complete mess of everything' [interview with Bill Wyman], *Guardian*, 10 March 2006.

'Hefner weds model', *Herald Sun* [Melbourne], 2 January 2013, p. 15.

"Helga", 'Curious Christian names', *Notes and Queries*, 19 March 1904, p. 236.

David Hey, *Family Names and Family History*, Hambledon and London, London, 2000.

David Hey, *Yorkshire from AD1000*, Longman, London, 1986.

Rosalind Hicks, *The Mary Westmacotts*, not dated, online.

Robin Hilmantel, 'How men REALLY feel when you keep your last name', *Women's Health Magazine*, 8 August 2013, online.

Patrick Hitler, 'To Hell with Hitler', in Shaun Usher (compiler), *Letters of Note*, Canongate, Edinburgh, 2013, pp. 48-50.

David Hunt, *Girt*, Black Inc, Melbourne, 2013.

Allan Hunter, 'Rod Steiger', *The Scotsman*, 11 July 2002.

N. Ibery, P.M. Patel & P.J. Robb, 'Do surgeons wish to become doctors?', *Journal of the Royal Society of Medicine*, vol. 99, 2006, pp. 197-199.

Icelandic Ministry of the Interior, *Personal Names Act No. 45 of 17th May 1996*, not dated, online.

Internet Movie Database, *Biography* [various film stars], 1990-2016, online.

Internet Surname Database, 2016, *Last Name* [various surnames], 2016, online.

"J", 'Curious Christian names', *Notes and Queries*, 27 February 1904, p.171.

Jonathan Jackson, 'Why I changed my last name when I got married—even though I have a penis', *Huffington Post*, 12 March, 2013, online.

Kris Jenner, *And All Things Kardashian*, Simon & Schuster, New York, 2011.

Charles Jennings, *A Brief Guide to Jane Austen*, Constable & Robinson, London, 2012.

Gary Jennings, *World of Words*, Atheneum, New York, 1984.

David R. Johnson & Laurie K. Scheuble, 'What should we call our kids? Choosing children's surnames when parents' last names differ', *Social Science Journal*, vol. 39, 2002, pp. 419-429.

Amy L. Juhala, 'Ruthven, Alexander, master of Ruthven (1580?–1600)', *Oxford Dictionary of National Biography*, Oxford University Press, 2004, online.

Justin Kaplan & Anne Bernays, *The Language of Names*, Touchstone, New York, 1999.

Chris Karsten, *Charlize: Life's One Helluva Ride*, Human & Rousseau, Cape Town, 2009.

Michael T. Kaufman, 'Gary T. Rowe Jr., 64, who informed on Klan in civil rights killing, is dead', *New York Times*, 4 October 1998.

Sam Kean, 'What's in a name?' *New York Times Magazine*, 28 October 2007.

Lisa Kelly, 'Divining the deep and inscrutable: toward a gender-neutral, child-centered approach to child name change proceeding', *West Virginia Law Review*, vol. 99, no. 1, Fall 1996, pp. 1-80.

Giles Kemp & Edward Claflin, *Dale Carnegie: The Man Who Influenced Millions*, St Martins Press, New York, 1989.

Myleah Y. Kerns, 'North American women's surname choice based on ethnicity and self-identification as feminists', *Names*, vol. 59, no. 2, June, 2011, pp. 104-17.

Rosie Kinchen, 'Do you take this man's name?' *Sunday Times*, 7 July 2013.

Stephen King, *Frequently Asked Questions*, Official Stephen King website, not dated, online.

Stephen King, 'Why I was Bachman', in *The Bachman Books*, Hodder and Stoughton, London, 1986.

Ann Kirk, *J.K. Rowling: A Biography*, Greenwood Press, Westport, CT, 2003.

Mark Knowles, *The Wicked Waltz and Other Scandalous Dances*, McFarland & Co, Jefferson, NC, 2009.

Elisabeth D. Kuhn, 'Rethinking Ms', *Women and Language*, vol. 30, no. 1, 2007, p. 4.

Susan J. Kupper, *Surnames for Women*, McFarland & Company, Jefferson, NC, 1990.

Sharon LaFraniere, 'Not on our list? Change it, China says', *New York Times*, 20 April 2009.

Kay Lagerquist & Lisa Lenard, *The Complete Idiot's Guide to Numerology* (2nd edn), Alpha Books, New York, 2004.

Simon M. Laham, Peter Koval & Adam L. Alter, 'The name-pronunciation effect: why people like Mr.

Smith more than Mr. Colquhoun', *Journal of Experimental Social Psychology*, vol. 48, 2012, pp. 752-756.

Bruce Lansky, *The New Baby Name Survey Book: What Impression Will Your Baby's Name Make?*, Meadowbrook, New York, 2007.

Carlton F.W. Larson, *Naming Baby: The Constitutional Dimensions of Parental Naming Rights*, UC Davis Legal Studies Research Paper Series Paper No. 241, 2011, online.

Jerome Lawrence, *Actor: The Life and Times of Paul Muni*, GP Putnam's Sons, New York, 1974.

Edwin D. Lawson, 'Personal names: 100 years of social science contributions', *Names*, vol. 32, no. 1, 1984, pp. 45-90.

Carol A. Lawton, Judith E. Owen Blakemore & Lesa Rae Vartanian, 'The new meaning of Ms: single, but too old for Miss, *Psychology of Women Quarterly*, vol. 27, 2003, pp. 215-220.

Sharon Lebell, *Naming Ourselves, Naming Our Children*, Crossing Press, Freedom, CA, 1988.

Michael Levin, 'Vs. Ms.', in *Sexist Language: A Modern Philosophical Analysis*, Mary Vetterling-

Braggin (ed.), Littlefield, Adams and Co, 1981, pp. 217-22.

Steven D. Levitt & Stephen J. Dubner, *Freakonomics*, Penguin, London, 2005.

Ren Lexander, *The Secret Meaning of Names*, Letgo Publishers, Carlingford Court, NSW, 1999.

Stanley Lieberson & Kelly S Mikelson, 'Distinctive African American names', *American Sociological Review*, vol. 60, no. 6, Dec. 1995, pp. 928-946.

Stanley Lieberson, *A Matter of Taste: How Names, Fashions and Culture Change*, Yale University Press, New Haven, 2000.

Stanley Lieberson, Susan Dumais & Shyon Baumann, 'The instability of androgynous names', *American Journal of Sociology*, vol. 105, no. 5, March 2000, pp. 1249-87.

Donna L. Lillian, 'Ms. as a courtesy title: variation through time and space', *Lacus Forum*, vol. XXXIII, 2006, pp. 211-218.

Mike Lipton, 'All adding up', *People*, 18 April 2005.

David Lodge, *The Art of Fiction*, Penguin, London, 1992.

Graham Lord, *James Herriot: the Life of a Country Vet*, Carroll & Graf Publishers, New York, 1997.

Irvine Loudon, 'Why are (male) surgeons still addressed as Mr?', *British Medical Journal*, vol. 321, 23-30 December 2000, pp.1589-91.

Lucy Stone League, not dated, online.

Joseph H. Lynch, *Godparents and Kinship in Early Medieval Europe*, Princeton University Press, Princeton, NJ, 1986.

Priscilla Ruth MacDougall, 'The right of women to name their children', *Law and Inequality*, vol. 3:91, 1985, pp. 91-159.

Kelly A. Malcolmson & Lisa Sinclair, 'The Ms stereotype revisited: implicit and explicit facets', *Psychology of Women Quarterly*, 2007, vol. 31, pp. 305-310.

'Male novelist who could be first man to win romantic novel award since 1960', *Independent*, 13 February 2014.

Stephen Manes & Paul Andrews, *Gates*, Simon & Schuster, New York, 1994.

Kate Mansey, 'Boom time for name swappers', *Sunday Times*, 16 October 2011.

M. Marqusee, 'Sport and stereotype: from role model to Mohammad Ali', *Race and Class*, vol. 36, no. 4, 1995, pp. 1-29.

Marriage Certificate Could Include Mothers' Name, BBC News, 4 July 2014, online.

C.M. Matthews, *How Surnames Began*, Lutterworth Press, 2007.

Alexander McCall Smith, *Corduroy Mansions*, Polygon, London, 2009.

Caroline McClatchey, *'Why Are More People Changing Their Names?'*, BBC News, online.

David McCullough, *Truman*, Simon & Schuster, New York, 1992.

Fiona McElduff, Pablo Mateos, Angie Wade & Mario Cortina Borja, 'What's in a name? The frequency and geographic distribution of UK surnames', *Significance*, vol. 5, issue 4, December 2008, pp. 189-192.

David McKie, *What's in a Surname?* Random House Books, London, 2013.

Richard McKinley, *A History of British Surnames*, Longman, London, 1990.

Tamara McLean, 'A devil of a name put on NZ banned list', *Age*, 20 July 2011, p.12.

Barbara McMahon, 'Parents lose custody of girl for naming her Talula Does the Hula From Hawaii', *Guardian*, 24 July 2008.

ndy McNab, *Biography*, not dated, online.

James M. McPherson, *Battle Cry of Freedom: The Civil War Era*, Oxford University Press, 1988.

Sandra W. Meditz and Tim Merrill. *A Country Study: Zaire (Former)*, Federal Research Division of the US Library of Congress, 1993, online.

H.L. Mencken, *The American Language*, 4th edn (abridged), Routledge & Kegan Paul, London, 1963.

'Misc, or Mx: a gender-neutral title', *Genderqueer in the UK*, 2011, online.

Franklin G. Mixon Jr & Richard J. Cebula, 'More is more: some economics of distinctively-named white kids', *Atlantic Economic Journal*, vol. 40, 2012, pp. 39-47.

Marilyn Monroe, *My Story*, Cooper Square Press, New York, 2000.

Patrick Montague-Smith, *Debrett's Correct Form*, Kelly's Directories, London, 1971.

Jeanmarie O'Keefe Moore, *Big Book of Grandparents' Names*, Silver Halo Press, 2009.

Cole Moreton, 'The dark family secret that drove Ben Kingsley to success', *Mail Online*, 21 May 2010.

David Morris, 'The rise of Christian names in the thirteenth century', *Nomina*, vol. 28, 2005, pp. 43-54.

Stilian Morrison & Gary Smith, 'Monogrammic determinism?' *Psychosomatic Medicine*, vol. 67, no. 5, 2005, pp. 820-824.

'Mr A Pothecary is a chemist', *International Express*, 11 June 2014, p. 16.

Kay Muhr, 'Irish and Scottish Gaelic family names', in *Dictionary of American Family Names*, Patrick Hanks (ed.), OUP, Oxford, 2003, pp. xxxvi-xlii.

Michael Munn, *John Wayne: The Man behind the Myth*, Robson Books, London, 2003.

'Naming Committee accepts Asia, rejects Magnus', *Iceland Review Online*, 12 Sept 2006, online.

Leif D. Nelson & Joseph P. Simmons, 'Moniker madness: when names sabotage success', *Psychological Science*, vo. 18, no. 12, December 2007, pp. 1106-1112.

New York City *Popularity Of New York City Female Baby Names By Ethnicity, 2012*, online.

New York City *Popularity Of New York City Male Baby Names By Ethnicity, 2012*, online.

Frank Newport, David W. Moore & Lydia Saad, *The Most Important Events of the Century from the*

Viewpoint of the People, Gallup, 1999, online.

'Notes on the Fishers of the Scotch East Coast', *Blackwood's Edinburgh Magazine*, vol. 51, March 1842, pp. 296-305.

Alana Odegard, 'And the name is . . .', *Icelandic Review Online*, 15 Feb 2010, online.

Karla Oosterveen, Richard M. Smith & Susan Stewart, 'Family reconstitution and the study of bastardy', in Peter Laslett, Karla Oosterveen & Richard M. Smith (eds), *Bastardry and Its*

Comparative History, Harvard University Press, Cambridge, Mass, 1980.

George Orwell, *The Collected Essays, Journalism and Letters of George Orwell: Volume I: An Age Like*

This 1920-1940, Penguin, Harmondsworth, 1970.

Hywel Wyn Owen, 'Welsh family names', in Patrick Hanks (ed.), *Dictionary of American Family Names*, Volume 1, OUP, 2003, pp. xlii-xliv.

Mario Pei, *The Story of Language*, George Allen & Unwin, London, 1952.

B.W. Pelham, M.C. Mirenberg & J.T. Jones, 'Why Susie sells seashells by the seashore: implicit egotism and major life decisions, attitudes and social cognition', *Journal of Personality and Social Psychology*, vol 82(4), April 2002, pp. 469-487.

Naomi Pfefferman, 'A nice Jewish porn star', *Jewish Journal*, 29 November 2001.

K.C. Phillipps, *Language and Class in Victorian England*, Basil Blackwell, Oxford, 1984.

Benjamin J. Pitcher, Alex Mesoudi & Alan G. McElligott, 'Sex-based sound symbolism in English-language first names', *PLoS ONE*, vol. 8, no. 6, online.

Select Bibliography

Bradley Pitt, 'A quick £33 and I'm Brad Pitt; next week I'm Tom Cruise', *Sunday Times*, 16 October 2011.

George Plimpton, 'John le Carré, the art of fiction No. 149', *Paris Review*, no. 143, Summer 1997.

Daniel Pool, *What Jane Austen Ate and Charles Dickens Knew*, Simon & Schuster, New York, 1993.

'Pope Francis reveals why he chose his name', *CatholicHerald*, 16 March 2013.

Peggy Post, Anna Post, Lizzie Post & Daniel Post Senning, *Emily Post's Etiquette: Manners for a New World*, 18th edn, HarperCollins, New York, 2011.

Dave Postles, *The North through Its Names*, Oxbow Books, Oxford, 2007.

David Postles, 'The distribution of gender? Women's names in the thirteenth century', *Nomina*, vol. 19, pp. 79-89.

Simeon Potter, *Our Language*, Penguin, Harmondsworth, 1966.

PR Newswire, *TheKnot Releases 2013 Wedding Statistics*, 2014, online.

Fiona Swee-Lin Price, *Success with Asian Names*, Nicholas Brealey, London, 2007.

Dominic M Prümmer, *Handbook of Moral Theology*, Mercier Press, Cork, 1956.

J. Ambrose Raftis, *Warboys: Two Hundred Years in the Life of an English Medieval Village*, Toronto, Pontifical Institute of Mediaeval Studies, 1974.

William Raspberry, 'What's in a first name?', *Washington Post*, 20 December 1993, p.A25.

P.H. Reaney, *A Dictionary of British Surnames*, Routledge and Kegan Paul, London, 1966.

P.H. Reaney, *The Origin of English Surnames*, Routledge & Kegan Paul, London, 1968.

George Redmonds, Turi King & David Hey, *Surnames, DNA, and Family History*, OUP, Oxford, 2011.

Ruth Rendell writing as Barbara Vine, *A Dark Adapted Eye*, Plume, New York, 1993.

Robert M. Rennick, 'Hitlers and others who changed their names and a few who did not', *Names*, vol. 17, no. 3, September 1969, pp. 199-207.

Robert M. Rennick, 'The Nazi name decrees of the Nineteen Thirties', *Names*, vol. 18, no. 2, June 1970, pp. 65-88.

Myra Reynolds, *The Learned Lady in England, 1650-1760*, Peter Smith, Gloucester, Mass, 1964.

Eric Richards, *Britannia's Children*, Hambledon and London, London, 2004.

Randy Roberts & James S Olson, *John Wayne: American*, University of Nebraska Press, Lincoln, 1997.

Edward G. Robinson, *All My Yesterdays: An Autobiography*, Hawthorn Books, New York, 1973.

Jennifer Robison, *Feminism—What's In A Name?* Gallup, 2002, online.

Alice S. Rossi, 'Naming children in middle-class families', *American Sociological Review*, vol. 30, no. 4, August 1965, pp. 499-513.

J.K. Rowling, *J.K. Rowling's Statement Regarding 'The Cuckoo's Calling' by Robert Galbraith*, not dated, online.

J.K. Rowling, *Transcript of National Press Club Author's Luncheon*, 1999, online.

John Sandford, *About the Author*, 2016, online.

Scott Sayare, "Mademoiselle' exits official France', *New York Times*, 23 February 2012.

John Scarborough, 'John Wyndham', in Richard Bleiler (ed.), *Science Fiction Writers: Critical Studies of the Major Authors from the Early Nineteenth Century to the Present Day*, 2nd edn, Charles Scribner's Sons, New York, 1998.

Janet Schwegel, *The Baby Name Countdown: 140,000 popular and unusual baby names*, 6th edn, da Capo, Philadelphia, 2008.

James C. Scott, *Seeing Like A State*, Yale University Press, New Haven, 1998.

Eliezer Segal, *Who Has Not Made Me A Woman*, My Jewish Learning, not dated, online.

Michael Sherrod & Matthew Rayback, *Bad Baby Names: The Worst True Names Parents Saddled Their Kids with—and You Can Too!* Ancestry Publishing, Provo, UT, 2008.

David Shipman, *The Great Movie Stars*: The Golden Years, Hill and Wang, 1979.

Raphael Silberzahn & Eric Luis Uhlmann, 'It pays to be Herr Kaiser', *Psychological Sciences*, vol. 24, 2013, pp. 2437-2444.

'Singer Lily Allen on mum Lily Cooper—and vice versa', *Gloucester Citizen*, 11 March 2014.

Scott Smith-Bannister, *Names and Naming Patterns in England 1538-1700*, Clarendon Press, Oxford, 1997.

Dale Spender, 'The ancient history of wifeliness', in Dale Spender (ed.), *Weddings and Wives*, Penguin, Ringwood, 1994, pp. 3-63.

Dale Spender, *Man Made Language*, 2nd edn, Pandora, London, 1985.

Bob Spitz, *The Beatles: The Biography*, Little, Brown, New York, 2005.

A.J. Splatt & D. Weedon, 'The urethral syndrome', *British Journal of Urology*, vol.49, April 1977, pp. 173-76.

Diane Stafford, *60,001+ Best Baby Names*, Sourcebooks, Naperville IL, 2008.

Una Stannard, *Mrs Man*, Germain Books, San Francisco, 1977.

Victoria Starr, *k.d. lang*, Random House of Canada, 1995.

Daniel Stashower, *Teller of Tales: The Life of Arthur Conan Doyle*, Henry Holt and Company, New York, 1999.

George R. Stewart, *American Given Names*, Oxford University Press, New York, 1979.

Pearl Stewart, 'Who is kin? Family definition and African American families', *Journal of Human Behavior in the Social Environment*, vol. 15, nos. 2-3, 2007, pp. 163-181.

Will Stewart, 'Found: Helen Mirren's Russian relatives', *Mail Online*, 15 October 2006.

Harry Stone, 'What's in a name: fantasy and calculation in Dickens', *Dickens Studies Annual*, vol. 14, 1985, pp.191-204.

Christopher M. Sturges & Brian C. Haggett, *Inheritance of English Surnames*, Hawgood Computing, London, 1987.

Christina A. Sue & Edward E. Telles, 'Assimilation and gender in naming', *American Journal of Sociology*, vol. 112, no. 5, March 2007, pp. 1383-1415.

Anthony Summers, *Goddess: The Secret Lives of Marilyn Monroe*, Sphere Books, London, 1986.

John Sumser, 'Not just any Tom, Dick or Harry: the grammar of names in television drama', *Media, Culture & Society*, vol. 14, 1992, pp. 605-622.

John Sutherland, *How to Read A Novel*, Profile Books, London, 2007.

Julie Szego, 'True badges of survival', *The Age* [Melbourne], 13 October 2010, p. 26.

J. Randy Taraborrelli, *The Secret Life of Marilyn Monroe*, Grand Central Publishing, New York, 2009.

Humphrey Taylor, *Mrs, Miss or Ms: Which Do Women Prefer?* Harris Poll, 1999, online.

Rex Taylor, 'John Doe, Jr.: A study of his distribution in space, time, and the social structure', *Social Forces*, vol. 53, no. 1, September 1974, pp. 11-21.

Jenny Teichman, *Illegitimacy: An Examination of Bastardy*, Cornell University Press, Ithaca, NY, 1982.

W.M. Thackeray, *The Book of Snobs*, D. Appleton, New York, 1852.

Donald Thomas, *A Long Time Burning*, Routledge & Kegan Paul, London, 1969.

Katheryn A. Thompson, 'Tussle over titles', *ABA Journal*, 8 January 2006, online.

Rachel Thwaites, *Women, Marriage, and Selfhood: How Names Impact upon Gendered Identity*,

University of York PhD thesis, 2013.

'The top 500 British surnames', *Observer*, 15 April 2007.

Nigel Tranter, *Rob Roy MacGregor*, Neil Wilson Publishing, New York, 2012.

Laura Troubridge, *The Book of Etiquette*, The World's Work, Kingswood, Surrey, 1931.

D. Kenneth Tucker, 'Increased competition and reduced popularity: US given name trends of the twentieth and early twenty-first centuries', *Names*, vol. 57, no. 1, March 2009, pp. 52-62.

Ken Tucker, 'What happened to the UK 1881 census surnames by 1997', *Nomina*, vol. 27, 2004, pp. 91-118.

Jean M. Twenge, '"Mrs. His Name"', *Psychology of Women Quarterly*, vol. 21, 1997, pp. 417-429.

Select Bibliography

Nicholas Tyacke, 'Popular Puritan mentality in late Elizabethan England', in Peter Clark et al. (eds),

The English Commonwealth 1547-1640, Leicester University Press, 1979.

UK Deed Poll Service, 'About the title Mx', not dated, online.

UK Government, *Informative Note: Explanation of Change of Name in the United Kingdom*, 2015, online.

US Marshalls Service, *Facts and Figures 2014*, online.

Vicki Valosik, 'For same-sex couples changing names takes on extra significance', *The Atlantic*, 27 September 2013.

Vatican, *Code of Canon Law*, 1983, online.

Anthony Richard Wagner, *English Genealogy*, Oxford University Press, London, 1960.

Martyn Waites, *About Tania Carver*, not dated (online).

Alexander Walker, *Stardom: The Hollywood Phenomenon*, Penguin, London, 1974.

Barbara G. Walker, *Woman's Encyclopedia of Myths and Secrets*, Pandora, London, 1995.

Timothy Wand, 'The 'Sister' title: past the use by date?', *Collegian: Journal of the Royal College of Nursing Australia*, vol.11, issue 1, 2004, pp. 35-39.

Booker T. Washington, *Up From Slavery: An Autobiography*, 1945 (originally 1901), OUP, London.

Daniel J Watermeier, 'Actors and acting', in Don B. Wilmeth and Christopher Bigsby (eds), *Cambridge History of American Theatre, Volume II, 1870-1945*, Cambridge University Press, 1999.

Laura Wattenberg, 'Aydin, Jaden and Zayden: newborn names all sound the same', *The Age* [Melbourne], 18 May, 2010, p. 11.

Laura Wattenberg, *The Baby Name Wizard*, 3rd edn, Random House, New York, 2013.

Richard Webber, *Names: A Source of Customer Insight*, Experian, London, 2008.

David W Webster, 'Scottish surnames and Christian names', in Robert Blatchford (ed.), *The Family and Local History Handbook*. 7th edn, York, Genealogical Services Directory, 2003.

Sarah Westcott, 'George makes comeback as parents copy Wills and Kate', *International Express*, 20 August 2014, p. 5.

Mary Westmacott (Agatha Christie), *Giant's Bread*, William Collins Sons & Co, London, 1985 (originally 1930).

What Can You Name Your Baby?, BBC News Channel, 1997, online.

What Does My Name Mean?, Psychic Readings, 2014, online.

'What's a Ms?', *Ms*, June, 1972, p. 4.

W.M. Williams, *The Sociology of an English Village: Gosforth*, Routledge & Kegan Paul, London, 1956.

Natalya Wilson, 'Meet Bill Spence, the man behind Jessica Blair – 60 years on', *York Post*, 13 February 2013.

Stephen Wilson, *The Means of Naming*, UCL Press, London, 1998.

E.G. Withycombe, *Oxford Dictionary of English Christian Names*, 3rd edn, Oxford University Press, Oxford, 1977.

David L. Word, Charles D. Coleman, Robert Nunziata & Robert Kominski, *Demographic Aspects of Surnames from Census 2000*, US Census Bureau, online.

Patrick Woulfe, *Irish Names and Surnames*, Genealogical Publishing, Baltimore, 1967.

Michela Wrong, *In The Footsteps of Mr. Kurtz: Living on the Brink of Disaster in Mobutu's Congo*. Perennial, 2001.

Malcolm X; *The Autobiography of Malcolm X*, Hutchinson, London, 1966.

'You have called me doctor for 10 years', *Dentistry.co.uk News*, 14 February 2006, online.

Ian Youngs, 'JK Rowling or Robert Galbraith: how to pick a pen name', *BBC News*, 15 July 2013, online.

Frank Zappa with Peter Occhiogrosso, *The Real Frank Zappa Book*, Picador, London, 1990.

Maurice Zolotow, *John Wayne: Shooting Star*, WH Allen, London, 1974.

INDEX

Notes: an entry such as 'Abigail (g)' indicates that this is a reference to the use of the name as a given (or Christian) name. An entry such as 'Anderson (s)' indicates that this is a reference to the use of the name as a surname. All known pen-names, stage names, aliases or birth names have been cross-referenced.

Index

Index

Index

HELLO
my name is
NEIL
BURDESS

← AN ENGLISH NICKNAME
FOR ENGLISH MERCHANTS
WHO IMPORTED WINE
FROM BORDEAUX..

The author's given name, *Neil*, is one he shares with the first man on the moon. He would like to claim that he was named in honour of Neil Armstrong, because he would then be 20 years younger. Unfortunately, this is not the case. However, he was part of the trend that saw the name Neil climb into Britain's top 50 most popular names in the 1950s.

The author's surname, BURDESS, is not a typo. The much more familiar Burgess is a different name. There are less than 300 people with the surname Burdess in Britain, most living in northeast England, centred on the perhaps unfortunately named town of Crook, where the author was born.